All for Nothing?

My Life Remembered

C. G. Tracey

WEAVER

—PRESS—

Published by Weaver Press, P.O. Box A 1922, Avondale, Harare. 2009

Typeset by TextPertise, Harare
Cover Design by Danes Design, Harare
The Endpapers were sourced from Digital Globes
Printed by Précigraph Ltd., Mauritius

ISBN: 978 177922 079 0

Contents

Prologue

This book covers four generations and a period of nearly ninety years. It is a story of the beginning and the end of an era.

Conditions in the early days of Rhodesia (now Zimbabwe) were fairly primitive. It was several years before we owned a car. There were no telephones. There was no electricity. After eighty years of 'progress', once again there is a major shortage of electricity, and telephone services have been severely prejudiced.

All my life I have been a farmer and have been fascinated by national and international affairs, particularly in banking, marketing and the improvement of agriculture. I am privileged to have served and contributed to the development of the country in many different ways. However, it is with great sadness that at the end of my story I have to relate how Wendy and I lost our farm under Robert Mugabe's 'land reform' programme.

I am no scholar or historian. I have tried to check facts, but please forgive me if what I remember may not always be entirely accurate or if your memory differs from mine. What I have tried to do is tell my story. In doing so I have referred to a variety of documents and books in my private collection, from some of which, as you will see, I have quoted on occasion.

When, after considerable persuasion, I agreed to write this autobiography at the age of eighty, I never anticipated how much work would be involved. The book has taken a considerable time to write because I was so often interrupted by the political and security traumas of the last five years of life in Zimbabwe, by illness, and by the death of my wife, Wendy. Had I known what a massive undertaking it would prove to be, I might never have started. But I have been fortified in the decision to proceed because the recollections of many of my generation will be lost forever unless they are recorded now.

C. G. Tracey
Harare, 2007

Acknowledgements

There are many people who I wish to thank most sincerely for their help, time and advice.

My good friend Much Masunda read and commented on several drafts of the book. Bert Rosettenstein, a very good neighbour, historian and lawyer, has been generous with his time and read the entire book from a legal perspective. Regretfully, the old adage applies: the greater the truth, the greater the libel.

Alex Masterson, our lawyer for two years following our eviction from our farm, was succeeded, at Coghlan, Welsh and Guest, by Kevin Arnott. Both were superb lawyers, and without their knowledge and ingenuity we would never have achieved as much as we did with the Mount Lothian court case. Our advocate, Adrian de Bourbon, has a mighty reputation and specializes in these difficult land legalities. Nokuthula Moyo, also a lawyer with Coghlan, Welsh and Guest, gave generously of her time to look at a later version of the manuscript and advise on various issues.

Michael Hartnack, a widely respected journalist, was a treasure chest of knowledge and had a prodigious memory. It was he who urged me not to give up. Sadly, he died early in 2007 after a sudden heart attack and is greatly missed.

My thanks go to the late Lady Angela Greenhill, who kindly gave me permission to use her poems, and to the staff of the United Nations Records Library.

I am greatly appreciative of Heather Hahn, my private secretary, who has looked after me with patience and skill for 23 years. She worked long hours after normal working hours to organize the manuscript and helped with a great deal of the editing.

Lyn Taylor did all the original typing and drafting, a consuming task which she had to fit in with her own very busy life.

Jill Day, herself a writer, helped me initially in gathering all the many strands of my story together and wove them into a better, more sequential and orderly manuscript. I greatly appreciated her advice.

My heartfelt gratitude to Venetia Winkfield, who picked up where Jill left off and worked long and arduously on my story to ensure that small details were as correct as we could make them, and that the text had a sequential flow.

Professor Ray Roberts of the University of Zimbabwe also kindly read the manuscript and helped to check historical facts.

It was an honour that Weaver Press agreed to publish these reminiscences. I realize that Irene Staunton's wisdom and experience have greatly improved the book.

Particular thanks also go to Roger Stringer of TextPertise, who not only did the layout but followed up on many tricky queries. I very much appreciate his technical skill and pursuit of accuracy.

Finally, I would like to give particular thanks to my family: Timothy de Swardt, my grandson, who read and commented on several of the earlier drafts; and my daughter Diana, with whom I now live, for not only has she been looking after me but she has had to bear my daily inquisition on the progress of this book. I am deeply grateful.

Many other people have helped me in many ways. To them all I express my true thanks.

In the Beginning

My parents arrive in Gutu • Hugh Tracey and African music
• Handley Cross farm, Chakari • Tracey family history
• Everyday life • Guinea pig racing • Ruzawi
• Blundell's • Wartime farming • The chapel

My father, Leonard Tolcher Tracey, was born in Devonshire, England, and educated at Blundell's. Just before the First World War he had begun a medical degree at St Bartholomew's Hospital in London but he signed up and served with the Gunners in the First Devonshire Regiment. He was wounded three times and awarded a Military Cross. During the war there was a Rhodesian in his regiment and my father became fascinated by his stories. He abandoned his medical studies and travelled out to Southern Rhodesia.

My mother, Evelyn Winwood-Smith, had been in the office of Air Marshal Lord Trenchard, head of the Air Force during the war, and was awarded an MBE for her work. When the war ended, she wanted a complete change and decided to visit Southern Rhodesia. Leonard's life and her own came together in unromantic circumstances on the Gwelo railway station platform.

Leonard went to a farm near Rusape, belonging to Barnes Pope, for a six-month familiarization with agriculture, and the romance blossomed. They were married in Rusape towards the end of 1919. He and nine others had been allocated completely undeveloped and unpopulated soldier-settler farms near Gutu in the south-east of the country. My father called his farm Willand, after the Tracey family home, and he and Evelyn decided that their honeymoon would be the journey to their new farm.

They bought a big buck-beam wagon with steel-rimmed wooden wheels and spokes and a framework covered by a tarpaulin, a span of trek oxen, a few cows for milk, and other livestock. The next fourteen days were spent on what our family calls the honeymoon trek, travelling across country as there was no direct route to Gutu. The journey of over a hundred miles

The honeymoon trek – crossing the Ruzawi River.

The first thatched hut my father built on arrival at Willand in Gutu.

took a fortnight, crossing large rivers like the Sabi and the Ruzawi. When they arrived they continued to live in the wagon and set about cutting timber to make pole-and-daga huts in which they lived until the house was completed. They made their own bricks using anthills for clay, which was ideal, and they burnt them in kilns in the usual way and thatched the roof. This was quite a change for my mother from a hospital, the war and the Air Ministry. The house my father built was occupied from 1919 until 2003, when it was looted and destroyed by Zimbabwean 'settlers'.

Martin was born in 1921 and I was born on the last day of 1923, arriving earlier than planned. Taken unawares, my mother was 60 miles from a hospital, doctor or nurse; we had only a pony trap. Our next-door neighbour's wife, Mrs Nelly Nel, came across to lend a hand and all went well. Women on farms in Rhodesia had to be tough and courageous, although after two births at Gutu my mother returned to London for my sister Bridget's birth.

Oom Gert Nel, undoubtedly the leader of the community around Gutu, attended the 1954 RNFU Congress in his capacity of area chairman and asked the president for permission to propose me for the vice-presidency. He jokingly said, 'Mr President, my wife should have taken the opportunity, on delivering CG, to throttle the little bugger, and then we probably wouldn't have the problems we now have.'

My parents were both strong supporters of the monarchy. Both had served with distinction in the First World War. When the King and later the Queen gave their Christmas address to the nation, we stood up as a mark of respect. We also stood up whenever the national anthem was played.

My father's younger brother, Hugh Tracey, came from England to join us in Gutu, and quickly became a versatile linguist. He later did a lot of work for both the Ford and the Carnegie Foundations and recorded many hundred pressings of pure, unadulterated African music, from as far afield as Kenya and Rwanda. (His collection was subsequently housed at the African School of Music at Wits University in Johannesburg, but was later transferred to Rhodes University.

The Ford Foundation asked him to speak on African music at a university in each of the 51 American states. Later, he received a letter that resulted in the following story. About six generations earlier, a Mississippi cotton planter had bought a girl in the slave market to nurse his children, and she had taught her charges an African lullaby. Later, she looked after the cotton planter's grandchildren; and her daughter became nurse to the third generation. Thus, the lullaby was passed from generation to generation. Now, the family had written to ask Hugh if he could identify the slave-girl's origin, and he asked them to write the song as a musical score. The School of African Music, at which he taught, was attended by musicians from all over Africa, but no one could identify the source of the lullaby. So, they suggested that it might help if a descendant of the slave-girl could sing the song. And old lady did so and when it was played to Hugh Tracey's team of musicians, one recognized it as coming from an area in the south-east of Rhodesia and into Mozambique, where it is still sung today. This story shows that slaves were procured for America from as far away as the east coast of Africa.

In 1925 my father moved to Handley Cross from Gutu, where the isolation and the fact that the soils were unsuitable for arable farming made it almost impossible to be a successful arable crop farmer. The prospect of developing a beef herd on the Gutu farm was too long-term for him. Of the original ten settler farmers there, none lasted more than three or four years. My father was advised to move to Chakari, which was at the apex of a triangle north of Hartley and Gatooma and about twenty miles from each. Both of these small towns were on the line of rail and on the main Bulawayo–Salisbury road.

The new farm provided a complete change of environment, with its big stretches of red soil, good arable land suitable for maize, cotton and other crops. Nobody had lived there because of a lack of surface water so it was virgin. My parents started all over again. Again, while the new house was being built, they lived in pole-and-daga huts, this time abandoned by a small-worker who was mining a gold reef a couple of miles away.

My father would spend every day making bricks, cutting roof timbers and building our house. Once again there were no builders and he laid every brick himself. He had to sink a well and install a windmill. If we had a couple of windless days we had to be careful how much water we used. There was no electricity, no telephone and no water-borne sanitation; we used a 'long-drop' for many years.

My earliest memory dates from this time. When I was about three, my father went up every morning to the brick-making and building sites. At the end of the day my mother would take my brother Martin and me in a pushcart, to fetch my father back home. It was always fun and I remember trying to be the first one to spot the evening star.

As our workforce laboriously stumped and cleared the land, we started to grow small acreages of crops, including tobacco, which, because the red soils were rather too fertile for it, resulted in a rather heavy leaf. The world

Where did our family come from?

King Henry I, as Duke of Normandy, exercised his 'droit de seigneur' for the favours of Mademoiselle de Tracy. The son of Mademoiselle de Tracy, who was the progeny of that occasion, took his mother's name and was either knighted or granted a baronetcy, with the title Sir William de Tracy.

In AD 1170, King Henry II was holding court in his Duchy of Normandy. The Archbishop of Canterbury of the time, Thomas à Becket, continually spoke out against the King's anticlericalism. The King, in a rage, is reported to have said, 'Who will rid me of this turbulent priest?'

William de Tracy and three other knights took that remark as an order and set off for the coastal port of Calais, where they boarded a ship, taking their horses, to cross the Channel. On arrival in England they rode straight to Canterbury. They found Archbishop Becket in the sanctuary of his cathedral, where they murdered him. They came back to face their trial some four or five years later and were found guilty. Their sentence was interesting – what was described as 'an indeterminate sentence'. They were ordered to make one yard of rope from sea sand. Obviously that was impossible and, try as they might, they were unable to make their yard of rope, so they continued to serve their sentence until they were eventually discharged.

Among other measures, the Church of Rome called down a curse, particularly on William de Tracy, intending to prevent him from embarking on a crusade to the Holy Land to expiate his crime. This ecclesiastical embargo held for William and his son. Their every attempt to set sail for the Holy Land was frustrated by contrary winds blowing them back to England. This led to a saying of the time, 'The Tracys, the Tracys have the wind in their faces'.

William's grandson eventually managed to get to the Holy Land, but on the return voyage he was captured and held for a high ransom. However, when no one produced a ransom, his captors eventually let him go. But this was not the end of his problems. There was a law that anyone who failed to return from a Crusade within seven years was declared 'missing, presumed dead'. Consequently, on his return to England he found himself officially a dead man. Worse, his wife, presumed a widow by now, had married again and all his lands at Tawstock in Devon, which his grandfather had been given, were now the property of somebody else.

This grandson bought estates in the North of Devonshire called Mortehoe and settled there, only to move to another estate nearby a little later. And subsequently the family bought the estate Bovey Tracey in the centre of Devonshire and settled there for many decades. Later, the land was disposed of through inheritances and although the village of Bovey Tracey remains, our family now has no connection with it. Wendy and I visited Sir William's grave in Devonshire.

When my brother Martin was given a farm by our father in 1945, he decided, as the oldest descendant of Sir William de Tracy in our generation, to name it Tawstock, to rectify this matter after the passage of several centuries. During the centuries we have added an 'e' to our name somewhere along the way.

On 8 August 2002, Martin was evicted from Tawstock by another unscrupulous ruler. The story, however, has not yet ended.

depression of 1929–31 put paid to the tobacco venture, however, as prices fell to an all-time low. So the main crop we grew was maize (Hickory King and Salisbury White varieties). My parents also started a small Friesland dairy herd and established our small herd of pigs.

For refrigeration we made a coolbox of charcoal with hessian walls, which were always wet from the tank on top. As the water dripped through the charcoal it evaporated and this kept the inside temperature relatively cool – enough to keep milk and meat fresh for a few days. My mother made her own soap, often from pig lard after a pig had been slaughtered. We had to be completely self-sufficient and she made our bread each day. Shopping expeditions took place every couple of months and a visit to Salisbury was a rare event, a journey of five or six hours. We had to plan carefully for food, medicine and other necessities.

Mail was delivered once a week and letters from Britain, which usually went via the mail-boat to Cape Town, took three weeks. At Chakari, three miles away, there was a post office, a one-man police station and a couple of Greek-owned stores providing goods for the indigenous population.

My mother taught the three of us through the government correspondence course. This was established by the Ministry of Education for children in remote areas. Every fortnight a canvas bag would arrive via Rhodesia Railways and the Road Motor Service from Gatooma to Chakari, which contained the next two weeks' work and the previous two, marked and appropriately commented upon. It was always an exciting moment.

School work required a good deal of input and discipline from both of us. I remember doing my work, sitting on the veranda behind the dairy, away from the distraction of the workshop and livestock; in fact, everything on the farm was much more interesting than my school work!

Every few months the Ministry of Education inspector, Mr Lenfesty, would make a visit, which I always looked forward to, and he was most encouraging.

At the age of nine and a half, I joined Martin at Ruzawi, an Anglican preparatory school founded by the Revd Robert Grinham and Maurice Carver near Marandellas. A coaching inn and a staging post to change mules on the road from Salisbury to Umtali had been built there many years before. These buildings were then converted into Ruzawi School in 1929. Originally Ruzawi had only fifty boys, until the Beit trustees and others funded the construction of a new school on the same site in 1937. Because of my excellent home education I went straight into Standard 2.

On the farm, any surplus funds were used for equipment, development, for buying our first Model T Ford, and for Martin's and my education. I do not know how my parents managed to send us to Ruzawi, where the fees were £100 a year and maize was fetching only six shillings a bag at the time.

One of our sidelines was my mother's Handley Cross cream cheese. We had the contract to supply the Rhodesia Railways catering department; it brought in a small but regular income. The cream cheese was packed attractively into proper cardboard punnets. It started its journey from us to Gatooma by the railways' Road Motor Service and from there went to Salisbury and Bulawayo for distribution to all the passenger trains running from Beira through to Umtali, Salisbury, Bulawayo and Victoria Falls. The balance was sold to three big grocery department stores – Meikles Brothers, Maltas and Divaris.

Additionally, my mother made butter from surplus cream. Because of the high temperatures in the summer, it was difficult to get the butter to come, which meant she had to get up at half past four most mornings to make the butter before the day warmed up. This was just another small contribution which she and lots of other farmers' wives made towards their pretty meagre income at that time.

Our first car was a Model T Ford. I'm on the left on the running board, and Martin is next to me, with our mother and father.

We took it in turns with our neighbours to slaughter a lamb, calf or pig and each family sold their surplus meat to the others. Occasionally my father shot a small buck or guinea fowl for the pot. Although even our nearest neighbours were three miles away, we kept in touch by foot, bicycle or on horseback. We always had horses on the farm and I rode from a young age. Although I have no recollection of riding lessons, we spent much of our time on our ponies.

John Masefield, the Poet Laureate, wrote an epic poem, nearly a hundred pages long, about the Grand National, 'Right Royal'. As I was so interested, my father read it to me when I was not quite seven, and I memorized almost the whole of the hundred pages. Later, at Ruzawi, I would be given the question paper for the English exam, 'Quote 20 lines from any poem you like', with a handwritten note on my paper 'except Right Royal'. The names of several of the runners from the poem were given to my own ponies.

These ponies formed the basis for Martin's and my great interest in riding in our adult lives. In the 1940s we started breeding thoroughbreds. Later, we both played polo at our small Chakari Club and, although there were very few players, we still managed to win a number of tournaments. My interest in horses continued and I used to ride as an amateur jockey, with no great distinction, on a couple of my own horses at the Belvedere racecourse in Salisbury.

Belvedere racecourse is now the site of the Magistrates' Courts, the Zimbabwe College of Music and the Rainbow Towers hotel, and I never drive down Rotten Row without remembering the collecting ring under the big shady trees, the seven furlong start on the edge of the Showgrounds, the straight past the hotel and the bend by the College of Music.

We were so far away from our neighbours on the farm that we had to create our own entertainment. We played with the children of our workers and learnt to speak Shona and ChiNyanja. As my father had always been interested in horses, we had a copy of *Whittaker's Almanac*, which, among other fascinating information, listed the winners of the Derby and the Grand National for the previous fifty years. We did not have any horses to race, so instead we developed a new sport of training and racing guinea pigs, many of whom were named after these winners. These delightful little animals took to their training extremely well. The racecourse was made up of a 100-metre circular course with proper jumps, including a water jump, every ten metres The guinea pigs learnt exactly what to do and they jumped like stags.

My father had been left a stopwatch, which he used to time each

Martin, left, Bridget and me with our racing guinea pigs.

guinea pig accurately. Originally we would run three or four together but, with no stipendiary steward, too many arguments resulted from bumping and boring. My father decreed that from then on each guinea pig would run alone and would be timed. We would buy guinea pigs from each other, especially those that we thought had good potential. We made our own jumps, which were nine or ten inches high, from planks which came from the boxes my mother used to take the cream cheese to market. We cut brush and stuffed it into the gaps, and it was a great sight to see these well-trained guinea pigs taking their jumps, urged on by their owners.

We had many small gold-mine workings in the area. One was operated by an Englishman, Mr L. K. S. Robinson, who had been the first Member of Parliament for Fort Victoria, and he became a close friend. He was intrigued by the guinea pig races and generously donated a trophy called the Robinson Plate, which was a silver inkwell and stand, suitably inscribed. The last time we competed for the trophy was in 1935 and it was won by one of my guinea pigs called Gay Devil.

Gay Devil safely over the last when winning the Robinson Plate.

By that time Ruzawi and other interests had overtaken guinea pig racing although we have the inkstand to this day. I wrote a short article about our guinea pig racing for *The Field* in the UK. The editor not only published the article but paid me a guinea – I was rich! I also appeared on Children's Hour on Durban radio in South Africa and spoke on the same subject.

At that time Lord Baden-Powell was the Chief Scout. Ruzawi had an active small scout pack and we were very excited when, towards the end of his life, the Chief Scout came to Southern Rhodesia and to Ruzawi. We met him and he told us some of his stories.

Every boy scout in Southern Rhodesia was first of all taught to honour his king and country and, second most important, what to do in the case of snake bite. One Sunday afternoon our patrol was returning from trying to make a small dam on the edge of the Ruzawi river when I felt a very sharp pain in my ankle and saw that I had been bitten by a snake, variety unknown. Everybody knew what to do for snake bite and so I was thrown to the ground and the area around the snake bite was cut open with a boy's scout knife, to get the blood to flow. One boy went off at scout pace – alternately fifty yards running and fifty yards walking – to call for help about two miles away, and the remainder fixed up a stretcher with staffs and coats and set off carrying me home. The doctor had been summoned and, on arrival, I was promptly injected with anti-venom. I showed no ill effects, except that the knife which cut my ankle open to induce the blood flow must have been pretty unhygienic and I suffered more from infection than I did from the snake bite.

I entered newspaper ownership when I was at my prep school at Ruzawi. The school did not have its own magazine and, when I was twelve years old, I thought an opportunity to produce such a magazine was too good to be missed. The groundsman of the school had an ancient typewriter and so I borrowed it to produce a school magazine. It was run on business lines and we sold it for sixpence a copy. I invited a couple of influential senior boys to join my editorial board, partly as protection against possible interference from staff and also to stimulate circulation.

The headmaster of Ruzawi, the Revd Robert Grinham, a pretty good headmaster generally, was immune to new ideas. He became aware of my project and warned me about the risk of subversion. I assured him that it was our policy to provide a service and make a bit of money and that with my editorial board we were unlikely to publish anything inopportune. After two terms, however, his continuous worry resulted in a summons to appear, and he told me that the magazine was going to be taken over by the staff, with the help of some boys. I enquired about compensation to be paid for the acquisition of a profitable going concern and I was tersely told there would be none. I don't think the headmaster understood what I was asking for.

The magazine limped along for a little while until eventually they were able to produce a proper magazine on good paper with photographs. Because of this experience, I have always been a strong opponent of any form of nationalization.

My first memories of Christmas were of a fairly quiet occasion, just with the family and presents from my aunts and uncles in Britain. We always went to church in Gatooma on Christmas morning. For the workers, it was a time of merriment. They all received a utility present – clothing, kitchen utensils and the like – from my parents. There was always tribal dancing in the afternoon when our workers came up to the house (and, clearly, beer had been consumed over Christmas lunch). This happened every Christmas and it was a time we particularly enjoyed.

When I was older, the Christmas paper-chase started. We would stop off on the way home after the Christmas church service at a farm owned by Mr Aubrey Green. He had been an only child and had had a governess. Strangely, when he grew up, he married her. There was a mounted paper-chase at his farm each year, followed by Christmas lunch. The horses had been walked across from Handley Cross in time for the paper-chase, with competitors of all ages and exciting brush jumps. While we enjoyed our lunch, the ponies would be walked back and by the time we got home they were in their stables. We were able to give them their evening feed, some hay and settle them down for the night.

Those were paper-chases, but the Delta hounds were a pack near Marandellas in about 1935. The master was a man called Tarrant. They hunted not foxes but leopards. The longest 'point' they ever had was fifty-eight miles. Keen supporters were John Rutherford, whose son Bobby later became president of the Commercial Farmers Union, and Mrs Molly Rutherford. The hunt folded at the beginning of the Second World War.

One of our neighbours was a South African called Percy Rushforth who had a medium-sized farm on the Suri Suri River. He became increasingly exasperated by both maize thefts from their big shed and rats in the grain store. So he went out and caught a 2½-metre python, which was put into the shed and all the exits blocked up. The python enjoyed the rats; the maize thieves gave up their quest and Percy was delighted.

For one of our first holidays, we went down to Beira by train and then by boat to Durban and back. On another occasion, we went to visit our grandparents in the UK. This entailed a three-day journey by rail to Cape Town, where we boarded a Union Castle mail ship bound for Southampton. The voyage took fourteen days, and after we had spent three or four weeks in Britain we began our long return journey.

On the way back to school one term, our family had lunch at Sanders restaurant on First Street. Three boys returning to another school had the same lunch, and all of us went down with typhoid a week later. In 'the san' I was delirious – the only thing I was conscious of was the cricket net practice below, the sound of the ball on the bat.

At fourteen I finished Ruzawi, having won my colours for cricket and soccer. I was head of Fairbridge House and won the Victor Ludorum for athletics, the year after I had had typhoid.

That year, 1947, we again travelled by sea to the UK where I entered Blundell's, my father's old school, a public school founded in about 1570. My brother Martin had already been there a year. Because the Rhodesian school year ended in December, I had missed the first English term: their school year had started in September. My father couldn't get away from the farm in the early part of the growing season, January to March, so we only reached Britain in April. I therefore had just one term of that first year's curriculum. The headmaster said that, if I could catch up those lost two terms, I could move up with the class to the Upper Fifth, which was the school certificate and matriculation form.

I enjoyed Blundell's enormously and managed to complete the year's curriculum as well as play in the junior Colts cricket team.

During that summer I was one of two boys from Blundell's who were selected for special coaching in London. We played our cricket on the top of Selfridge's store in Oxford Street, in an area completely enclosed with netting. We had coaching from top English cricket players, including a number of test players. This stood me in good stead, as the next season I was made captain of the senior Colts and had the advantage of being given some special coaching by Frank Champain, a cricketer of note who had been an Oxford blue. He was determined that I should captain Blundell's in the next year.

I managed to get a day off from Blundell's, hopped on a bus and went to Taunton, where I saw the legendary Don Bradman, the captain of the Australian team, in the match against Somerset, where he scored 204.

After four terms at Blundell's, I obtained good results in my Oxford

School Certificate and matriculation exemption. Neville Gorton, my head-master, urged me to write my Oxford University entrance exam at the same time. Having got through, as a reward I was given the whole term off. Because at sixteen I was too young to go up to Oxford, I sailed back to Africa on a Union Castle ship, the *Llandovery Castle*. I recall the fare was £17 for the cheapest cabin, over the screw. In rough weather, when the boat pitched the propeller came out of the water and made an infernal din.

The next part of the trip was a three-day journey by train from Cape Town to the farm in Rhodesia. A month after I returned, the Second World War broke out. I could not get back to Britain and therefore was never able to go to Oxford, although I was offered a place after the war when I was already married to Wendy. I have always felt the loss of that opportunity deeply – and with only four terms of secondary education, I always put the words 'uneducated' in my CV.

Farming was regarded as an essential service and thus I was not allowed to enlist to fight in the war, although I tried several times. A number of Royal Naval Volunteer Reserve officers, who had immigrated to Rhodesia after the First World War, farmed in the area surrounding Chakari. Soon after the outbreak of war, many of them left their farms without management and returned to serve in the Navy. My farming life began at sixteen when I stepped in to help.

Within a few days our livestock manager had been called up. I took over the pigs and dairy cattle initially, but soon became involved with the crops as well. My father was appointed to the National Food Production Committee because Rhodesia had been given the responsibility of growing food for the region, which reduced the time he could spend at Handley Cross.

My brother Martin moved across to Newbiggin, the next-door farm, whose owner, Frank Crackenthorpe, had been called up by the Royal Navy Reserve. Two years later Martin joined the Gunners and, after training at King George VI barracks in Salisbury, he was commissioned in North Africa. By this time I was running our three family farms and two farms for neighbours in the Royal Navy, with help from my sister Bridget, who looked after the dairy cattle. She also left school earlier than usual owing to the circumstances.

Two years after their invasion of Singapore, intelligence had been received that the Japanese were planning to launch an invasion of Madagascar and to use this as a jumping-off point, first into Rhodesia and then into

South Africa. Plans were made, in the event of an invasion, for the white population to be evacuated to South Africa, leaving 450 able-bodied men who would live off the country and harass the Japanese. I was one of these 450 men. We had several training camps, learning to live completely rough in the bush, finding our own food, catching guinea fowl and rabbits, perfecting the art of silent night movement and then the technique of unarmed combat. I know how to take a man's foot and with one twist put him on his belly, fold his legs up over his backside and quickly turn him outwards and down. If this is done too vigorously you will split him up the middle, so when practising we had to be careful. Once the Japanese had started to retreat, our training was discontinued. It was tough, but very interesting.

At Handley Cross, after the war, our local policeman was Claude Hunt. He had worked on *The Times* in London, got the cheapest fare to South Africa and moved to Rhodesia to join the British South Africa Police (BSAP). He was one of the five people at my wartime 21st birthday party.

After training, Claude had been posted to a remote station near Beit-bridge on the Limpopo, which was the main entry point from South Africa into Rhodesia. In those days, being young and a bachelor, he didn't get much pay and so he used to go out on some evenings and shoot a guinea fowl or duiker for the pot.

Late one afternoon he went out with his 'black watch' (a black non-commissioned police officer) and heard some guinea fowl chattering in one of the big acacia trees. He stalked them slowly and carefully and got sufficiently close to the birds so that, when he fired, he was almost below them. A bird fell to the ground. As they were picking it up, an oldish man with a goatee beard appeared from the far side of the tree and indignantly accused him of being a thoroughly bad sport for shooting a sitting guinea fowl instead of flushing it and taking it on the wing.

Claude Hunt looked at this chap and said, 'I imagine that you are from the other side of the river. You have no right to be here and you certainly should not have a shotgun'. He took the gun away and handed it to his 'black watch'. The stranger protested, 'Do you know that I am General Smuts?' Disbelieving, Claude Hunt put his hand out and said, 'Welcome General, I am the Archbishop of Canterbury.' The old man said he really was General Smuts, he knew he shouldn't be in Rhodesia and that he was staying at a safari camp on the opposite side of the river with the Governor-General of South Africa (then the Earl of Clarendon), Lady Clarendon and a party of VIP guests.

Claude Hunt recalled that he had heard some talk about this some time ago. In apprehension, he asked General Smuts if he could accompany them to their camp to provide his identity. Smuts was charming, and agreed to do that, if he could take his gun out of the hands of 'that black policeman' and wouldn't Claude like to stay and have dinner with the Government House party? Honour was satisfied, they got back over the Limpopo, Smuts identified himself and they had a splendid dinner.

My father, who was a great churchman, built a small church, what we called 'the chapel', on the farm. Constructed of farm bricks with a mopane pole thatch roof, it seated about twenty-five people and was situated among the farm buildings. Depending on the wind direction, we called it either St Stephen's in the Sties or St Martin's in the Maize. The Bishop of Mashonaland, Edward Paget, cousin of the famous English general, consecrated our chapel.

On a typical Sunday morning we had to work efficiently and quickly. We tested the arsenic solution for the cattle plunge dip and dipped the whole herd against tick infestation, which had to be done weekly. Immediately afterwards we had to write up the work tickets for everyone employed the previous week and finally tidy and ready ourselves for church.

Once a month the parson in Gatooma travelled some twenty miles to celebrate matins or communion here with a congregation of neighbouring farmers and miners. Our Anglican priest was responsible for a parish of about 2,500 square miles. The building lasted about twenty-five years before termites destroyed the roof, and then my brother and I rebuilt it.

The Anglican Cathedral in Salisbury had been built of granite blocks but when funds ran out ordinary cement blocks were used. A small group, including Humphrey Gibbs, Sir Ronald Prain and my father, raised the funds to complete the building with stone and to erect the bell tower. The bell came from a Royal Navy destroyer.

– 2 –

Early Years on Handley Cross

Sunn hemp-maize rotation • Maize • Ploughing match • Cotton
• Suri Suri dam • Irrigation • Hand-over of the farm

I have already mentioned that Handley Cross had a high percentage of arable land with deep, rich red soil, but no surface water. Boreholes were not very productive. The whole area had been prospected by small-scale gold miners but, because of the absence of electricity and pumping equipment, the miners could not go much deeper than sixty feet before they ran into water problems. They would then move on to another reef.

Chakari is notoriously prone to drought, and if there were two droughts in succession, we could not rely on maize for our main income and it became difficult to survive financially. Some form of diversification was essential and after the war we started to use the water from the gold mine shafts for small-scale irrigation schemes. These disused mine shafts gave us a good water supply.

Over the years we cleared and stumped about 1,000 acres. We continued for some time with the dairy herd and the cream cheese project and became one of the first producers of hybrid seed maize.

There was no compound fertilizer as we know it today. All we could get was raw rock phosphate which came straight out of the phosphate mine. Superphosphate was not available and the phosphate release to the growing crop from raw rock phosphate was very slow. Later, the milled rock was treated with sulphuric acid to increase the availability of the phosphate once in the soil.

Rates of phosphate application were low and we had no potash or nitrogenous fertilizer, so we grew a crop called sunn hemp (*Crotolaria* spp.). This is a legume capable of fixing nitrogen from the air and transferring it through its root system into the soil, and it was our substitute for nitrogenous fertilizer. It was a very tall, dense and prolific plant and when we ploughed it under in the autumn it helped to keep up the humus level in the soil, although its effect did not last more than one or two seasons.

We used to do a rotation of one year's maize and one year's sunn hemp to try and keep the fertility levels correct and the soil texture friable. The whole sunn hemp crop was then ploughed under. It was a difficult job with disc ploughs, as the plant was some six or seven feet high. The decomposition of this mass of vegetable material was valuable, and it was a great sight to see a span of sixteen oxen pulling a three-disc plough, turning it into the soil.

My father with his team of 16 oxen and three men,
'ploughing under' the crop of sunn hemp.

The oxen were inspanned at about 4.30 a.m. and worked for three or four hours, after which it became too hot and they were outspanned. We would start again in mid-afternoon and, in good conditions, a span could plough about three acres a day. A youngster, called a *makokere*, led the span, keeping the front oxen straight in the furrow. Seated on the plough was the ploughman (called a *fielerman*) whose job it was to ensure that the plough depth was deep enough and to steer the plough along the last furrow. Then there was the driver, who knew each of his oxen by name and with his long whip kept them all leaning into the yoke. If the driver spotted one not pulling his weight, that ox would get a crack of the whip a couple of inches off his ear, which helped him to concentrate on the task in hand. The three-disc ploughs – the Dragoons and the Hussars – that we used were made by Ransomes, Simms and Jefferies of Ipswich, UK.

In October, about a month before the usual onset of the rains, we had to prepare the land for the planting of maize. We used to 'check-row' the land with hand labour, which entailed using a light wire chain, 70 yards long. The land was laid out accurately and geometrically in blocks of 70 yards by 70 yards with a line every yard, so a block equalled an acre. Along the chain a hole was dug at three-foot intervals. These holes were sufficiently large to be able to catch rainwater and to act as a marker where the seed could be dropped and covered. When the crop had emerged, you could see how accurate the check-rowing had been. When it had been done correctly, the lines would be quite straight and you could see across at 45° and even at 22.5° across the land.

It was important to be accurate in setting the ox-drawn cultivators which killed the weeds mechanically between the lines of maize. This left only a few inches around the plant to be hand-hoed. Sometimes, when the weeds were bad, we cross-cultivated the lines in the opposite direction. The cultivators, most of which were made by Avery in Australia, were drawn by a couple of oxen with a leader. We fastened a wire-mesh nosebag on to the oxen to prevent them snatching too many of the young green maize plants as they went down the line. This cultivation was an effective method of weed control, leaving a minimum of hand work to be done.

When the crop was mature, workers cut the maize plants by hand and put them in stooks. Each stook line across the land was 50 to 60 yards apart. Once the maize dried, a gang of reapers stripped the cobs from the stooks straight into grain bags.

We had a small trailer which carried a two-hole maize sheller, powered by a small diesel Petter engine made in Yeovil, Somerset. Reapers would hoist the bags on to the trailer and tip the cobs down the two chutes into the sheller drum. The shelled cob went out one side and the clean grain was bagged on the other side. The trailer had a scale, and once a bag weighed two hundred pounds it was sewn up.

In the evening we loaded that day's shelling on to a six-ton ox-drawn sprung-tyre trailer made for us by I. K. Lockie, whose forge was immediately opposite the cathedral in Second Street. The trailer travelled for about six hours to the first point, which was half way to Hartley, where the team of oxen outspanned to rest, and a second span took it straight away to Hartley station, arriving in the early hours of the morning. The maize was off-loaded and a third span already there made the return journey to the halfway point, while the second span had a day's rest in Hartley. The rested first span then took the empty trailer back to the farm. So there was a continual trailer circulation 24 hours a day, which enabled us to dispatch our daily output of reaped and shelled maize.

In the 1930s, Southern Rhodesia had a special niche market and was able to produce 100 per cent guaranteed white maize for the Brown and Polson cornflour company in Britain. Product supplied to them had to be pure white and could not be contaminated with yellow maize. The extra price that our pure white maize fetched was so valuable that legislation was introduced prohibiting the production of yellow maize in the grain-growing areas of the country, to rule out the risk of cross-contamination. That regulation lasted for many years, but yellow maize is now grown in the country for stock feed.

In 1937, my father decided that it would be fun to have a ploughing match. These took place all over the world but so far not in Rhodesia. Competitors came from neighbouring farms, loading their ploughs on to a wagon and transporting them to Handley Cross. On the morning of the great day, each competitor ploughed a small piece of land, which took about two hours.

The judge, who came from a different district and knew none of the competitors, took into account the straightness of the furrows, their depth and the general neatness and speed with which the job had been done. There was great excitement among the workers from the different farms who came to support their teams, and in the evening there was much merriment and feasting with plenty of beer. The next day the ploughs were loaded up and everyone went home. It became an annual event until war broke out. After that, with the advent of tractors, the ploughing matches changed from ox-drawn to tractor power.

The *Rhodesia Herald* of 24 April 1968, reported that the first ploughing match with tractors was to take place. Mention was made of the original Handley Cross ox-ploughing match organized by my father. In that article, my father paid tribute to the part the trek oxen had played in the history of the country.

In the second year, the competition was widened to include a reaping bee. After the starting shot, each competitor set about reaping his cobs, bagging them and, when 60 minutes were up, his cobs were carefully weighed. The competitors worked energetically, and often one hour's production almost equalled a normal day's work.

Cotton became an important part of the cropping programme on Handley Cross, together with certified hybrid seed maize, maize for livestock feed, and soyabeans. In the early 1950s we expanded our cotton production until we were growing 300 acres – but that was after we had installed our new irrigation system. The frequent droughts made arable farming hazardous,

We built on Handley Cross a Norman pigeon house, of most unusual design. The photograph shows it was hollow and the pigeons had entry points at little doors all the way round, and then made their nests inside. The whole building was hollow in the centre and one could climb up and put a hand in from the opposite side when there was a demand for some squabs. Our biggest predators were the owls which came in through the little doorways. There are many such pigeon houses, or pigeon lofts, in Normandy and with a different design, some huge ones in the Middle East, housing up to four or five thousand pigeons in caves.

Our Norman-style pigeon house.

and it was essential to find a substantial water source to augment our three irrigation schemes of between five and fifteen acres each, run with water from disused mine shafts.

Some years later we had our first cotton-reaping competition on Handley Cross, an idea received with great enthusiasm by farmers and pickers alike. Competitions were held in the different districts, with each area bringing their top pair of reapers to the finals. It was remarkable how much cotton a nimble pair of hands could reap in the two-hour period. The cotton was spread on a grading table and marks were deducted for contamination by leaf or stem.

Government hydrological engineers did a survey to site the Suri Suri Dam, which was seventeen miles away on a reasonably reliable river. Its main purpose was to ensure water supply for the Dalny Mine, still one of the highest yielding gold mines in the country. They built the dam, and a canal was made to take the Suri Suri water by gravity as close as possible to the mine.

The canal ran through Handley Cross. The water then went into a small holding dam and was pumped to the Dalny Mine. Fortunately, this was close enough, so we were able to pump water from the holding dam into our underground piping reticulation system. Water meters were installed so that our off-take was measured accurately.

The difference in construction costs between a two cusecs canal and a ten cusecs canal was marginal, because the bulk of the cost of the canal was for land clearing along its route and excavation and was much the same for both. So Water Affairs built the larger canal and we benefited.

Large-scale irrigation was new in our area and farmers were reluctant to participate or to support and guarantee the scheme financially. We therefore guaranteed to take 80 per cent of the water for twenty years, and so the income generated by the mine and ourselves justified government's expenditure and helped to realize Dalny's full potential.

We now had the chance to put virtually our entire arable acreage under overhead irrigation. It was a major investment, but we decided to go ahead and installed two 250-horsepower electric pumps. Wright Rain, our contractors, then had to plan how to distribute the water. They used asbestos pipes for the main underground reticulation, from which we had off-take hydrants every sixty yards. The water was taken from these hydrants via moveable aluminium piping to the overhead sprinklers. Fortunately, the big blocks of land were so flat that it made sub-division quite simple.

A farmer in the UK, Jack Wright of Ringwood in Hampshire, had been developing sprinkler irrigation systems. He had won a Nuffield scholarship, which took him to America to study new irrigation techniques. Being a dynamic person, he carried out his own research and development in Britain, and having set up a thriving company there he sought opportunities elsewhere. He came to Rhodesia and established the Wright Rain (Rhodesia) group, which pioneered overhead irrigation systems from Mozambique to Northern Rhodesia. He flew throughout the region, from project to project, but was tragically killed in a flying accident. His company lives on, and 50 years later we are still using Wright Rain products.

In 1946 my father took a most generous decision to hand over his farms to my brother Martin and me and to retire, if you could call it such, to Salisbury. Here he embarked on a different career, consulting for major companies such as the copper mines in Northern Rhodesia, who asked him to advise on the likelihood of that country being able to feed itself.

My father wrote a comprehensive book called *Approach to Farming in Rhodesia* as a gift to the returning soldiers from the Second World War who were going to start farming and needed some wise and practical advice. This book is quoted sometimes even today. One of my grandsons recently found a copy in the library at Columbia University.

After he retired from Handley Cross, my father was determined to keep

My father, L.T. Tracey,
at the end of the war, when he
retired from Handley Cross.

Evelyn and Leonard Tracey
in retirement.

one pace ahead of his two sons and decided at the age of 56 to take his private pilot's licence. He succeeded in this and, although he flew very little, he was very proud of his achievement.

In 1964 he was asked to chair the Freedom From Hunger movement in Rhodesia and also the local branch of the international charity Oxfam, both of which are still very active today.

My father also chaired a number of farming companies, some of which were British-owned. These investors were excited by the prospects in Rhodesia and wished to farm on a large scale here, but they needed strong local direction.

When my mother was well into her eighties, she could not be left alone for long periods. My father, like his grandfather before him, took up wood-carving. He made a beautiful mantelpiece, which later had pride of place in our living room at Mount Lothian, our farm in the Enterprise farming district.

At the age of fifty, my father could still have continued on Handley Cross for many years, but he believed that Martin and I should be given our heads, which was the most generous start two young men could have. At the time, I remember reading a verse that I thought was particularly appropriate. To this day it hangs in a frame on my bedroom wall.

'Old man,' cried the fellow passing near,
'You are wasting your strength by planting there.
Your journey will end with the ending day
And you never again will pass this way.
You have crossed a chasm deep and wide –
Why plant a tree at eventide?'
And the planter raised his old grey head,
'Good friend, on the path I have come', he said,
'There followeth after me today
Two youths, whose feet will pass this way.
They have not come to twilight dim.
Good friend, I am planting a tree for them.'

Anon

– 3 –

Wendy

Marriage • Our first daughter

In 1946, on 10 August, Wendy and I were married in the Cathedral of St Mary and All Saints in Harare. Her father, who had served in the trade section of the British Foreign Office, had moved around the world, and his longest posting before he came to Rhodesia was in Cape Town. Wendy had started her education in Cape Town and finished it when she came to Salisbury. She then joined the nursing service at the Salisbury General Hospital where, in 1946, she duly qualified as an SRN.

She had been born in Trinidad, where her father had been posted, and we always teased her about her birth certificate. Apparently in Trinidad when something unusual happens it is recorded on the birth certificate and in her case, stamped in capital letters across the birth certificate is the word 'legitimate'. In response to our teasing she always challenged me and asked me to prove my own legitimacy.

Our wedding, 10 August 1946.

We met through a distant cousin and friends. Wendy and her parents used to come down to the farm fairly frequently. But my visits to Salisbury were few and far between and I have always regretted that we didn't have a traditional courtship and engagement because of distances and the war.

Father Victor, who was dean of the Anglican Cathedral in Salisbury, a member of the Community of the Resurrection and a family friend, married us. Compared with weddings nowadays it was a very low-key ceremony – so many people were away, fuel was still very difficult to obtain, and I think we had only about thirty people in the Cathedral. The shops were empty and a large proportion of our wedding presents was Pyrex glassware, which was about the only thing you could buy.

We borrowed my father's Oldsmobile and set off for our honeymoon late that afternoon, stopping at the Mvuma Hotel for the night. I don't know how many minus stars the Mvuma Hotel had at that time, but it was nothing like what the young expect nowadays.

The next day we motored on to the Mountain Inn in Louis Trichardt in the Northern Transvaal, through the pass in the mountains. The old Oldsmobile lost its headlights along the way and a kind motorist agreed to drive in front of us so that we could follow his light, and we travelled twenty or thirty yards behind. When we went back the next day to see where we had driven, we were horrified at the precipitous drops and bends. If we had known, I think we would have stayed on the side of the road until sunrise.

The Mountain Inn in the Soutspansberg mountains was lovely and cool. The next day we drove down through Tzaneen with miles and miles of gum and pine trees to the first camp in the Kruger National Park, where we spent four or five days. We had forgotten to put a can opener into our picnic basket and had to use a sharp quartz stone to prise open the first tin, which served as the kettle to make tea once we had eaten its contents. The cooking part of the beginning of our married life had had a somewhat inauspicious start, but we bought the missing equipment at the next village stall. And so we came back to Handley Cross ten days before the Salisbury Show and together went straight into farming.

So many people have paid great compliments to Wendy for the way in which she graduated from a nursing career and city life to Handley Cross. She quickly picked up whatever reins were loose and entered wonderfully into the farming activities.

Our first daughter, Elizabeth, was nearly three weeks overdue and Wendy became impatient and asked our GP, Dr Bellasis, what he was going to do. He cheerily advised her to take a couple of tablespoons of castor oil when she went to bed that night and he was sure everything would start conveniently the following morning. But he was wrong. At 2.30 a.m., Wendy dug me in the ribs and said that we had better get a move on and get to the maternity home quickly.

We were in the middle of a very wet spell, the gravel roads were atrocious and there was a lot of storm water lying about. Five miles from home, we came over a rise to find that rain had flooded the road and we were faced with sixty yards of 18-inch-deep water ahead of us. There was no alternative but to pray that we would get through. The car surged into the water, the splash soaked all the spark plugs and the engine died on the spot. I leaped out, got the bonnet up, dried the spark plugs with my handkerchief, pressed the solenoid to start the engine – it was still dead. I whipped the top off the distributor and found there was water there, which I dried and, thank the Lord, the engine responded and we got going again; otherwise, Elizabeth would have been born in a ditch on the side of the road. Wendy's urgings gave speed to my wings and we got to the maternity home in Gatooma with only five minutes to spare before Elizabeth arrived. The good thing was that Elizabeth was born not on 29 February (that year was a leap year) but on 1 March, so she continues to have proper birthdays.

The rest of the children were born in far more normal surroundings and had a wonderful farm upbringing, coupled with excellent education here, in South Africa and in Britain. The first of our grandchildren was married shortly after Wendy's death, and two more of our grandsons were married in October 2006. I am hoping that the arrival of great grandchildren will not be long delayed but it seems that the younger generation are more interested in getting their careers established and starting a family a little later.

Wendy feeding one of the orphaned duikers at Handley Cross.

– 4 –

Farming at Handley Cross

Seed maize • Soya beans • Vegetable and flower seed • Tomatoes • Mint •
Jerseys, Charolais and Limousins • Wiltiper sheep • Pigs • Pigs to Greece
• Jack Malloch • Locusts and disease • Salisbury Show • Farm managers

During the Second World War, in 1943, the renowned maize plant breeder Harry Arnold asked me to work with him in a small way with the first production of hybrid seed maize. Shortly after the war, Alan Rattray, who had a degree in plant breeding from Cambridge, joined him. The industry grew and grew, stimulated by the improved yields from hybrid seed; new hybrids were continually developed at the Salisbury experimental station. The expanding use of hybrid seed led to a marked improvement in yields in the commercial maize sector.

Alan Rattray bred a hybrid called SR52 which at the time was acknowledged to be the best white hybrid maize cultivar in the world. It won major awards at international shows, particularly at the Toronto Royal Winter Fair. These two men will never be forgotten for their research. Alan Rattray was later awarded the Farming Oscar for his work.

In the early 1980s, growers decided it would be better to control and

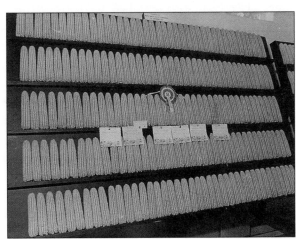

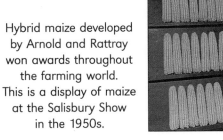

Hybrid maize developed
by Arnold and Rattray
won awards throughout
the farming world.
This is a display of maize
at the Salisbury Show
in the 1950s.

own their own research and breeding programme. A plant-breeding station was established in the Enterprise Valley, not far from our Mount Lothian farm. As a tribute to these two men, it was called the Rattray Arnold Research Station and it now also does work on other crops such as soya beans, sunflowers, sorghum, millet and groundnuts. This independent and grower-owned station was and still is funded by the Seed Maize Growers Association.

In 1946, when my father handed Handley Cross over to me, I could not understand why the plant breeders in our Ministry of Agriculture dismissed the opportunities to develop soya beans, which are such a valuable source of edible oil and protein. Only two varieties were being grown in this country at that time and no breeding work had been done for years.

Soya beans were being widely grown in the USA and Brazil, in exactly the same areas as they also grew maize. One of the reasons for our not growing soya beans was low yields as we did not have varieties suitable for our day length. Soya beans are photosensitive in that each variety will produce seed only if the number of daylight hours is suitable for that variety: a variety bred for 14 hours of sunlight will not produce if it is grown in a 12-hour sunlight zone. I found a variety that grew well in the southern states in America, the closest to our day length. If that variety had been grown further north, it would not have been daylight-compatible and yields would have been reduced.

I got in touch with the soya breeders at Beltsville, the major USA research complex near Washington, but there was not much research being done on soyas grown in other countries at a similar latitude. We went ahead with our own plan and imported four cultivars from the southern states. The plant breeders had recognized the importance of having the pods set three or four inches above the ground so that, when the combine knife cut the plant, none of the seed was left below. Moreover, because a period of three to four weeks is normally needed to harvest a crop of soyas, it was important that the mature seed would stay on the plant for that time without shattering and losing its grain.

Two people in government here – Ned Kerr, who was head of the Seed Services Department, and Jack Humphreys, in Research and Specialist Services – were very encouraging and helped us to lay out trials of the varieties which we had brought not only from America but also from Colombia, Brazil and West Africa. The work we did on Handley Cross stimulated the government plant breeders, who then stepped up their efforts and developed new varieties.

Soya beans can be harvested mechanically and, because of the demand, prices were usually good; soyas' yield was half that of maize but the price was usually at least double. Soya beans are now the most important oil-seed crop in this country. Soya supplies a large part of our edible oil as well as soya cake for livestock.

We were farming seed maize, maize for livestock, and soya beans, but we needed an extra crop. One day Ned Kerr, who was well acquainted with the English seed market, approached us. He told us that Suttons, one of the oldest of the vegetable and flower seed houses in the UK, wanted a very small area of their latest variety tomato release to be grown in isolation. They offered such a good price per gramme that we wondered whether it was a seedless tomato. It was not, of course, but they grew well. That seed crop helped establish us with Suttons and other companies in the seed market in Britain.

At the same time we had an approach from one of the British vegetable seed breeders and distributors, Tozer and Co., enquiring if we could produce a lettuce seed guaranteed to be free from the seed-borne mosaic virus. This virus is carried by aphids and in between lettuce crops can infect a different host plant; then a later generation of aphids can infect the next lettuce crop. It is impossible to prevent cross-infection. But, as no lettuce grew within miles and miles of Handley Cross, we were virus free. We exported enough seed to plant hundreds of acres of greenhouse lettuce in Europe. Our lettuce seed, however, was a victim of British sanctions against Rhodesia in 1965. We could no longer export and had to stop production.

Sanctions led to currency restrictions and Rhodesia could no longer import canned tomato goods from companies like Heinz, Schweppes or Campbell's soups. We were approached by our Ministry of Industry, who asked if we could open a small canning factory, concentrating on tomato products to replace the lost imports.

I had never done this before and had to start from scratch. I visited Britain, where the people from Heinz took me to Britvic, the biggest tomato juice factory in the UK. Its only rivals were in Spain and Italy. I was taken aback by the extent and quality of their processing equipment and wondered whether we in Rhodesia would be able to afford to import all the stainless-steel equipment we would require, or whether we could manufacture it.

Next, I visited the tomato canning factories in the northern Transvaal and then had their tomato cutters, pulpers and screening units copied in this country, which they helped us to do. The tomatoes were passed under high pressure jets of water to clean them. Then they went into the cutter, which crushed the whole fruit, and the pulp was passed over the first of two screens, which eliminated skin, stems, seed and any foreign material. Next, the juice went through a coil of circular stainless-steel tubing, which was inside a hot-water tank. Immediately after we heated the juice we canned it in sizes varying from a small retail pack to a can that held just less than a gallon. We had a seamer or can-closure unit made up by the Metal Box Company which gave an air-tight seal. Because the juice went in hot, it contracted as it cooled and created a vacuum. The cans then went into a huge autoclave where the final sterilization took place. After being subjected to high temperature in the autoclave, the cans were put into a cold-water shower to drop the temperature as fast as possible. This gave the product a shelf life of at least twelve months.

We had to learn this process the hard way, making mistakes as we went. We grew the tomatoes ourselves and so had the advantage of picking fruit in the morning and canning it the next day. This gave us an edge over the big factories, whose tomatoes were older by the time they could be processed. We grew an Italian variety of tomato, Roma, which produced a kidney-shaped fruit, with less flavour but higher solids than a salad tomato. After cooking and canning, it was superb.

You may have noticed that a bottle of tomato juice which has stood for some time often has half an inch of clear liquid at the top of the bottle, which is undesirable. This occurs when there is a delay between extracting and heating the juice, which allows an enzyme to develop. To neutralize it, the juice must be heated as quickly as possible after extraction.

The products in demand ranged from tomato juice and tomato cocktail to whole peeled tomatoes, tomato soup, and tomato purée. The workers in the plant suggested that we make a product that would appeal to them, so we put all our slightly blemished fruit, together with 10% of chopped onions and one red hot chilli, into each can. This produced a very tasty relish. We had our own labels printed for this relish, which in Shona is called *tsumo*. Subsequently other factories made *tsumo* and until recently you could buy it in any Zimbabwe supermarket. In order to produce this range, we soon found ourselves working an extra shift.

Because of sanctions and the consequent dearth of imports we had a monopoly, but we did not believe we could withstand competition from the international brands that had so many advantages over us. Consequently, when I was in the UK in 1971 and heard Sir Alec Douglas-Home speak in the House of Commons about the Home–Smith agreement, I heard warning bells that a political settlement, which could result in the removal of sanctions, might be reached. I could not see how our tomato-processing plant could possibly survive such a development, so I started looking for a buyer for our factory and recipes, which we found and the plant was moved to Salisbury. In fact, I was premature because sanctions went on for another nine years, but so came to an end an interesting part of our farming.

Flower seeds were another major part of our irrigated production. We were contracted to big, international seed houses in the USA. Compared with First World countries, our labour was inexpensive so we concentrated on crops that could not be harvested mechanically, where labour costs put our competitors at a disadvantage. We produced seed of zinnias, calendulas, petunias, morning glory and marigolds.

As I have said, we used an old, deep mine for water, which enabled us to irrigate seven or eight acres. Bringing the water to the land entailed running it down a steep earth furrow. The fast-flowing water eroded the furrow and we had to do something to check the velocity. Mint grew very well in my mother's garden, so we planted mint in the furrow every twenty yards. It grew well there too, and provided just the right barrier to check the speed of the water. In fact, it grew so well that we had to cut it back regularly, throwing away the excess.

One day I saw an advertisement in the newspaper seeking a supplier of herbs for the government's dehydration factory, which produced soups and stews for the army. From then on we cut and air-dried the mint from the furrows. Our production fell far short of the factory's requirements so we planted another small area, which grew well. When the war ended, the dehydration factory closed and so did our market.

I asked the Federation of Overseas Farmers' Co-operatives in Fenchurch Street, London, if they could help us to find a market. They said there was a substantial demand for high-quality dried mint and would we send them a sample. This we did. It fell short of their standards, but they then sent us a sample and said that, if we could match this quality, it would be worth our while.

We had some technical help in the drying process from the Electricity Supply Commission and replaced our ambient air-drying system with heated air-drying in barns, with fans and a heat-exchange unit to reduce energy consumption. Once the mint was dry, we then had to 'rub' it to remove the leaf from the stem, making sure that the final product was not contaminated with small bits of stem lest these found their way into Crosse & Blackwell's mint sauce bottles.

To achieve this quality, we bought a gravity separator or shaker from the UK, which removed all small pieces of stem and any mint dust. The market proved lucrative, and at one stage we had over ten acres growing ten tons of leaf a year; and the price at £400 a ton helped enormously to bridge the gap in our cash flow caused by droughts. We packed the dried mint in special hessian bags lined with tar paper to keep out any moisture, all part of the demanding standards we had to meet, and shipped it via Beira to London.

In 1953, at the time of the Suez crisis, Egypt was our biggest competitor for sales of mint. They started subsidizing their production in order to market it and obtain the foreign exchange. Faced with their substantial price-cutting, and unable to find another market, we had to stop production for the time being. Mint had been an interesting crop, had a lovely smell and our sheep eagerly consumed the stems. We almost produced mint-flavoured lamb!

The land was put back into vegetable production and we supplied the large mines nearby, for their labour force.

Our livestock was a very important part of Handley Cross. We had a pedigree Jersey herd which did well. They were lovely cattle but not as profitable as some other breeds as they produced less milk. Originally we were paid a standard price, regardless of the butterfat content, although Jerseys have the creamiest milk. We negotiated a significantly higher price for Channel Island milk, which was sold in bottles with gold caps. The dairy remained a fairly minor part of the farm but it was one of the parts we loved the most.

The dairy was Wendy's responsibility, and all our children, from when they were in their prams, grew up in the dairy. Elizabeth learned her arithmetic by being in charge of counting out the scoops of food for each cow. At the age of five she knew every one by name. We gave all our daughters a heifer each. Elizabeth was very proud of hers: they bred well and she exhibited them successfully under her own name at the Salisbury Agricultural Show.

One of the saddest moments of our farming life was when we had to say goodbye to the last of our Jerseys, which had to be sent off Mount Lothian after we were evicted in 2002. We knew each other intimately and they were our friends.

Elizabeth with her own Jersey cow, Olivia's Royal Beauty,
imported from Jersey and several times a champion cow, with her calf.

The herd started with ten foundation cows from a top breeder near Cape Town. From the island of Jersey we imported a couple of top-class cows and a young bull, who travelled by sea. A little later, we imported a one-week-old bull calf, by air. I collected him from the airport and put him on the back seat of our Austin Westminster, suitably blanketed.

Driving through Salisbury town centre, I had to stop at a traffic light and a car drew up alongside. The driver glanced at my car and I enjoyed the expression on his face. He leant out and asked:

'What the devil is that in your car?'

'It is a young bull calf just arrived by plane from Jersey,' I said.

'Good Lord! Now I've seen everything!' he exclaimed.

During the early part of sanctions, we had a bit of money rattling around in our bank in the UK. As the sanctions officials were in hot pursuit, we thought we had better change this investment from banknotes to pedigree cattle. Initially we sent our refugee funds to France and went over to select a nucleus of ten in-calf Charolais heifers, which travelled by sea, and we gradually built up our herd. Our biggest problem was in calving, because the calves were so massive. Many cows needed help with calving and ranchers who used Charolais bulls, where cows calved far from home, were at risk. As a result, a prejudice developed against the breed.

They were lovely animals. The continental beef breeds, in addition to Charolais, were the Simmentals, Limousins and Salers. The European breeds were well known for their ability to produce a carcass with a high lean meat content and a minimal amount of fat, which is what the consumers wanted, and the cattle were fast growing.

As a result of the prejudice against Charolais, we disposed of the Charolais herd and started to develop a Limousin one. This breed also originally came from France, although our breeding stock came from America. They were lovely big cattle, brick red in colour and with a high lean meat content, and they grew quickly with beefy conformation. We created the whole herd by importing embryos for transplanting into donor mothers, instead of bringing in live animals.

In America, fertilized ova were taken from top cows. These cows had been inseminated with semen from top bulls. Four days later, the fertilized ova were removed from the uterus and deep-frozen. Sometimes it was possible to get a batch of seven or eight fertilized ova from one insemination. The deep-frozen embryos (fertilized ova) from America were flown to Rhodesia and were each inserted into the uterus of one of our ordinary beef cows. It had to be done at exactly the right period of the oestrus, so we treated our cows with hormones to synchronize ovulation.

We achieved a 60 per cent conception rate through this method and we could bring, albeit expensively, embryos from some of the best Limousin cows in the United States. They were really splendid animals and the herd grew and grew. We were successful with them at the shows, the bulls sold well on the annual sales and the breed grew in popularity with the ranching community. It is interesting to note that, a couple of years ago, there were more cows inseminated to Limousin semen in Britain than any other breed except Simmental.

We wanted, as a new venture on a nearby farm, to develop another Limousin herd. When I was in the United States a couple of years ago I made arrangements to import some more embryos to restart our herd. However, there are alas no qualified embryo transfer technicians left in Zimbabwe to conduct the very delicate and difficult procedure.

When the 'war vets' invaded Mount Lothian and we were given 48 hours' notice to leave, we had to dispose hastily of the entire beef herd, which I believe ultimately went to an abattoir.

The indigenous sheep of Rhodesia and those from the drier parts of South Africa are called Black Head Persians. They originated in the Middle East and are short-haired, slow-growing and have an enormous fat tail, which suits the needs of the Arabs. Under good management they produce a reasonable carcass, except for the excessive fat.

The reason why exotic breeds of sheep did not thrive in Rhodesia was because they all had woollen coats and a lot of our grasses have a sharp, barbed seed. Once this seed got into the wool it penetrated deeper and deeper into the coat. Because the barb could not come out the way it entered, it penetrated the skin, causing tiny pustules. The challenge was to design a breeding programme which would combine the hardiness of the indigenous sheep and the quality carcass of the exotic breeds, without too much wool.

My brother Martin, my sister Bridget, who was on Handley Cross at the time (she started her own farm near Salisbury later on), and I decided to see if we could, under guidance from a geneticist, establish a new breed with those characteristics. At Cambridge University in the United Kingdom I discussed this with the famous animal breeder, Sir John Hammond, a world legend at that time.

In Britain, there is one breed of sheep, the Wiltshire Horn, that, unusually, has no wool at all but a coarse covering called kemp. This fibre is largely hair with little wool and we wanted to use that characteristic and the good mutton conformation by putting them together with the hardiness of our local sheep. We imported a Wiltshire Horn ram and some ewes and started putting the Wiltshire Horn on to the local sheep. The progeny of that breeding was called the F1 generation. Thereafter we were told to breed the F1s in a closed group, with no further introduction from either parent. The geneticists know that generation as the F2 generation. We continued breeding the sheep in the same way, with strict selection at each generation, until after four or five generations we had a high percentage of sheep with the desired traits. We then used that fifth generation as a base for the new breed.

We needed skilled guidance on the whole breeding–selection process and we were introduced to an old Dutch geneticist from Holland who was so interested in what we were going to do that he offered to become involved. He would be able to spend three or four months each year in Rhodesia, so we built him and his wife a small house and he lived on the farm. He was Dr Haagedoorn, recognized internationally for his work in genetics, and we were fortunate to have access to his skills and services.

After about twelve years, sheep specialists visited the farm, examined our records, checked on the different generations of animals and declared themselves satisfied that the resulting breed was now stable and could be recognized as a breed in its own right. We called them Wiltipers, a name combining the two parents, the Wiltshire Horn and the Black Head Persian. They became well known in Rhodesia and were quite widely used. The five or six pedigree flocks, scattered in different parts of the country, were lost with the 'war vet' and land re-settlement problems after 2000. So much work, initiative and expertise were destroyed.

The first job I was given at the outbreak of the Second World War was to take over the running of the pig herd on Handley Cross. My father had started it in 1934 with some English bloodlines that he acquired from Natal, and I had become so interested that I decided we should register the pigs as a pedigree herd and import more bloodlines from South Africa.

At the end of the war, after my return from taking the pigs to Greece (which I will describe later), I spent some time looking at the best pedigree herds in Britain, where, for £45, I was able to buy a top-class young boar from John Ryman's herd. We also bought a young gilt and they were both shipped to Cape Town.

While I was in Britain, I had the good fortune to spend a day with Sir John Hammond, who had helped us initially with our Wiltshire Horn flock of sheep. He had just returned from Canada, where he had seen what he thought was the best Large White herd anywhere, and he encouraged me to obtain a gilt from that source. He gave me a letter of introduction to the principal of McDonald College of McGill University in Ontario. Normally their pigs were used only for experimental purposes and they did not sell breeding stock, but, with the benefit of the introduction from Sir John, they agreed to let me buy one gilt in pig, but they would be unable to send her until the ice on the St Lawrence waterway had unfrozen. This river is the exit to the sea for all ocean transport in that part of Canada and on this particular occasion it took longer to thaw than usual.

As our gilt, McDonald Princess, was too heavily pregnant to get to Rhodesia in good time to give birth, she stayed in the Cape Town quarantine station at the Cape Town docks, where she farrowed. When the piglets were five or six weeks old, they travelled with their mother to Rhodesia. She was an outstanding gilt and her descendants were

McDonald Princess, from Canada, the best pig we ever imported.

sent all over the region and competed successfully at the Rand Show in Johannesburg.

At the same time, technical developments enabled us to use frozen pig semen. There was another good herd in America which was progeny-tested. The Connaught Research Station produced pigs for one of the major pharmaceutical research companies, because there is a great similarity between the stomach and digestive systems of pigs and humans. Thus many drugs are initially tested on pigs. We were able to bring out frozen semen from this herd in canisters of liquid nitrogen that held the temperature at about -40° C and inseminate some of the sows on Handley Cross, widening our bloodlines.

We imported a few more pigs from Britain and were the first breeders in the region to import from Sweden the Scandinavian Landrace pigs, famous for their carcass qualities. We subsequently imported more of these from other parts of Europe and so we had two herds, one of Large White and one of Landrace. These we then developed into a herd of 300 breeding sows.

Handley Cross pigs competed successfully at the Rand Easter Show in the breeding-stock classes which went hand in hand with the sale of breeding pigs. The Rand Spring Show had only young sale boars and gilts and carcasses, which competed first of all live and then, after slaughter, two days later in the carcass classes. We swept the board with champions in both baconer and porker classes. We were up against the cream of the South African herds, and consequently there was wide demand for Handley Cross breeding stock from the region. We sold well at the twice-yearly auctions in Johannesburg, where for many years we held the record for the highest price on sale.

The annual show season was important in our lives each year. The two main show societies were in Salisbury and Bulawayo but there were smaller shows in Marandellas, Sinoia, Gatooma and Umtali. We concentrated on the Salisbury Show, although we occasionally exhibited at one or two of the others. In addition to pigs we showed our Jerseys and Wiltiper sheep. The pigs, however, were our main focus and we would have a full string of Large White and Landrace pigs in the classes for animals under 9 months, 9-12 months, 12-18 months and over. Competition was strong, with up to ten exhibitors. There would be a judge from South Africa or overseas. We did a great deal of work so that our exhibits would look to best advantage in their classes, and we started preparing two or three months before the show. This extra care and attention paid handsome dividends.

Our pedigree pigs won many prizes in local and international shows.

Handley Cross Field Marshal 96th, a Large White, won Supreme Champion in his year at the Salisbury and Bulawayo Shows and the Rand Easter Show in Johannesburg. This pig broke South African price records at the Easter sales. He was bought by the noted breeder Montagu Simpson, and his progeny won the breed championships every year for the next five years.

We put time and effort into training our cattle and pigs to show themselves to best advantage. I remember going to Johannesburg for our first Spring Show where only younger pigs under a year were shown and all were sold on the auction. Additionally, there was a slaughter stock section for cattle and pigs. We had entries in the classes for baconers and porkers. The animals were judged on the hoof and then taken to the abattoirs, slaughtered and judged on their carcass quality, depth of back fat, proportion of lean, and firmness of fat.

Our pigs did not fare too well in the live classes, as they were deemed to be 'unfinished'. I remember telephoning Wendy and saying that we had only come fourth and fifth, but I was confident that we would do much better with the carcasses. The livestock judge kindly came over to me, a young newcomer from Rhodesia, and asked how I had fared.

'Sir,' I replied, 'I came fourth or fifth.'

'OK,' he said. 'I'll give you some tips on what to do in future.' And he did, a great number, for which I was most grateful.

On the Monday, I went in some trepidation to the hall for the carcass competition. The carcasses were arranged in order all round the hall, and there was a table for the speaker at the top. On each side of it was the champion baconer and the champion porker flanked by the best baconer and porker pens. We had swept the board, winning every category. The judge was openly embarrassed and came across to say that he saw now that I was not in need of his advice. But I was grateful to him just the same. Having won all the carcass competitions was a great boost to our sale pigs, which fetched extremely good prices in the subsequent auctions.

We sent the pigs to the Transvaal by rail, making a little bedroom in the railway wagon for Julius the stockman, who knew exactly what to feed them and how to look after them on the journey, and they arrived in good shape. We showed in Johannesburg for a couple of years with remarkable success.

I was always happy to challenge competitors so that we could measure our achievements against other countries. We decided to send some of our pig carcasses to Britain to compete at the 1953 Smithfield Show. We bred four of our best sows simultaneously, to give us some thirty-two weaners of the same age. From this group in due course we selected the eight best pigs, at the correct weight, which we would send to Smithfield. These pigs were slaughtered in Bulawayo, where the first selection of carcasses took place. They were transported in a refrigerated truck, normally used for beef exports, to Cape Town and thence by sea to Southampton. On arrival, they were sent to a bacon factory and the cured carcasses were subsequently sent to Smithfield. Although there were not many entries, we were delighted to win the Commonwealth class for the best four baconers and the best single carcass. The British carcasses competed separately, except in the classes for single baconers, where our best carcass won third prize. We lost by a narrow margin, the scores being 76%, 75.5% and our score of 75%. It was a great achievement and very exciting for us.

We had no help from our own authorities and had to make all our own arrangements and pay our own way. At the conclusion, all the costs were added up and I received a cheque for the balance of four pounds, ten shillings and sixpence for the eight pigs, which just covered our transport, curing and exhibition costs. But the increased prestige was well worth it.

We sold breeding stock all over the region. One consignment flew on a DC4 to Kenya and, with the legendary Jack Malloch at the controls, I flew in a Dakota to Nairobi with thirty pigs, half from our herd and the rest from John Strong's. We also sent two big consignments, each of 200 pigs, by air to farms in Angola and, with more conventional transport, to Natal, the Cape and Transvaal in South Africa, Mozambique, Northern Rhodesia, Nyasaland and the Congo.

Our pigs went even further afield. I learnt that, during the course of the German retreat from Greece in the Second World War, almost the entire population of pigs and cattle had been destroyed. I was faced with the financial responsibilities of my marriage to Wendy, which encouraged me to seek every opportunity to make money. I had an idea and wrote to the director-general of the United Nations Relief and Rehabilitation Agency (UNRRA), who, under the Marshall Plan, was helping to rebuild Europe. I told him that, without any background knowledge, I understood that the pig population had been decimated in Greece. As we had a wide genetic base in Rhodesia, I offered to supply them with a nucleus breeding herd to re-start that industry.

To my surprise and delight UNRRA accepted the idea, on condition that I did the whole job myself, from selecting the stock, chartering a ship and delivering the herd to Thessalonika.

They wanted 40 boars and 360 gilts. Payment was to be a government-to-government agreement. Most countries in the West had pledged to contribute a percentage of their GDP to UNRRA. The cost of the operation formed part of Rhodesia's contribution, so the financial arrangements were between ourselves and our government.

I was 23 years old when the order was approved. I had to find out about ship chartering and managed to charter the whole top deck of a collier going from Durban to Thessalonika. I arranged with Hunt, Leuchars and Hepburn, a big timber firm in Durban, to construct pig pens, which covered the whole deck. They were built of substantial wood, with a malthoid roof, with single pens to accommodate the boars and larger pens which took twenty gilts.

We bought pigs from different herds to supplement our own supply. When we were ready to travel, we had a carefully synchronized plan, whereby pigs from the western side of the country gathered in Bulawayo, were transported to the Midlands where they combined with pigs from this area, and all these were taken to Salisbury to join up with the rest.

At this stage we heard that the ship had not sailed. The crew had gone on strike, because they were not enamoured of the fact that their large air ventilation inlets were plumb in the middle of some of the pig pens. They could not be sure what might come sliding down into their living quarters – and who could blame them? The police promptly arrested them for striking and in the end the ship's owners compromised by offering a bonus of 'smell money' to undertake the trip. The strike was resolved and the boat sailed for Beira.

Consequently we had had the pigs in trucks in Salisbury for 48 hours awaiting news of the ship's departure for Beira, with difficult feeding conditions and no space to off-load them. It was with great relief that we set off for Beira by rail to link up with the ship. The voyage took 28 days.

On the way, a sudden huge wave came up on the starboard and crashed down on top of the timber pig sties. Three pens with twenty gilts in each of them were smashed to smithereens, but fortunately the pigs were washed by the wave towards the centre of the boat and into pens on the opposite side and we didn't lose one pig. One sailor and I were right in the path of the wave and had to really hold on to avoid being washed into the sea ourselves!

Pig skin is very sensitive and our pigs, having been completely soused with salt water by the big wave, came up a beautiful beetroot pink. I had taken the precaution of taking 400 gallons of Carron oil, which is a blend of lime water and linseed oil and very soothing. Within an hour, all the pigs were back to normal.

The pig pens smashed by the huge wave, on our way to Greece.

We sailed through the Red Sea where we thought the temperatures might cause heat stress, but luckily we didn't lose any pigs.

After the Suez Canal, I went to Cairo to report to the head of the UNRRA mission and found to my dismay that no one knew anything about a shipment of pigs going to Greece. No arrangements, such as selecting a farm or organizing food supplies, had been made. I had taken six weeks' reserve of food for the pigs, so this was useful after their arrival in Greece.

Then we set off through the Mediterranean, trying to avoid uncharted minefields. I learned that, if the look-out saw a mine ahead, the captain would not veer to port or starboard, because so doing would quite possibly swing the stern of the boat into collision with the mine. We saw a drifting mine and steered only slightly out of its path. I could see the wretched thing bobbing along as we passed it, about thirty yards away.

Thessalonika had been badly bombed. We could see a number of sunken ships whose masts protruded from the water in the harbour and the quays were badly damaged. After we had docked, I asked the UNRRA official how far the pigs would have to go. He said that the journey would be about three miles beyond the eastern outskirts of the city, six miles in all. I told him how many three-ton trucks we should need to ferry the pigs this distance. To my astonishment, he said that, as pigs had a low priority for motor transport, they would have to walk.

I forewarned the official of the problems associated with animals that had been cooped up for a month, and which were unaccustomed to being herded, let alone walking through an urban centre. If he wanted to do it his way, he would have to sign receipts for all the pigs then and there: I would take no responsibility for marching 400 pigs through Thessalonika. The city was growing fast and there was a great deal of traffic, buses, trams and pedestrians.

During the early afternoon I went into the city to sign off the documents, prior to spending the night on board before flying out to the UK on RAF transport. Returning to the ship with the head of mission, we ran into a traffic jam and waited rather a long time for it to clear which, he said, was unusual. Suddenly the reason for the traffic jam dawned on me – and, sure enough, around the back of the bus in front of us appeared a few of my dear pigs, followed by the rest of the 400, all making their way through the city centre. Hundreds of enthusiastic, cheering supporters were following the herd with catcalls and wolf whistles.

The oestrus cycle for pigs is about 21 days and so about forty of our gilts were ready for service. The boars had been celibate for a month and needed no encouragement, which added to the excitement. The sight of forty gilts, with boars on top of them walking on their hind legs through

Some of our Handley Cross pigs on the quay in Thessalonika.

the city centre, was something that had never happened before. The Greeks were vociferous in their encouragement.

I caught my RAF flight to London, but this was 1946 and the civil war in Greece had just started. We were diverted to Athens where there was shooting within earshot of my hotel, the Grande Bretagne, and that did worry me as I thought I might be stuck there. It took longer than expected to return home but we managed to fly out the next day.

There was another memorable occasion when I transported pigs to a different country. Jack Malloch had been a wartime fighter pilot and had settled in Rhodesia, where he ran his own commercial air charter business. He was a remarkable man, who flew whatever commodity his clients required to many different parts of the world.

In 1957 the Kenya authorities allowed the importation of Swedish Landrace pigs. We had had this outstanding breed in our own herd for about four years. There had been concern about the possibility of bringing disease from Europe into Rhodesia and thence to Kenya. The veterinary regulations were very strict, which was why Kenya was so far behind Rhodesia in allowing pigs originating from Scandinavia to come into their country. In Scandinavia they have a disease, rhinitis, which seriously affects the economic performance of the pig and it takes a long time to eliminate the disease from a herd. But Rhodesian pigs were clear and eventually the permits were granted.

We asked Jack Malloch to fly a Dakota full of Landrace pigs to Kenya. They could take only one attendant, and it was either John Strong, the other breeder and great friend, or me, and I pulled the long straw. We could not get all the pigs on to one flight and so we sent up a few pigs on the previous week's plane with a mixed load of cargo and passengers. Jack Malloch arranged a canvas partition so that the passengers sat in the front cabin and the pigs behind. It was hoped that the pigs would settle down and not get through to the passenger section.

At one stage, a large gilt emerged from the 'pig cabin' and, as pigs are wont to do, worked her way forward and started snouting underneath the passenger seats, to the alarm of the lady passengers, who felt their seats rocking backwards and forwards. Most passengers rushed forward to the aircraft loo. Jack Malloch then radioed Ndola to ask if the veterinary department could look after the pigs until the next week when I would be on the plane. So they landed, took off the offending pigs and completed that flight uneventfully. When I flew up the following week, we landed at Ndola, collected the wayward animals and proceeded equally uneventfully.

I remember that flight exceptionally well. It was in February and the Zambezi had the greatest flood it had ever known. Construction of the great Kariba Dam had started. A circular coffer dam about 250 feet high had been built across the river from one bank to the other, with the water flow diverted around this and through diversion tunnels on either side, allowing construction work to proceed within it.

In spite of the flood, the contractors continued to work within the coffer dam. One final surge of floodwater arrived, however, and the river rose above the height of the coffer dam and submerged it completely. This caused a major delay in the completion of the whole project. Jack flew me over the site to see the fury of that great river going over the coffer dam.

André Coyne was the designer of the dam at Kariba. He was a Frenchman, famous for the big dams he built around the world – sadly also famous for two of his dams which in later years collapsed. He had a shock of white hair and a great sense of humour.

He stayed at Meikles Hotel and at a dinner one night criticized the barbaric behaviour of Rhodesians. He said that he had bitterly complained at being woken by a servant in the hotel at 6.30 a.m. with a tea tray. He preferred, he said, to work late and to sleep late and this bad tea habit was destroying his rhythm. Two days later, in the back of a cupboard, he discovered a notice, 'Please do not disturb', which could be hung outside his door. 'You are', he said, 'an interesting people. I thought I would now escape the horrible morning tea but to no avail because the next morning, after the knock on the door, I received instead a tray with two cups.'

I got to know an outstanding South African engineer, Henry Olivier, very well. He had been head boy of the Umtali Boys High School while his father was working there. He qualified as an engineer in Edinburgh and began a long and outstanding career. His first job was on a hydro-electric scheme in the Scottish Highlands. He was involved in the design and construction of the Mulberry harbour used at Arromanches in Normandy in 1944 by the invading Allied forces. He was also engineer for a major hydro-electric dam in the north of Scotland and was the engineer in charge of Kariba and also Cabora Bassa. His first project in Africa was as the engineer for the Owen Falls dam at the headwaters of the Nile in Uganda and he worked on the giant Indus dam in India. In addition he was very much involved with the Orange River scheme in South Africa.

Back to Jack Malloch, who formed his own company, Affretair, for commercial cargo charter. Regularly he flew to Gabon. The president of

Gabon was a man called Omar Bongo and the country had a seat at the United Nations. When in need, our government could rely on the Gabon vote in the United Nations Assembly. Regularly the Rhodesian government paid him support money in foreign currency, flown up by Jack.

Jack Malloch took cargoes of all sorts around the world, pedigree cattle from Rhodesia to Uruguay, prawns from Mozambique to Spain, flowers and vegetables to Covent Garden, frozen meat to the Middle East.

Angola had become independent and civil war between the two factions was raging. Rhodesian aircraft were forbidden to enter Angolan airspace but that did not trouble Jack, whose aircraft was on the register of Gabon Airways. On one occasion our Minister of Foreign Affairs, Piet 'P.K.' van der Byl, was curious to meet President Bongo and flew up with Jack. They had just entered Angolan air space when Angolan air traffic control told Malloch that he was infringing their air space and should get out. Typically, he proceeded on course, receiving a second warning, which he also disregarded. Fifteen minutes later, air traffic control called to say that two fighter MIG aircraft would now escort him to Luanda because of his transgression of Angola's territorial rights. Almost immediately, two MIGs arrived on the scene. They were more than a match for an old Dakota, but Jack, using his wartime skills, managed to slip and slide through the clouds, evaded them and got out of Angolan air space just in time. The Dakota contained one very frightened Minister of Foreign Affairs, who had suddenly realized that he could have become a prisoner of the Angolan government. Anyhow, all was well. They delivered the cash as a thank you to Gabon for their support when necessary at the UN, but they thereafter always carefully avoided Angolan air space – and van der Byl's curiosity had been satisfied.

Some years later, Jack meticulously rebuilt an old Spitfire almost from the start in a hangar in Harare. He test-flew it and it performed perfectly. He earned the admiration of Air Force men for what he had done and his Spitfire was a source of great interest. One day in March 1982 he took off in the company of Wing Commander Bill Sykes who was flying a Vampire and flew into a cumulus cloud. Nobody knows what happened inside the cloud, but his Spitfire crashed into the ground near Goromonzi and disintegrated, and Jack Malloch was killed. He was a great loss.

Government took over Affretair after independence and provided an incompetent service for the export of flowers, fruit and vegetables to London and Holland. At the take-over, there were three aircraft. They soon stripped one down for spares, leaving two, then cannibalized the second, which left them with only one aircraft and, when that aircraft succumbed to poor maintenance and could no longer fly, Affretair had no aircraft left and went into liquidation.

Jack's nephew, Mike Kruger, then founded the MK air freight company flying Zimbabwean products all around the world. They had a substantial carrying capacity. One of their planes later crashed in Canada just outside the Arctic Circle and another in Nigeria, but otherwise they had an excellent record and their freighters flew many millions of miles.

The constant problems that we had on Handley Cross included swarms of locusts which used to come in the early part of the growing season. If a swarm descended on a crop of young maize, by morning there would be only bare soil. If the maize was only, say, a month old, however, it would grow again. The only way we could try to keep a swarm moving was by burning smudges of brushwood around the land: the smoke would drift across and help to move them on. If you could start burning the smudges early enough, it might even prevent the locusts from landing. Some of the swarms were four or five miles long, and sometimes they laid their eggs when they arrived, which hatched later into 'hoppers' which rapidly grew into adults, giving a double problem. We used to cut brushwood or maize stover before planting maize, and put piles of this around the lands.

The main breeding area for locusts in East and Central Africa is the Rukwa valley between Tanzania and Uganda. Later on, the East African locust control operation was able with aircraft to deal with swarms emanating from Rukwa. Locusts are a thing of the past in Zimbabwe now, because of better international control.

I never experienced the dreaded cattle disease, rinderpest. This could wipe out all the cattle in an area and it broke many farmers. In Zambia some of the Jewish farmers, such as the Wulfsohn and Barnett families, employed hundreds of 'skinners', who went through the stricken areas skinning the dead cattle and drying the skins. Many fortunes were founded on this very unpleasant and smelly initiative.

Lack of knowledge and control of foot-and-mouth disease was a serious problem in the 1920s and is still a problem as I write this in 2007. My father bought a batch of young feeder cattle from Dick Dott of the Angus Ranch near Fort Victoria. Between the time of striking the deal and sending the cattle, foot-and-mouth broke out in that area and all movement ceased, so we had paid for the cattle and could not take delivery of them. The deal had been done through H. Shapiro and Company. Mr Shapiro, an honest man, returned the cheque and said that he hoped my father would come back for another deal when the restrictions were lifted.

Mr Shapiro's son-in-law, Robbie Isaacson, followed in his footsteps running the cattle auction company and was highly regarded in the farming community. Shapiro and Company was later turned into a partnership with the Cattle Co-op Limited. Now operating under the name of CC Sales, they are the main cattle-auctioning business for what remains of the cattle industry. They used to cover the whole country but now most of their sale pens have had to close down.

Between 1970 and 1975, Vec Hurley and I used to lease large tracts of land in the south of the country adjacent to the 2,5 million acre Nuanetsi Ranch, which was owned by the South African Imperial Cold Storage Company. It was very dry country, the grazing was sweet and cattle did well. Our agent who helped run this venture used to buy cattle at the communal area sales and we put them on to the leased land. I recall that one of the people from whom we rented land was a Chinese lady. These cattle did well and we marketed them six or eight months later when they were in prime condition. Vec Hurley had a single engine Cessna and we used to fly down to these rented ranches every month.

In the early days, about 1946, when we participated in the Salisbury Show, we had to take our animals twenty miles to Gatooma by truck and transfer them to rail cattle trucks for the journey to the Salisbury Show Society siding. We had to load all the food, bedding and tack into those trucks and the next day we took our seven-ton truck with all our camping gear and the most special animals by road, arriving in time to meet the train and then walk the animals from the show siding to their pens.

A magnificent yarding of weaners and feeders at the Marandellas Sale Pens.

The Bedford truck was given a thorough spring-cleaning and we set up camp. We ran a tarpaulin up the side, over the top of the truck and down the other side, which provided good shelter. We had two or three beds on the truck itself and the others were on the ground. Wendy, the three girls and I therefore had a wonderful base, close to our animals, for the duration of the Show. We took our old cook, Zuze, who cooked all our meals at the camp, and many of the exhibitors came for a quick fried egg and bacon breakfast, with Jersey milk from our cow exhibits. Quite frequently an exhibitor would ask me to keep an eye on a cow on the point of calving. Professional breeders always liked to have a cow at the Show who was on the point of calving or had very recently calved, to show off her full udder development.

The children had the time of their lives, wandering around the show-grounds, helping with the washing and preparation of the animals, and looking at other exhibits. When they were tired they would kick off their shoes and take a rest, and then head back into the fray. Our eldest, Elizabeth, said that Show Week was, for her, the best time in the whole year.

Pigs used to be judged on a Monday because there were a number of exhibitors who could not cope with their cattle and pig exhibits simultaneously. On the Monday evening we all attended the Show cocktail party, which traditionally was held at Government House. President Banana continued the tradition for a couple of years after independence and then it fell away.

Captain Alec Hampshire came to Rhodesia in the early 1950s and married one of the famous Meikle daughters. Alec and Joan were successful pedigree Shorthorn cattle breeders. When the president ceased hosting the show cocktail party, Alec and Joan stepped in and Meikles Hotel became the new venue. A couple of hundred guests from all aspects of the show fraternity, and diplomats and others, would gather there for a lovely evening. This tradition continued until the land settlement eliminated almost every pedigree herd.

The history of the Meikle family would fill a book – the family still has a large stake in Kingdom Meikles Africa, which owns the five-star Meikles Hotel, and Thomas, Joan's father, was responsible for all the department stores in the country. To this day, the Meikles group is one of the major conglomerates quoted on the Zimbabwe Stock Exchange.

On the Tuesday, each of the cattle breeds was judged separately, and on the Wednesday, the interbreed classes were judged, with the beef separate from the dairy breeds. Only those animals who had fared well in their own breed classes went through into the interbreeds, and there was always a large attendance of interested breeders and farmers to watch the judging. The competition was intense.

Over the years, we won our fair share of male and female championships, with pigs and cattle and their progeny groups. On one occasion, we exhibited our Jersey bull, Cordwell Flying Meteor, which we had imported from Britain and who was Champion Dairy Bull All Breeds and Reserve Champion when competing against the beef breeds. This was a great milestone for us.

Cordwell Flying Meteor.

Many times Breed Champion and Supreme Dairy Interbreed winner, Goldie, bred at St Ouens in Jersey.

We met a man from Jersey who had showed his cattle at the island shows and he gave us a very good tip: half an hour before the bulls joined the line-up for the parade, we drenched them with a couple of quarts of good beer. It put a sparkle in their eyes. You had to time it carefully, in case they became sleepy during the parade, and once they were back in their pens it was not long before they were lying down and fast asleep.

We never won the Thousand Guinea Trophy for the champion bull. Successive droughts and East Coast fever in 1910–13 had had a seriously debilitating effect on the Matabeleland cattle industry and the fortunes of the Bulawayo Agricultural Society. Louis Dechow put forward a plan to fund the cost and crafted a magnificent trophy to be awarded annually to the champion bull of Rhodesia. An Australian, he had been struck by the grandeur of the Melbourne Cup and decided to produce a similar trophy valued at a thousand guineas. His original idea was to get 40 donations of 25 guineas each; in the end, they raised £1 200 from 68 subscribers, of which 20 were firms and organizations, the others individuals. The trophy subsequently manufactured contained over 175 ounces of gold.

On the Friday, the Salisbury Show was opened officially by an overseas or South African dignitary. It was a magnificent spectacle to see so many top-class pedigree cattle on parade on the green grass in the main ring before the grandstands, breed by breed. After the parade, the interbreed judges determined the champion bull and cow from all the breeds, both beef and dairy. Many of the animals were world class.

As a result of the land grab, there remain only half a dozen pedigree herds. There are no pedigree cattle classes at the Harare Show and there is no traditional cattle parade.

The Thousand Guinea Trophy.

The grand cattle parade at the Salisbury Show.

Thousand Guinea Trophy stolen

The Thousand Guinea Trophy was stolen during the night of Wednesday, 18 February 1998, from the Bulawayo National Museum. ... the theft made headline news in the City, and a reward for $10 000 was immediately offered for information leading to the arrest of the culprits. This amount was later increased to $150 000.

In what appears to have been quite a well-planned robbery, some of the gang responsible probably remained behind in the building from the previous day's public hours, before breaking open the display cabinet around 2.00 a.m. Ropes left trailing from a first-floor balcony would suggest that they made good their escape that way, complete with a very large and heavy bag containing the trophy.

In the process of removing their prize they appear to have triggered a silent alarm, which was apparently responded to some five minutes later by the security company responsible for monitoring its signals, but neither they, nor the guard from another security firm tasked with patrolling the Museum grounds, found any sign of the thieves.

Eight days later, however, according to newspaper reports, six men were arraigned before the courts, charged with stealing the trophy. Three of the men were from the one family – Michael Kim Handson , and two of his sons, Sebastian Kim Handson and Gerald Leslie Handson. The other three charged were Brett Dereck Ball, Marven Charles Ismail, and Tremayne Paul Williams.

The State case against them, based largely on finger-print evidence from the crime scene, on the fact that there were confirmed reports of them having purchased the getaway ropes from a particular shop a few days prior to the theft, and on abrasion marks found on the hands of two of the suspects, appeared very strong. Despite several applications for bail, one of which went to the High Court, they were detained in all for eight months pending further investigations.

Then, on 5 October 1998, they were freed when the State announced its intention to withdraw the charges before plea, while further investigations, 'which were expected to take some time to complete', were carried out. The men were warned that they were free for the time being, but would be summoned to court once the State was ready.

Over a year later [1999] it would appear that the State is still to complete its investigations. The culprits remain free, and the Thousand Guinea Trophy would appear to have gone forever.

Whether in the end Handson and Co., or someone else entirely, will be found guilty of this theft, it is clear that they will have achieved a level of historical notoriety quite beyond their wildest imaginings!

Extract from John McCarthy, 'The Thousand Guinea Trophy, 1914–1997', *Heritage of Zimbabwe* No. 18 (1999), pp. 88-100.
That article was based on Chapter Three of Robin Rudd's book, *Show Business: The History of the Bulawayo Agricultural Society* (Bulawayo: Bulawayo Agricultural Society, 1997), pp. 38-54.

In 1948, I was asked to stand for election to the Show Council, and I became the youngest council member by far. I joined a number of positive, enthusiastic people – farmers, accountants, lawyers and business folk – who gave the council a good spread of interests. My first chairman was Col. Sir Ellis Robins, who was later elevated to the peerage for services rendered to our part of Africa (and it was he who had donated the Victor Ludorum trophy I won for athletics at Ruzawi school). Sir Ellis Robins was chairman of the British South Africa Company and later of the Anglo American office in Rhodesia. He was a good chairman, who encouraged initiative.

It was wonderful to see how the Show organization grew. It was without doubt one of the best agricultural shows in Southern Africa. We raised funds to build breed pavilions around the main Smithfield judging arena and also built commercial halls for non-farming exhibits as well as trade and commercial stands for organizations such as the electricity authority, the Tobacco Hall, and halls for fertilizer and chemical companies. Exhibitors of machinery and vehicles used the bright green lawns, and then there were the livestock, including rabbits and poultry, and the industrial, commercial and motor stands. The show was a combination of nearly all sectors of the economy, except mining.

In 1996 HRH Prince Edward presented Wendy and me with a silver rose bowl for exhibiting at the Harare Show for fifty consecutive years – a record never surpassed at any major show. Hamish and Jean Smith jointly held the record with us and a similar presentation was made to them.

HRH Prince Edward presenting Wendy and me with the silver rose bowl for exhibiting our livestock at the Harare Show for 50 consecutive years.

But, since 1997, the Show has been a travesty of its former glory. Because of the seizure of nearly all commercial farms, lack of veterinary control as a result of lack of discipline and mismanagement by the Ministry of Agriculture, and the consequent spread of foot-and-mouth disease, there are no livestock exhibitors. No breeding cattle. No fat bullocks. No pigs. No sheep. By 2007 most pedigree breeders had been forced off their land. The years of care, improvements and selective breeding displayed at the Harare Show have been blown away in the ill wind of the Land Acquisition Act. The breeders' pavilions were bulldozed and that area is completely devastated.

Now the Show has drum majorettes, some gymkhana events and a medley of commercial stands and parastatal exhibitions. Enthusiasm from the farming side has understandably evaporated. I handed in my resignation as a life vice-chairman of the Show Society. The Show is now a commercial and industrial exhibition, quite different from the agricultural show where we exhibited for so many years.

Meanwhile, at Handley Cross we had been well served by several really good managers.

Ben Driver came from Selby in Yorkshire to join us. He had been working on the Pig Industry Development Association testing station at Selby and had been highly recommended to us by Dr Alex Calder, who was by this time the director of our Pig Industry Board. Ben married, came to Handley Cross, took over the livestock, and made a first-class job of it. He worked for us for over twenty-five years. He gradually gained experience of other sectors of the farm, was promoted to general manager, and was much involved in the development of our Wright Rain irrigation scheme and the cropping programme.

He had been walking along an irrigation canal one day when a dog sprang out from behind the pump house and bit him badly. He went off to the Dalny Mine Clinic nearby to have the wound stitched. The nursing sister gave him an injection, which turned out to have been anti-tetanus instead of anti-tetanus and rabies. She stitched him up and sent him home. Ben told me he had had the necessary injections. But ten days later he started to sicken. He rapidly became seriously ill and was taken by ambulance to Harare, where almost immediately he was diagnosed with rabies. It is said that, once the symptoms have appeared, only one person has ever recovered from rabies. Ben was put into a special quarantine room, which was padded because of the dreadful convulsions that happen to rabies patients. Doctors going in to treat him were heavily body-protected, but they had to go in to give him tranquillisers. No one else, not even close family, could go into the room. He died a few days later.

His wife, Ethel, could not go into the ward and could only see him through a glass window. She said she felt so hopeless seeing Ben inside like a caged animal and knowing that nothing could be done for him. Immediately after the diagnosis was confirmed, Wendy and I and anybody else who had been in contact with him had injections against rabies. It was a tragic occurrence and it happened only a few weeks after Wendy and I had made a special presentation to him for his excellent service to Handley Cross over twenty-five years.

Bob Vetters joined us from Britain, where he had been working on a large poultry-breeding farm. He was a congenial Scotsman, and worked well in developing our poultry section. On my return from Johannesburg one day, I found a tragedy had occurred. Without enough knowledge and experience, Bob Vetters had attempted to braze a vehicle petrol tank, which he should never have done. It exploded in his face, shattered his goggles and severely damaged his eyes. He had already gone to hospital, but they could not say whether he would ever regain any of his sight. After a year, he was sent to the Moorfield Eye Hospital in London, where they were able to repair one eye, to give him three out of ten vision, but the other eye was blind. Immensely courageous, he continued to work for us in other fields, but he could not read precision instruments such as thermostats in dryers or incubators. He wisely married his nursing sister. She was a lovely person, and they eventually went back to Britain.

Shortly before Bob's accident, we had become accredited breeders for the 'Chunky Chick' hybrid organisation near Berwick, which was one of the first of the huge poultry-breeding operations in the United Kingdom. To help us, they sent out a young man, David Cameron, who had been working in their team. We built him a house and imported the first lot of day-old chicks by air – initially from New Hampshire, USA, and then from Scotland. Their carcass conformation, speed of growth and food conversion were greatly superior to the birds that we had been using to produce our broilers.

Then Chunky Chick was taken over by a big group, Ross Trawlers, and we would either have had to join a competitive poultry farm here, as ordinary multipliers, or withdraw, which we did. We closed down our poultry division, because we knew that our ordinary flock could never complete with a hybrid, and David returned to Britain.

In the 1970s I approached the principal of Mlezu Agricultural College, Fritz Meyer. Mlezu was an agricultural college near Que Que, catering for indigenous students, mainly from communal areas. Fritz Meyer was a good principal and Mlezu had a heavy emphasis on practical teaching. The youngsters going through the college went home, after the two-year course, well equipped with a good basic knowledge of farming. I was impressed and asked Fritz Meyer to identify his best student in the second year, and simultaneously I offered that youngster employment on Handley Cross, together with a scholarship to pay for his second year's education.

The student he selected was Ignatius Mangombe, who came top in his final exams. Every year thereafter, for many years, Ignatius would go on my behalf to Mlezu and, with Fritz Meyer, would select a candidate for a scholarship from Handley Cross. Part of the agreement was that the selected students would spend most of their holidays on Handley Cross, fine-tuning the technical agricultural aspects of farming. With the benefit of that extra experience, they almost always came top of their class.

Ignatius started on the livestock, but the aspect of jealousy in African culture very soon reared its head. After three months, he said he could not continue working on Handley Cross because the untrained and often older men that he was working with resented him. I emphasized that, if he was to succeed in life, he must not run away from problems and that he should stick it out. Fritz Meyer wrote him an excellent fatherly letter and Ignatius did stay.

Gradually Ignatius worked himself up from livestock into the cropping and management side, and ultimately he became general manager of the farm after Ben Driver's death. Ignatius was with us for twenty-five years and retired only because he developed diabetes. He came with us to Mount Lothian where he was much involved in all the new developments, and we were sad to lose him.

We had a bright young man called Zuwanai working on Handley Cross, operating the market garden tractor, who had an interesting background. His mother, Marshu, married, but after two years there was still no sign of any offspring. As often happened in such cases, and with no modern laboratory techniques, she and her husband accused each other of being responsible for failing to produce a child.

The husband had paid *lobola,* the bride price which a young man has to pay before he is allowed to marry the girl. He alleged that, because she was infertile, he should get his *lobola* back. The girl's family, of course, said that the fault was entirely his, so the dispute went to the local headman for resolution.

African custom is often quite logical. The headman discussed with the elders who was the best family man in the area and she was ordered to go and live with him for three months. He had already had eleven children and his ability could hardly be challenged. The local family man made no objection to the arrangement. At the end of three months the old wise women in the village made their examination and declared that she was pregnant to the family man. From that evidence, the headman decreed that the fault was with the husband and that he would not get his *lobola* back. In due course a son was born to Marshu. When this baby, Zuwanai, grew up, he worked on Handley Cross as our market garden tractor driver. The actual father of the child was a driver called Jakalaas, who had come up with my parents from Rusape and then worked on Handley Cross for many years.

Not far from Handley Cross was a group of farms that had been bought by Sir Abe Bailey, the mining magnate. Managers were put on the farms and it was quite a substantial company farming operation, with section managers on each farm. In due course Sir Abe decided to disinvest in agriculture and the managers were given the option of buying, on generous terms, the farm they were managing. One of those men was a man called Frank Cadiz. Cadiz is a Spanish name, and the story goes that, on a ship from the Spanish Armada which was wrecked on the Irish coast, was a man named Cadiz. He settled in, married an Irish girl and the name persisted. His descendant, Frank Cadiz immigrated to Rhodesia and worked in our area for a long time.

Something which remains in my mind from those days is the magnificent exhibition as part of the 1953 Rhodes Centenary celebrations. Her Majesty the Queen Mother opened the exhibition at the National Gallery in Salisbury. That exhibition still amazes me, that these wonderful paintings should have been lent to our Gallery, paintings by Gainsborough, Reynolds, Augustus John, Turner, Brueghel, van Dyck, Rembrandt, Constable, Rubens, El Greco, Corot, Degas, Monet, Renoir and Picasso.

– 5 –

Wider Interests

RAF training scheme • Nuffield scholarships • The RNFU
• RNFU Labour Committee • Agricultural Research Trust •
Pig Industry Board • Coffee • Farming Oscar • Margaret Strong's speech

Shortly after the outbreak of the Second World War, the Royal Air
Force chose Rhodesia and Canada as prime sites for air training
schemes for their pilots, navigators and air-gunners. Rhodesia had more
hours of sunshine than most countries and Rhodesia and Canada had the
two biggest training schemes. The RAF quickly established nine separate
stations in this country, with full-length aerodromes and with housing,
albeit thatched buildings with hessian sides. They commandeered the
Salisbury show grounds.

There were three separate elementary flying schools, three intermediate
and three advanced. These were at Cranborne, Belvedere and Mount
Hampden near Salisbury, Moffat, Guinea Fowl and Thornhill around
Gwelo, and at Heany and Khumalo near Bulawayo. The trainees were, of
course, unlikely to have friends or relations here. Farmers and townsfolk
gladly put them up during their short spells of leave and many good
friendships developed.

The young men selected for training had been through a very rigorous
selection programme. Only the cream – in terms of IQ, reaction time,
fitness, mentality and personality – were sent to Rhodesia. Many of them
returned to settle after the war.

Academic success, however, was not always a sure indicator. A cousin
of mine joined up in Salisbury, despite having a grave disability when
writing examinations. When he was twenty, his parents thought he should
give up trying to pass his school certificate and accept the reality that he
was not academic. Consequently, he was sent to 'the Colonies' and joined
his Uncle Leonard on Handley Cross, where he proved a rather mediocre
farm assistant. We moved him on to another farm and, after his third
job, war broke out. Within days, he was in the Air Force. He rose to be a

squadron leader; he was in the Pathfinders, did eighty trips over Germany in Bomber Command and was awarded the DFC.

One man whom we got to know well was Group Captain Tap Jones, a fighter pilot, who had led the two British wings in Greece at the time of the Allied evacuation. After a number of kills in the Western Desert, he was shot down with a bullet through his neck. Miraculously, he was not seriously injured, but it was thought best for him to leave the war zone, so he was sent to the headquarters of the Royal Air Force Training Group (RAFTG). His wife and two children had been living in Egypt, but, because of the German advance on Cairo, they had been evacuated to South Africa. When Tap Jones joined the RAFTG his family joined him and they frequently stayed with us. He eventually became Air Marshal commanding the Royal Air Force.

Lord Nuffield, who began life as Mr William Morris, owned a bicycle shop, but expanded rapidly into the motor-car business: he produced the Morris. He amassed a fortune and, being a philanthropist, began the Nuffield Trust, which, among other projects, inaugurated Nuffield farming scholarships to benefit farming communities in the Commonwealth.

The Trust's operations in Rhodesia began in 1946 and Humphrey Gibbs was its first chairman. One or two Rhodesian, and later Zimbabwean, scholars were selected every year from successful men of the younger generation who could disseminate what they had learned.

The Nuffield programme assembled students from around the world, each hosted by an English farming family. For three months, the students were familiarized with farming practice in the UK, and visited the head-quarters of the National Farmers' Union and many different farms. Next, they visited Europe to learn about their marketing systems and better understand the impact of European farming on world agriculture. They then returned to the UK where they spent a week at the annual Royal Agricultural Show.

Afterwards, the scholars separated, each to study an aspect of farming that particularly interested them. They could go anywhere in the world: cotton in Israel, irrigation in the arid areas of the Middle East, or the beef industry in Australia.

Each returning scholar came back with a thorough knowledge of a particular sector; consequently, we developed a core of farmers who were familiar with their subject internationally and who could pass on their experience to others in the farming community.

Funding came partly from within the country, though each scholar had to make a substantial contribution. The Nuffield Trust bore the brunt of costs after the students arrived in Britain. Our young people met scholars from many Commonwealth countries and established lasting friendships.

Nuffield selected Zimbabwe for its biennial world conference in April 1992. This caught the imagination of the private sector, who generously provided the finance required to host it. The conference lasted a week and brought together many previous international Nuffield scholars and worldwide farming leaders. It was opened by Denis Norman, Zimbabwe's first Minister of Agriculture.

Afterwards, the delegates went on a week-long bus tour, visiting cattle ranching, feeding projects, dairies, pigs, tobacco, maize, and the sugar estates. Each night, the delegates stayed with different farming hosts.

In 1980, Mike Butler, our first Nuffield scholar in 1946, took over the Nuffield chairmanship from Sir Humphrey Gibbs. Our relationship with the parent trust had been interrupted by UDI in 1965, and we remained suspended until independence. Then our links were restored and Zimbabwean farmers began to participate again.

No fewer than 42 Rhodesian and Zimbabwean scholars have enriched our community with their knowledge. They were a great addition to the ranks of organized farming and many of them rose to high office. There was strong competition to be selected, and potential scholars had to have a good record in farming as well as being natural leaders. Mike Butler, for instance, became my vice-president on the Cotton Association and went on to lead the Rhodesia National Farmers Union, of which I was a trustee. He served with distinction on many agricultural, banking and other boards and remained an inspiration to us until his death in November 2003.

Nuffield forms a remarkable bond of farming fellowship. If an ex-scholar wants to visit a member country, he only has to let the UK headquarters know and former Nuffield scholars in any country will always assist. The value of Lord Nuffield's fellowships cannot be over-estimated.

The economic collapse in Zimbabwe since the beginning of 2000, with the mortal damage suffered by the farming community as a result of the land resettlement programme, has sharply reduced the number of potential scholars. Inflation and a falling currency have also put the cost of such visits out of reach of most candidates and the scheme has gone into mothballs - just at a time when new farmers need a broadening experience.

Before the 1940s, the farming community in Rhodesia had a number of disparate farming organizations, but during the Second World War it became apparent that we needed a countrywide, all-embracing body.

Humphrey Gibbs, later to be knighted, who was farming in Matabeleland, and John Dennis, from England, who was farming on the edge of Salisbury, were tasked with forming the Rhodesia National Farmers Union (RNFU), covering all areas and all commodities except tobacco, which had its own separate body. John Dennis was the first president with Humphrey Gibbs as his deputy.

The union divided the country into seven provinces, giving wide geographical representation, and also had commodity associations covering crop and livestock production as well as representatives for development projects, labour matters and finance. The RNFU had a president, two vice-presidents and a council elected from the regions and from the different commodities. Government was supportive, as it gave them a single organization to deal with and communications and price negotiations were greatly improved.

The International Federation of Agricultural Producers (IFAP) was formed in 1946. This was a kind of 'agricultural United Nations'. I was in London at the time and Humphrey Gibbs asked me to join him and C. L. Robertson, the Permanent Secretary for the Ministry of Agriculture, at the inaugural meeting. The first chairman was Lord Boyd Orr, who was also the first chairman of the Food and Agriculture Organization, established a year earlier.

When Jim Sinclair was president of the Commercial Farmers Union (CFU), as the RNFU became known after independence, he was elected one of IFAP's vice-presidents. Rhodesian and Zimbabwean commercial farmers derived considerable benefits from IFAP, which linked us to nearly every agriculturally important country in the world. Recently we have not been able to pay our membership fees, given the extreme shortage of foreign exchange. This is just another casualty of our current economic crisis.

> Tobacco farmers had formed their own organization in 1938, the Rhodesia Tobacco Association, RTA (later the Zimbabwe Tobacco Association, ZTA), which continues to this day. It is independent and self-funded, but works closely with the CFU on matters of common interest, such as labour.

I was a member of the RNFU council as Chairman of the Pig Breeders Association. After a few years, I was asked to chair the Labour and the Research and Development committees and shortly afterwards was elected one of the two vice-presidents. Initially, I served under Billy Evans, a very dynamic man who was farming in Zambia. I was about thirty-two at the time and threw myself into the job with enthusiasm, firmly believing in a structure for agriculture that protected and promoted farming as a whole and which could speak with a single voice to government.

The pattern was for a president to hold office for two years and to be followed by the senior vice-president. Following UDI, president Tim Mitchell chose to continue in office beyond the normal two-year stint. Politics had crept into the union, the Rhodesian Front (RF) government found him compliant and was anxious to keep someone in place who would support their policy come what may. Support for the Rhodesian Front, particularly in farming areas, was strong.

The president of the RNFU used to be elected from the floor at the annual congress. At the end of Mitchell's third year as president, pressure developed for change at the top, and I was proposed to follow him. I have never been a member of a political party, so there was some alarm in government circles at the prospect of a more independent president heading the union. This led to a lot of political lobbying and I lost the election by 65 votes to 67, but continued as vice-president. At the next election, the same thing happened.

The farming community had, in the meantime, recognized that it was better for a president to be elected by his peers on the council, who had a better knowledge of the ability of the man. The RNFU constitution was changed and, although I was under pressure to stand for election again, I declined.

As I have said, the RNFU/CFU represented the interests of all commodities except tobacco, and this on occasion called for diplomacy and sensitivity. For example, maize producers wanted the highest possible price, whereas beef producers, who fed their livestock a great deal of maize during the fattening process, wanted maize at the lowest possible price.

Politically, the very independence and sturdiness of the farming community made them conservative and, in some cases, very right wing. Most of them had developed their farms through their own initiative and were concerned by the advancing tide of developments which started in the Congo in the 1960s. At that time many white Belgian refugees passed through Rhodesia and told their horrific stories to the many farmers who helped them on their journey south.

In the 1960s, Rhodesia had a vigorous white community of 220,000. Unlike the whites in the northern territories – who, when they said, 'I'm going home', went to Britain on six months' leave – Rhodesian whites went home every night. Anxious about Harold Macmillan's 'winds of change' and supported by South Africa under the apartheid presidents Hendrik Verwoerd, John Vorster and P. W. Botha, they hoped to stem the flow of economic disaster taking place to the north. This resulted in increasing Rhodesian Front majorities and highlighted the breach between the RF and Britain. The farmers' fears that there could be a repetition in Rhodesia of the events to the north proved only too correct.

The RNFU was apolitical and we acted in the best interest of all commercial farmers, no matter what their political persuasion. One of my responsibilities as vice-president of the RNFU was to chair the Labour Committee. There were no trade unions in farming, but relations between farmers and their workers were, by and large, pretty good, although housing and other facilities urgently required upgrading. The cost of building was the main stumbling block. The politicians regarded farmers as paternalistic because they supplied free of charge all the basic food – maize meal, meat, vegetables and beans. The workers' families were well looked after.

In December 1979, government gazetted regulations on the minimum wage. This was to be paid as cash. Many employers who had previously given food as well as a small wage now had to pay a higher wage so they stopped providing the food. Most farm labourers were poorly educated and the concept of a budget was beyond them. The cash was spent on other things and less food was bought. As a result, poor nutrition became common. Most farm-workers would have preferred the old system of receiving food and a small amount of cash, as opposed to no food and more cash – paternalistic or not.

Wages were low and farm schooling was in its infancy. My brother Martin, a man of very good deeds, constructed the buildings for a primary school on his farm for nearly 400 pupils, which he handed over to the government who staffed and ran it. Martin's wife Jill was attacked and murdered on the farm, at the height of the farm evictions.

During Edgar Whitehead's government, the Minister of Labour was a lawyer, A. E. Abrahamson, who created some alarm by proposing legislation to establish farm-workers' trade unions. Confronted with this situation, the RNFU decided to see if there were any countries in Africa who had such unions. The only one was Kenya. I took a small group of my Labour Committee there, and we spent a useful week looking at the pitfalls, snags, pros and cons of farming trade unions.

The first thing we learnt in Kenya was that 44 per cent of all the organizers and union officials at grassroots level had either been or were presently jailed for having scooped the till clean of all the farm-workers' contributions. This was hardly an encouraging start. The concept of trade unions in an emerging democracy seemed premature and subject to corruption.

Some East African farmers elected to pay their workers' dues directly to the union headquarters, which was known as the 'check-off system'. Those who did not pay direct to the union found that the trade union officials were always getting at their workers, causing trouble and trying to persuade the workers to join the trade union for a fee paid direct to the organizers. It was clear that, if these unions were to succeed, a much better structure and administration were necessary. The workers, who did not understand what a trade union was and how it worked, needed transparency and a simple system.

It was during this visit that I met Tom Mboya, a prominent and forward-thinking young Kenyan politician. I had an hour of absorbing discussion, learning of their development plans for the East African region. He was a Luo, one of the minor tribes in Kenya, much smaller than the dominant Kikuyu. As in most parts of Africa, ethnic tensions were strong, and tragically he was assassinated in Nairobi in 1969. Kenya lost a very good man.

Kenya produced tea, coffee, pyrethrum and dairy products and farmers and corporates had a strong agricultural tradition. They grew excellent Arabica coffee and high-quality tea, and international companies such as Brooke Bond ran big estates right down to Kenya's western border.

In my team, as a tobacco representative, was Piet 'P.K.' van der Byl, who came from an upper-crust, old English/South African family, a fact which he was never reluctant to disclose. He was a great womanizer and spoke English better than anyone who had been up at Oxford. He was a dandy, but highly intelligent, and he knew some of the 'remittance men' in the aristocratic families in Kenya. They were so called because they lived off remittances from their families who did not want them to return and make a nuisance of themselves in Britain, and their regular remittances were just enough to keep them away.

When we visited Kenya, it had been independent for a few years and was recovering from its Mau Mau troubles. Tourism was developing fast. The seeds of corruption and disintegration, however, had been sown.

Having studied the situation in Kenya, my team felt that there were no advantages to having a farm-workers' trade union and that the time was not ripe then for us to follow Kenya's lead.

As a result of the visit, van der Byl, who was very right-wing, decided that he would enter politics to do his best for Rhodesia and to avoid what had happened in Kenya. He won a seat, became a Member of Parliament and thereafter Minister of Information and of Foreign Affairs. Not long after independence, he inherited his father's huge estates around Caledon, in the wheat lands of the Western Cape, so it was no surprise that he returned there permanently in the mid-1980s.

Shortly before independence, when affirmative action and drastic change within the Ministry of Agriculture were inevitable, a group of us felt there was a need to establish an agricultural experimental station where applied research, as opposed to pure research, could be carried out, which would be financed entirely by the commodity associations – maize, winter cereals (wheat and barley), oil-seeds (principally soya beans) and cattle. Producers paid a levy on their production to their parent association, who in turn made a block contribution to the Agricultural Research Trust (ART), which gave us invaluable financial independence and improved contact between farmer and research station. Field days at ART were always well attended and farmers were not slow to use the results from 'their' research station.

John Strong, president of the RNFU and a close friend, was one of the founders of ART, as was Keith Kirkman, who had been active in farming politics and has a very fine collection of Rhodesiana and Africana books. Keith was a Rhodes scholar and is a rare combination of practical farmer and research worker. David Stobart, a second generation Rhodesian with a master's degree from the University of Illinois, was the first chairman. (His house near Mount Lothian was subsequently burnt down by 'war vets'. His workers' houses were looted and they were violently ejected. David and his wife are now in the UK.) I was the fourth founder member.

Some of the associations' reserves were pooled and a farm just north of Salisbury was bought. The Agricultural Research Trust started from nothing. All the capital and recurrent expenditure were provided by the commodities and we never had to go to government for funding. We had to erect buildings, sink boreholes (because there were no dam sites) and employ staff.

Our forecast on the future of agricultural research in general was borne out and there were many personnel changes in the Department of Research and Specialist Services and many good experienced men left the country.

The ART staff were enthusiastic with a get-up-and-go attitude. Seed companies could have their varieties tested scientifically under our conditions and new cultivars from the Zimbabwe Seed Maize Association could be evaluated. The international seed houses were impressed with the quality of our work and were ready to pay substantial research and testing fees for these services.

In 1985, Richard Winkfield was appointed director. He had been in the conservation and extension branch of the Ministry of Agriculture. Richard is one of the outstanding people in Rhodesian and Zimbabwean agriculture and is also a practising Christian. (His son-in-law had a highly productive farm at the top of the Mazowe Valley. They produced 1,500 tonnes of maize, soya beans, wheat and paprika a year and fattened sixty bullocks. This farm was taken by a woman with no farming knowledge, but she was related to a provincial governor. No commercial crops are produced on that farm today.)

ART became self-sufficient through its own production and from fees paid by international organizations for the use of its testing facilities. It is respected throughout the region and overseas.

We have also used marginal land for pasture, buying in 200 weaner steers each year and finishing them on high energy rations and on irrigated vlei pastures.

In 1998 a modern pig unit with 100 sows was established at ART. Norman Kennaird, who had been closely connected with ART, and I were charged with the planning and construction and had great help from Peter Parsons, who had an immense knowledge of modern and scientific pig development. Colcom helped with some of the funding and ART contributed the balance from its reserves. The recording was immaculate. The figures relating to food conversion, speed of growth, minimum back fat have been recorded for every single pig, and we have been enthused by the fact that our results match the best international results in Britain.

The pig unit has made a significant contribution to the finances at ART, which, with the turmoil in farming generally, has come under similar stresses to other farms. Since then the number of commercial pig farmers has declined dramatically and there are now only four or five producers, of whom ART is one.

Nick Brooke is the current director of ART. His parents were murdered in a spate of violence at their farm house, and later the farm was taken away from Nick, who shortly afterwards became director of ART Farm, which remains an example of excellence, especially in contrast to other farms in the district these days.

During the Second World War, half a dozen breeders formed the Pig Breeders Association for pedigree breeds only. In this it was similar to the National Pig Breeders Association (now the British Pig Association) in the UK. I was its first secretary and was active in developing the fledgling industry.

It was my interest in this direction that led to my appointment to the Pig Industry Board at the age of twenty-five, my first public appointment. My father had been a founder member of the Board, retiring at the end of

1946. They were seeking a replacement and the minister of the day asked me to take his place. Subsequently, it was asked whether the producer representative on the Board was a hereditary appointment!

The Pig Industry Board when it was founded in 1937 consisted of E. R. Jacklin, a ministry official, with T. E. Preston from Nyamandhlovu, L. T. Tracey, my father, from Chakari, Frank Neil to represent the bacon factories, A. Hampson from the Chamber of Commerce on behalf of the retailers and grocers, and Dr A. E. Romyn from the ministry, a livestock geneticist. He had taken his degree at Iowa State University. When he arrived there he was told he needed to take a minor study as well as his major. From the list of subjects, he chose folklore or fairy tales, from which his children benefited enormously.

Arthur Cowie was the PIB chairman when I joined the board. He was a civil servant in the Department of Agriculture, liaising for government with the livestock, cropping and marketing sectors. We had representatives from the producers, the consumers and the bacon factories on the board.

The Pig Industry Board was funded by a levy. I soon discovered that none of the levy was actually being used to further the interests of pig producers and almost no research was being conducted. Our accumulated funds, increasing year by year, were being invested on a loan basis with a sister organization, the Maize Control Board. I could see little point in collecting a levy and not using it in the interests of the people who had subscribed to that levy. I had seen how the National Pig Breeders Association operated in Britain and suggested that we should use our own funds to establish a parastatal research organization. We drove the project hard, and the Ministry, who were not doing anything in this field, were relieved that somebody else would take over the responsibilities and costs.

Anchor Farm, in the Enterprise area, twenty-five miles from Salisbury, was bought on 16 December 1963. We paid £5,500 for 180 acres. From a greenfield base, we built the pig research station using accumulated funds, starting with the accommodation for pigs, housing for senior staff, a workers' village, and then putting the arable land under grain crops as food for the pigs. This was an industry helping itself and providing all the funding to do so.

In 1947, the director of the Pig Industry Development Authority in the UK was an outstanding Scotsman, Dr Alex Calder. He was fifty and, following his successful tenure there, was looking for a new appointment. We invited him to have a look and then offered him the job of director of our research station. Being independent, we did not have to conform to government scales and were able to pay him a lot more than even the

Secretary for Agriculture earned. We were fortunate to find Dr Calder, who was internationally recognized. His energy and enthusiasm quickly turned our station into probably the best in the region. The only other agricultural sector at that time to establish and fund itself was the tobacco industry.

As farm manager we appointed a man named Benny Brooks, who had been managing one of the Oppenheimer ranches in Shangani. He worked very well with Alex Calder, and a great deal of credit for the construction and running of the research station is his. At Shangani he had been getting the princely salary of £25 a month.

We built our station to the same specifications as the South African one. All the pig food was mixed at the same centre in South Africa and so it was possible to compare the results, such as food conversion, low fat percentage in the carcass, growth rate and fertility, which we used as a basis for improvement, particularly for the quality of our carcasses. We copied the British system of progeny testing and genetic improvements.

A few years later, I was asked to chair the board, a challenging and rewarding position I held for some twenty years. We had a very good team and we never had to beg government for funding.

After ten years, Dr Calder retired and we had a succession of directors, all of whom had done outstanding work in pig development and research in Britain and who wanted a job in the last few years of their career. David Bellis and Robert Johnson were two of the best.

In 1980 the first indigenous (or black) executive director was appointed. He resigned after it was found that he was using Pig Board food for his own pigs just up the road. Since then the testing station has fallen into disuse, the experimental and research work has largely lapsed and the station is now an ordinary pig farm, making very little contribution to the industry. It helps some new small-scale producers to learn basic pig production and it runs a farm butchery. Many small-scale communal farmers are starting to keep one or two sows, almost all for home consumption, which swells the total number of pigs produced but makes no contribution to exports.

In the early 1960s, Caltex, in conjunction with Harvard University, ran a couple of short courses for top management in the private sector and for very senior officers in the armed forces. I took it as a great compliment to be asked to participate. The courses were two weeks of highly intensive work, with few hours to sleep, and were a very valuable experience. It was interesting that the military participants were invariably at the bottom of the class. If it had been a military think-tank, perhaps we would have been bottom instead.

At about the same time, Robin Fennell and his family arrived in Rhodesia from Assam, where they had been tea planters. They bought land in the south-east of the country around Chipinga and began growing tea and, later on, coffee. Early pioneers such as the Phillips family had been growing tea on the Tanganda Estate in Chipinga since the 1900s.

There are two main coffee species, *Coffea arabica* and *C. canephora* or *robusta*. Arabica is a finer coffee, but robusta fills the demand at the lower grades. Fennell coffee was all arabica and, as they became successful, so other farmers in the area began to grow coffee. The climate, with very little frost, is ideal, as are the soils, and a profitable small crop burgeoned. The biggest coffee-producing country in the world is Brazil, where huge quantities of arabica are grown, but the berries are allowed to ripen and fall to the ground and are only collected at the end of the season. In consequence, they are desiccated and of a lower grade.

In Chipinga (now Chipinge), the coffee is picked day by day as it ripens. The red berries are put into tanks of water, where the fleshy covering of the coffee bean is fermented. Depending on the temperature, this process takes around forty-eight hours. The beans are then washed with fresh water, which removes the outer mucilage, leaving the bean itself. Any diseased beans – or floaters, as they are known – are removed, leaving the good-quality beans which sink to the bottom. The beans are then placed on mesh racks in the open to dry. Once dry, the beans are hulled, removing the outer skin or parchment, leaving what is known as 'green' beans. These are graded and go to a coffee mill, where they are roasted, ground and then 'liquored' to determine quality.

The liquoring process uses a small sample from each bag of roasted coffee. It is an astonishing sight to see a table with hundreds of coffee cups, each filled with a spoonful of coffee representing one sample. The coffee liquorer's job is to take a sip of coffee from each cup, swill it round his mouth and decide on its grade, quality and whether there are any off-type flavours or defects. He tastes each cup, notes the grade, spits out his mouthful and repeats this until he has finished that day's production. The liquorers become expert, and the proof of their competence is the reception our coffee receives from the international markets.

South Africa hardly produced any coffee and was therefore a convenient regional market. The quality of our coffee at the height of our agricultural industry was second only to the Kenyan and Colombian arabicas, and it became well known. Although the crop was small in volume, there was a strong demand and, beside South Africa, Germany became one of our biggest customers.

We shipped coffee to the port of Hamburg into the huge warehouses at the docks and we employed coffee brokers to on-sell our coffee. There was one particular broker, Baron von Zizzewitz, who had been a large landowner in Prussia and had lost his estates when that part of Prussia was absorbed into Russia. He had a lot of sympathy for us in the UDI days – very much a Prussian and very much a military man. He had the courage and skill to penetrate markets we could never have reached ourselves.

Coffee production grew after its introduction in the 1960s and the coffee growers formed a co-operative to market their coffee. However, it ran into cash-flow problems. They took the growers' coffee, but it was many months before it had been sold and the funds were paid to the growers, which meant the growers were short of cash for prolonged periods. The banks were strangely unwilling to fund or to provide sufficient bridging finance.

At this time, I was a member of the Agricultural Marketing Authority (AMA), which was the marketing and control authority for our main agricultural products except tobacco, coffee and tea. It was an organization which in many ways served the country well. It had an outstanding chairman, Bill Margolis, who was the son of a Lithuanian immigrant and who had built up his own family agricultural and industrial business which after independence he sold to Heinz.

Coffee growers were reluctant to surrender their individuality and be swallowed up by a large organization. I had frequently taken international visitors to that almost forgotten south-east corner of Rhodesia, a well-watered and fertile area around the Chimanimani and Vumba mountains, and had a good relationship with the producers. As a result, a group of farmers came to see me to discuss their problems. They needed to join the AMA for its financial muscle, but they were reluctant to lose their independence. They wished to meet the AMA chairman to discuss a possible trade-off. They would join the AMA on condition that I became the first chairman of the coffee board. It was a compliment to me but demonstrated their concern that they might be side-lined as the smallest commodity in a massive organization. The AMA was anxious to be an all-embracing agricultural marketing body, the ploy worked and coffee joined the AMA family.

Production grew and grew, but coffee, as a commodity, has always suffered from under- and over-production in the world markets so producers everywhere find themselves alternating from rags to riches. I enjoyed chairing that commodity immensely. Here were true pioneers putting their own money into their own research with enthusiasm and a get-up-and-go attitude. We were subsequently given meaningful help by the European Union.

However, in 2005 land invasions in the area escalated and farms were overrun. The European Union were funding a lot of the research and development work. In one week, two very good producers were ejected from their coffee farms immediately adjacent to the coffee research station. The European Union pointed out to government that they could not seize farms on the one hand and ask the European Union to do the research on the other. They said that should government persist in these acquisitions they would withdraw their support. Invasions continued, and four days later the European Union stopped all help to coffee research.

I asked Daniel the Jeweller to create a silver coffee branch with berries in cherry-red enamel – just as they would be at harvest time – which I presented as a trophy for the Coffee Grower of the Year. Judging included not only the yield and quality of the crop but also farm management. That trophy was awarded annually for 25 years, for the last time in 2004 to David Wilding-Davies, a Canadian Olympic rider, who shortly afterwards was forced to leave his farm.

In the early 1960s, when I was the senior vice-president of the RNFU, I approached two of my friends, David Worthington, who was the head of the Cattle Producers Association, and Bob Reynolds, who led the Loma-gundi region. I felt that there was a need for the farming industry to have its own awards to people who had made an outstanding contribution to agriculture, whether as farmers, in research and marketing, with the agri-cultural shows, the Rhodesia Tobacco Association, the Natural Resources Board, or the fertilizer and chemical companies. The three of us planned that a committee drawn from those bodies would receive the names of the appropriate people and in secret select an award winner. In order to create an element of surprise and suspense, the winner was only told of the award very shortly before the RNFU Congress, where it would be presented.

The first award was won by the Zambian farmer, Billy Evans, who was president of the Farmers Union. He was president for five years and helped to bond agriculture in Northern and Southern Rhodesia and was much respected.

We had not at that stage arranged for the creation of the trophy itself and so Billy was presented with a sporting rifle. Then a trophy was designed - a plough disc suspended from the overhanging branch of a msasa tree, which was a common way farmers erected their road signs. The tree was made out of hard wood and on the ground was a simulation of the cattle grids which were so widely used between paddocks, particularly in ranching areas. The plough disc was made in silver and engraved *Rhodesian Farming Award*. It very soon became known as 'the Farming Oscar' and the list of recipients over fifty years honours selfless men and women who have done so much for agriculture. In 1990, a book was produced, listing every winner to that date, with a photograph of the recipient and the text of the acceptance speech. The award continues to be made every year.

I was honoured to be awarded the Farming Oscar in 1972.

One of the most outstanding acceptance speeches was made by Margaret Strong in 1979 at the RNFU annual conference. Margaret accepted the award on behalf of her husband, John, who was unavoidably away at that time. It epitomized the role which many, many farming wives played in the difficult times of insurrection and serious security risks. This is what she said:

> Mr President, Honourable Minister Mr Mazaiwana, Honourable Acting Chief Justice, Honourable Ministers, distinguished guests, friends. I am sure John's ears must be burning, even in his sleep, at the nice things you have said about him tonight. David, I hadn't heard of his horsy experiences, but it obviously explains why he defines a horse as dangerous at both ends and uncomfortable in the middle!
>
> I have been looking forward to tonight as one looks forward to a major operation. I know I will feel much better when it is all over. So I ask you to bear with me. David, just for the record, we didn't get engaged in a GMB depot!
>
> When David Spain told John he was to be this year's recipient of the Farming Oscar, he was immensely proud and very surprised. But his immediate reaction was that there was someone – or, rather, a group of people – more worthy of the award than he. I refer to the farmers' wives of Zimbabwe Rhodesia.
>
> John realized that he would be overseas at the time of the

presentation, so he felt that this would be an ideal opportunity for me to receive the award, not only as his representative, but representing every farmer's wife, both black and white, in Zimbabwe Rhodesia today.

Speaking as a farmer's wife, John wanted me to give just a few impressions of the changes which the war has brought in our lives. These changes crept up on us so gradually that they are now an accepted part of our way of life.

First came the fences around our homes; an awful eyesore, we felt they would be. But who today would be without their fence? They give a limit to our gardens, which in the past have tended to encroach upon our husbands' farming lands. They are an ideal way of restraining our dogs from hunting, maxi-play-pen for small children, and a better support for sweet peas has yet to be devised.

After the fences came the grenade screens on the windows – a perfect excuse for not cleaning the windows. Our house staff loved them.

The next step was the protective walls around our beds. They may cut out the view, but are marvellous for hanging photographs and the endless posters with which our children surround themselves.

The final stage is wearing a gun belt round the waist; a great posture aid. It really makes you hold your tummy in.

The community spirit in every area has benefited enormously by the sharing of common security problems. Today people are drawn closer together than ever before and in so doing are strengthened by their mutual dependence upon each other. In our area we have Val, who gives the most practical and often blood-curdling first-aid lectures. June, who has the unenviable task of arranging radio duty rosters to suit everyone. Helen, who does so much valuable administration work for the Police, and Mary, who was instrumental in raising funds to convert the Women Field Reservists' house and that essential building, the pub, at the police camp.

The war has given us a completely new vocabulary. I don't only mean the language we overhear on the police radio duty, although our member-in-charge has a particularly descriptive vocabulary. We now refer confidently to 'sitreps' and 'sunrays', 'roger' and 'relay', and have learned such delightful terms as 'hayburners' used to describe the mounted PATU sticks.

Every area has its own special people, and in our area I would like to tell you about Barbara. Apart from a saga of family problems and sickness, they have had six landmines on their farm, four homestead attacks, tobacco burnt, maize burnt, maize stolen, and a seedbed pump blown up. When John visited them recently in his capacity as area co-ordinating committee chairman to discuss their future plans, Barbara was as adamant as her husband in their determination to stick it out – a real example and inspiration to us all.

The role of the farmer's wife has changed completely since the start of the war. Most of the farmers' wives used to consider themselves busy running the home, shouting at the children, arranging the flowers and fitting in time for tennis and bridge parties.

Looking back on those halcyon days, however did we fill in our time? Today farmers' wives are turning their hands to every aspect of farming while their husbands are on call-up. Mostly we have learned by trial and error, but the fact that we are still in business doesn't speak too badly for our efforts.

An added closeness has developed in our marriages because of this sharing of responsibilities. Sometimes, however, it can lead to problems. I remember one farmer's wife telling me how she resented her husband coming home and interfering in her grading shed.

David, if you were to ask any farmer's wife what is the greatest burden she has to bear in this war, she would tell you, without hesitation, that it is the burden of worry. Not the worry about the day-to-day running of the farm, but worry about the safety of her loved ones, not only in the bush, but on the roads, on the farms, and even in the home; that ever-present anxiety is never far from the forefront of her mind.

We pray with all our hearts that this war will soon end, and with it an end to all the suffering and bloodshed. In many cases we will face the future with a great burden of sadness, but surely each and every one of us will have been strengthened and even enriched by what we have endured.

Before John retired from the RNFU last year, David, he was given a piece of advice, a word of warning from his predecessors. He was advised to get away as soon as possible, to have a chance to relax and unwind. However, within five days of retiring from the union he found himself chairman of our local area co-ordinating committee, with little chance to relax or unwind. It is only now, one year later, that he has managed to get away for that much-needed break.

The warning he was given was that he would feel severe with-drawal symptoms when he stepped down from the presidency. On this trip to Australia he is looking forward with great anticipation to having sufficient time to sit back, relax and feel those long-awaited withdrawal symptoms.

Before I finish, David, I would like to read a message to you all from John:

I recognize that there is no higher honour that the union can award than the Farming Oscar. Its bestowal is a very singular act of recognition. My immediate reaction was a tremendous feeling of humility and inadequacy and a knowledge that there was someone who was far more deserving. This grew to a certainty that those who deserved this highest award this year were the farmers' wives – all farmers' wives. The fact that I cannot be present and that Margaret will accept this Oscar is not only especially gratifying to me and my family in recognition of the part she herself has played, but emphasizes the vital importance of the family unit.

Let her be the personification of my reason for accepting this high honour. Let it be seen as a symbolic gesture of dedication to all farmers' wives of this Farming Oscar. And so I dedicate it to all those wives and mothers who have lost their loved ones. I dedicate it to all those wives whose calm voices over the Agric-Alert during appalling attacks on their homes have inspired their friends and neighbours. I dedicate it to all our black compatriots, whose wives and mothers have been forced to witness the brutalities and obscenities of terrorism before their eyes. Above all I dedicate it to all those wives who have carried on their normal lives maintaining a sanity in our world, whose courage, compassion and resilience is the very fibre of our nation. To all our wives I pay my homage and I salute you.

– 6 –

Tobacco

One morning in 1975, George Pio, president of the Rhodesia Tobacco Association (RTA), together with his two vice-presidents, Gyles Dorward and John Strong, asked to see me. Their invitation, which came out of the blue, was for me to take over the chairmanship of Tobacco Sales Limited (TSL). Its chairman, Hubert Fox, had had an injury to his neck and spine in a car accident. His fellow directors were George Rudland, who had been a government minister; Sam Whaley; Harry Beak, who was managing director of Rhobank; and two nominees from the RTA.

I was asked to be prepared to take over at fairly short notice when Hubert's inability to continue in the job became apparent. They also wanted the new board to appoint Peter Dorward as the managing director of the group. Peter was a very able financial man, who had been at Cambridge, and had worked in Johannesburg for UAL, a leading merchant bank.

Hubert Fox had been a Member of Parliament, was on a number of boards and had a dynamic personality. A month after I was approached, Hubert's health deteriorated and he died soon afterwards.

However, George Rudland had his eye on the chairmanship and a tussle developed between him and the shareholders. The latter prevailed and fairly soon afterwards George Rudland himself was taken ill and left the board. Harry Beak decided to emigrate and, shortly after I became chairman, Sam Whaley resigned because of a conflict of interest as he had been appointed chairman of the Constitutional Commission. I was left with a somewhat new board, but had the good fortune to have David Lewis, who had replaced Sam Whaley, Strath Brown, who was a very successful tobacco grower and engineer, and the two RTA nominees.

TSL was a public company listed on the Rhodesian Stock Exchange. Its original and principal involvement was in the operation of the Tobacco Sales auction floor where our main rival was Tobacco Auctions. The RTA wanted to find a chairman who was non-partisan in the tobacco field. I didn't grow tobacco and I didn't smoke. It was helpful to be able to stand in the middle when difficulties arose between the growers' various districts, or the growers and the trade, or on the level of sales commission charged by us to growers on the sale of their tobacco.

There was a considerable variation in the styles of tobacco produced in the medium altitudes, as opposed to the higher. The medium, and therefore warmer, altitudes produced arguably the better-quality leaf, but yields tended to be lower than in the higher altitude areas of Harare East, Marondera and down into Manicaland.

I took over the helm at this old and well-respected public company and remained there for some twenty-two years. During that time I worked with the growers, the RTA (later the ZTA) council and president, and the link was of the greatest importance. I regard it as a great compliment that each successive president wanted me to continue, and together we were able to work through what was sometimes a minefield of problems.

At the centre of the industry was the Tobacco Marketing Board, a statutory board appointed by the government with members from all sectors of the industry. They did not handle tobacco at all, but were in control of the systems ensuring orderly delivery of tobacco to the floors from the farms. They advised the government regarding tobacco and trade-related issues, including the controversial subject of the commission paid by growers to the floor.

The ZTA's sister organization was the Tobacco Trade Association (TTA), which for many years was led by Tom de Chassart, who sometimes had to try to develop a common approach between growers and members of the trade, and between members of the trade themselves, many of whom had vested interests. Relationships were usually good between ourselves, the ZTA and the TTA. The ZTA had far-sighted men on their council,

Growers and the trade decided jointly to set up their own research station, which we were prepared to fund and staff to provide practical facilities for fundamental research. It was called Kutsaga (the Shona word meaning 'to search'). It was yet another example of the industry recognizing the need and refraining from looking for charity, just getting on and doing the job. Dr Stinson was the first Director, followed by Dr Ian McDonald, who became pre-eminent in the tobacco research world. They organized and planned was probably the biggest and best tobacco research conference in the region (see Chapter 10).

top growers in their own right. Some had a limited experience in public corporate affairs, but they provided a very good balance. So TSL was the central body in the chain with the TTA, the Tobacco Marketing Board and our rival floor, Tobacco Auctions.

There was strong rivalry for market share between ourselves and Tobacco Auctions, and we would anxiously await the news each afternoon when the Tobacco Marketing Board announced the percentage of the floor sales sold by each company.

With this responsibility, the strain of commuting between Handley Cross and Salisbury became excessive, and we bought a house in Orange Grove Drive in Salisbury. Wendy often stayed at Handley Cross but sometimes came to town with me, and I went home to the farm for weekends when I could.

Vec Hurley was the initiator and mastermind of the establishment of the Tobacco Training Institute on Blackfordby Farm, twenty kilometres from Salisbury. We at TSL gave this project our full support. It was imaginative and very practical. This training centre ran a basic tobacco-growing course over a full twelve-month season. The students themselves did every job on the farm, from the preparation of seedbeds to growing, reaping, curing, grading and selling the crop. Blackfordby was run financially as a practical school, but benefited from donations and grants from the RTA and the private sector. After a year at Blackfordby, the students were highly sought-after in the agricultural industry. They had learned how to run or manage a tobacco farm successfully. Some hundreds of skilled young men, black and white, found employment and made a considerable contribution to the growing industry.

Subsequently the City of Harare took over Blackfordby Farm for urban development. Pressure on land was such that the ZTA bought another farm north-east of Harare and moved the whole college, now known as the Blackfordby Agricultural Institute, which still offers a one-year diploma course in general agriculture, including tobacco, although the number of students has understandably shrunk.

Vec Hurley will be remembered not only as a good president of the RTA but also as the architect and founder of Blackfordby. He subsequently was awarded the Farming Oscar for his work there and also for his participation in the Promotion Council and African Farming Development.

At the time of the Second World War, Vec Hurley and a group of twenty men volunteered to serve in the South African army. There were not a great number of volunteer South Africans and they were reviewed by General Smuts, who told them that because they were volunteers they would have some choice of unit in which they would serve.

A few months after their arrival in Egypt, they were posted to the Pioneer Corps, which had the unpleasant chore of looking after the toilets, dirty baths and basins and keeping the area swept. Vec Hurley protested to no avail that they had not volunteered to come to Egypt to do that sort of job. They mutinied and were promptly put into the cooler for thirty days, after which they were court-martialled. At the court martial they explained their reasons, but the Colonel Provost Marshall told them that they had seriously compromised King's Regulations and they were guilty. He said he had no alternative but to sentence them, but nonetheless hoped that when they came out of the cooler they would serve under him in his regiment. He arranged for their transfer, and the colonel and the twenty South Africans served together under him right through the Italian Campaign. It was typical of Vec Hurley to stand his ground, a characteristic demonstrated later in difficult negotiations.

Tobacco Sales Limited started to acquire and develop subsidiaries and associates, and it was decided that, as overall chairman of the group, I would chair those companies. As chief executive of TSL, Peter Dorward was in overall executive command, which gave us a good team. The only exception was the Tobacco Sales Floor, where we were very well served by Strath Brown.

There were a number of highly successful men in different sectors of the tobacco industry. One of the longest serving was Ginger Freeman, who was originally on the TSL board and who then led the Tobacco Corporation after UDI, masterminding disposal of the crop. Two well-known men in the early tobacco industry were Red and Black Parham, so named because one had bright red hair and the other black. They had had experience of growing tobacco in Ontario and were instrumental in the first significant commercial tobacco production in the country. Working closely with them were Archie Henderson, Evan Campbell, Ted Jeffreys, Mansell Edwards, Don Bell and Fred Cooksey.

Evan Campbell was tobacco farming at Inyazura. He went on to the RTA Council, and became one of its most dynamic presidents for many years. After he stood down, he

> Archie Henderson owned a lovely farm, 'The Great B', in the Mazoe Valley. Subsequently, he generously donated the farm to the nation to become a government research unit. Today it is known as the Henderson Research Station.

was primarily responsible for the establishment of the Tobacco Export Promotion Council of Rhodesia, Tepcor. After retiring from Tepcor, he stood in the 1962 general parliamentary election against Winston Field, who defeated him. With great magnanimity, and recognizing his ability and wide international contacts, Winston Field, after becoming Prime Minister, asked Evan Campbell to become the Rhodesian High Commissioner in London. Campbell was always very opposed to the possibility of UDI and found it difficult to represent what his political masters from Salisbury wanted. So, just before UDI, he resigned and was replaced by Brigadier Skeen, a retired English army officer.

Evan Campbell

Evan then went on to a number of boards, including the chairmanship of the Standard Chartered Bank. He played a leading role in the private sector, including his useful contribution on the Rhodesia Promotion Council and later the Zimbabwe Promotion Council. One of his major successes was initiating and holding the Third World Tobacco Scientific Congress in Salisbury during his RTA term of office in 1963, a resounding success and attended by people from the tobacco industry worldwide.

Another of Evan's innovative achievements was the Tepcor Floating Tobacco Exhibition. Tepcor arranged to construct a Rhodesian Tobacco permanent stand on a passenger boat going up the East Coast of Africa and to the Far East. The first boat was the MV *Ruys*, which visited Japan, Hong Kong, Singapore and Malaya. The exhibition was a great success and in 1961 a similar exhibit aboard the *Tegelberg* visited South America. In 1962 the MV *Oranjefontein* went to Amsterdam, Bremen, Hamburg, Oslo, Stockholm, Helsinki and Copenhagen. In 1964 the floating exhibition was aboard the Royal Inter Ocean Line's MV *Boissevain*.

Colonel H. C. Bunnett, who had been the RTA's public relations officer, took charge of these floating exhibitions and was on board with Mike Garratt. While the boat was in harbour, local dignitaries and anyone interested could come on board, see the exhibit, and hear about the current situation and the plans for Rhodesian tobacco in the future. Tepcor's representative would get the exhibition started in each port and then fly on to the next, ready to receive guests. This project of course came to an end when UDI was declared.

Ted Jeffreys produced very high-quality tobacco. In his capacity as President of the RTA, he was bold enough to challenge Ian Smith on the dangers of UDI. Had this not been declared, we would, he said, have been the biggest tobacco exporter in the world by 1968. UDI was to be a serious set-back for the industry from which we would not recover for many years. It was courageous of him to take a stand against the government, but in the end he was proved right. Brazil would take over our markets and we would lose our position as one of the top two tobacco-exporting countries, Brazil being the other.

Don Bell, the chief executive of Rhodesian Leaf Tobacco, was a strong businessman and guided Universal (of South Carolina, the biggest tobacco company in the world) into being by far the largest customer for our tobacco. Universal were exporting our tobacco to many companies throughout the world.

Mansell Edwards, a tobacco man through and through, was managing director of our Tobacco Sales Floor for many years and was highly regarded. He had a major hand in the design and construction of the new floor which was opened in April 1986 by President Robert Mugabe. Edwards was one of the earliest winners of the Farming Oscar for the outstanding contribution he made to farming, specifically in tobacco.

The industry was highly disciplined to achieve control of deliveries from the growers to the floors and, when the growers had more tobacco than could be sold each day, a quota system was applied to ensure that they all had an equal opportunity to sell every ten days. Arbitrators would decide on disputes between buyers and sellers.

The Tobacco Sales Floor was at that stage the largest tobacco auction floor in the world, selling up to 18,000 bales of tobacco every morning through four simultaneous sales. Sales started at 7.30 a.m. and concluded about lunchtime. Buyers from the merchant companies were licensed and experienced and on average it took just six seconds to sell a bale of tobacco. The ticket marker had to record on the sales ticket the buyer and the price in the few seconds before the next bale was sold.

The tobacco came in daily from the farms, the bales were marshalled into the correct order of sale according to the grower's instructions and readied for the next day's sale. All tobacco received on one day was offered for sale the next day, with the auctioneer and group of buyers and support staff walking along line after line of bales, which were all laid out on trolleys. Each tow-tractor towed 28 bales, each on its own trolley. The bales remained on the trolleys after the sale and the whole line was then towed away to the delivery point. Buyers' or their agents' vehicles took control of their purchases at that point, when every bale had been sold. During the course of a day, the floor would be re-laid, sold and continuously replaced four times. In the afternoon, all the bales for the first lay of sales for the following morning were laid out.

Immediately after the auction, both seller and buyer had the opportunity to cancel the sale. This window was open for thirty minutes. The grower could cancel the sale by crossing the ticket if he was dissatisfied with the price and could bring that bale back for resale the next day or later. With advance market intelligence, growers would be aware of likely changes in price for the many different grades and could take a bale off, to bring it back when he thought the price would have risen. The buyer could examine the bale in more depth and, if it was found to be defective in any way or if the tobacco was mixed, the arbitrator had the final word as to whether the tobacco sale was to be consummated or cancelled.

At the end of the thirty-minute period, the tobacco was towed away. The bale tickets were removed and taken to the computer rooms. Within ninety minutes of the sale taking place, a grower would have his sale sheet for that day with all the relevant data – grower's number, weight, classification (which was done by Tobacco Marketing Board technical men), price paid for each bale, deductions for the Tobacco Association levy, weighing and auction fees. It was a very comprehensive document and all the data was consolidated into an updated summary for the whole season. This was valuable when discussing farm performance with bankers and obtaining facilities for the next season. It was a service as good as any of its kind in the world and we were very proud of it.

Our next development in the tobacco field was the formation of a wholly owned subsidiary, a company called BAK Storage, who stored, fumigated, and in due course dispatched merchants' tobacco. We had a series of large warehouses quite close to the original auction floor with our own railway siding and a mobile crane.

In addition to tobacco BAK handled other commodities such as black granite. That black granite, mined in the Mutoko area and cut into 30-tonne blocks, went mainly to the United States, where slices an eighth of an inch thick were cut with special saws, as cladding both for the inside and outside of buildings, including the whole of the outside of the Sears Tower skyscraper in Chicago.

Containers from all over the world were sent to the BAK container park awaiting filling and dispatch, including large shipments of fertilizer and

The 40-tonne crane at BAK Storage.

grain. We could accommodate 10,000 containers. BAK later developed another major storage site for a further 10,000 shipping containers, which came into Harare full and were then emptied and filled with tobacco or anything else to be shipped out.

Another company, Propak, was established jointly between auction floors and investors to provide a steady flow of tobacco paper and hessian for growers to pack their tobacco. When the bales returned with tobacco to the floors for sale, these used wraps went back to Propak and the grower was debited with a hire charge. The packaging was recirculated four or five times throughout the season. There were occasions when shipping problems delayed replacement hessian supplies from Bangladesh, which caused great problems for the growers.

When the Cotton Co-op went into liquidation, TSL took over the agreements which they had with the Sentrachem organization in South Africa. Sentrachem is a large chemical company linked with chemical giants in the USA, Britain and Europe. Agricultural chemicals were one of its main products, some of which were imported and others formulated in their factories. They had substantial export markets. We had a joint operation, which has stood the test of time, and we became the principal supplier of agricultural chemicals in this country. The company was floated on the Zimbabwe Stock Exchange and its shares have performed extremely well.

The company is now known as Chemco. It was a proud day when the Minister of Agriculture opened our own formulation plant. This enabled us to reduce the end cost of chemicals in foreign exchange by buying the chemicals and converting them into the finished product.

We also acquired Agricultural Buying Services from the Cotton Co-op, which farmers used to save themselves much shopping time in town, and the company thrived. Our timber operation in Harare, TS Timbers, provided construction timber for the building industry, and later we were able to acquire our own lumber from the forests we had bought from the Imperial Tobacco Company.

At TSL, we looked at an opportunity to enter the tobacco packing, merchandising and export sector, but we needed a technical partner. Just after independence, Imperial Tobacco, established many years before, became anxious about the future of the country and wished to disinvest. The Imperial Tobacco group owned a packing plant at Msasa in Harare and also had extensive forestry interests in Nyanga. We took over all their operations but felt the need to join forces with an international tobacco company in the ultimate marketing of our tobacco. We identified the large German firm of Gebrüder Kulenkampff in Bremen and our partnership worked well, to the advantage of both.

We bought into a printing company, Print Holdings, and developed their somewhat outdated equipment. Because of the foreign currency shortage, we accepted an offer from two indigenous Zimbabweans to become shareholders in the company on the understanding that they would bring foreign currency into the company. This was the first of some similar mistakes. As soon as they had a shareholding, they presumed that that gave them the authority to interfere with all management decisions, and Bryan Walters, the managing director of TSL, had a very frustrating time until the partnership was terminated. We were not the only business who met problems on becoming involved with shareholders who had a minimal understanding of corporate governance.

Later, a shareholding in Hunyani Pulp and Paper became available as the Standard Chartered Bank wished to disinvest. A long tussle ensued with one rival bidder, but, after a long and somewhat acrimonious negotiation, we obtained the key shareholding and gained control of the company. A new board was appointed, with Tim Rowett as chief executive.

The company was listed on the Zimbabwe Stock Exchange and its pulp and paper plant were at Norton. They bought in eucalyptus timber and their own gum plantations near Norton also provided a lot of timber.

They had a creosoting plant near Marondera, treating everything from electricity transmission poles down to fencing poles. Mount Lothian had a contract with them and they gave us a lot of technical advice. We had only 24 hectares of eucalyptus but, following their advice, it was becoming increasingly productive until we were evicted in 2002. The gums were felled in a four- to five-year cycle and grew again for a further cycle – an excellent renewable resource. After we had been evicted, the occupants proceeded to bulldoze a lot of them out to make way for soya beans. What a short-sighted decision.

When the decision was taken to dispose of the equity of TSL, we identified the origin of the funds that had been invested over the years by growers through their levy. It was, after all, their money which had contributed to the huge growth of the company. It seemed best to sell and distribute the proceeds in relation to the amount of tobacco that a farmer had sold (but only to Tobacco Sales Floor) over the previous ten years. This arrangement was warmly welcomed and substantial payouts were made, so after many years Tobacco Sales Floor ceased to be grower-owned.

– 7 –

Our Racehorses and Stud

Show-jumping • Polo • Race meetings
• Buying from Newmarket • The Queen's filly and sanctions breaking
• Twink Allen, Princillon, The Aga Khan and Alec Head
• Arrested at Heathrow, illegally to England • Exchange
• 'Shares' and 'legs' • David and Diane Nagle
• Jockey Club Rooms • Ecurie
• Visit to Argentina • Visit to Kentucky • Dispersal of our stud

When we were young children on the farm, our horses formed a very important part of our existence. Never would a day pass without our being with them, riding to different parts of the farm, finding gullies to jump and wading into the dams. As I mentioned earlier, my passion for horses and racing led my father to read me John Masefield's poem 'Right Royal', which I learnt by heart.

In 1933, my father bought me an unbroken country-bred filly which had come off a ranch in the north of the country. I called the filly Gavotte because, in 'Right Royal', Gavotte ran a very good race and was described as 'small, and with steel springs', which absolutely described my filly. It was the beginning of a love relationship. Gavotte had never been backed and so, aged nine, I had to break her and we bonded together. I played polo on her. She jumped like a stag and we won many jumping classes at the various shows, including winning the Open Jumping class at the Bulawayo Show in 1947. She was a wonderful mate.

I participated frequently in jumping and horse-riding arena events. My show-jumping career had been quite successful, but it was brought to a premature end by a bad fall in the Open Jumping at Salisbury Show in the 1950s. My horse, Hermes, took off too far out and straddled the double oxer, a big brush fence with rails on each side, and then he cartwheeled, coming down on top of me. The saddle tree broke, but my helmet protected me to some extent from the fall and his subsequent kick to my head.

Gavotte and I competing at the Bulawayo Agricultural Show in 1947.

I was badly concussed. Hermes was fine but too nervous ever to jump again. We smashed the jump and stretchers were sent for. I was taken out of the arena past the members' stand. Someone had put a hat over my face, which everyone took to mean that I was dead. They all stood to attention to pay their last respects. I came to in hospital five or six hours later and, in my muzzy state, had to be restrained by the nurses from returning to the competition.

Polo had been played since the 1930s, mainly in the farming districts and at one club in Salisbury. It was very popular and the club membership increased. Our best players were handicapped only slightly lower than the top South African teams and, in more recent years, occasionally beat them. We were short of players at Chakari. The tobacco growers were far wealthier than we were and could afford top-class ponies. I got up to a three handicap and we were able to muster a team to compete at the main tournaments, and were eventually promoted to the A Division.

These tournaments were huge fun. Once I broke a leg in the semi-finals. The orthopaedic surgeon patched me up and told me that if I wanted to play the next day, it was entirely at my own risk. But the rest of the team lent me their most manageable ponies and I put on a cricket

> The polo ground in Salisbury was next to Government House (now State House) and is now used as President Mugabe's helicopter pad.

pad and did manage to play. The opponents largely discounted me as injured and did not mark me. I managed a couple of goals and we won the tournament. I had to undergo surgery thereafter to straighten the bone – it was pretty sore but I reckoned it worthwhile.

John Lakin, brother-in-law of Lord Cowdray, was in 1965 an international polo player with a six handicap. He helped Patrick Kemple, our Rhodesian player in Britain who played for the polo team organized by the legendary Indian international Hanut Singh. Patrick was selected to play for the Commonwealth team in the World Championships in Argentina. A problem arose because the tournament was to be held just after UDI in 1965 and it was argued that Patrick should not be allowed to play for the Commonwealth because he was a Rhodesian citizen and Rhodesia was in rebellion to the Crown. The problem was overcome in a diplomatic way and Patrick played for the Commonwealth. The team was captained by the Australian Sinclair Hill, who had a handicap of ten – the highest in the world, matched only by half a dozen Argentinian players and one Australian. Patrick Kemple was a seven handicap, Lord Beresford a five, and Lord Waterford a four. Our team beat the American side but was no match for the Argentinians. It was great that a Rhodesian could be ranked as the second highest handicap player and be good enough to go to Argentina.

The Chakari polo team won the Senior Handicap in Salisbury.
From left to right: John Kemple, Ronnie Baines, Martin Tracey and C. G. Tracey.

At the same time, Country Districts, as the area around Marandellas and Salisbury was known, held race meetings, limiting entries to horses bred in the Country Districts. There were a couple of steeplechases on the cards and we raced at Marandellas, Banket, Umvukwes and Sinoia. These were the greatest of fun and led to my progression into serious racing.

I bought my first filly, named Santo, in 1943 for £50; she was a cast-off from Sir Digby Burnett, chairman of the BSA Company in Rhodesia. As my salary on the farm at that stage was £10 per month all found, I had to rely on a good slice of my bonus to buy her. We used to run in the amateur races at the Belvedere race-track, though we were seldom successful.

In about 1944, I bought another two horses, which were trained for me in Salisbury. I had to get up at two o'clock in the morning, drive from Handley Cross to Hartley station, get on the train at three o'clock in the morning, arriving in Salisbury at 6.30. I would have breakfast, go down to the racecourse and spend the day there. After racing, I would catch the train back to Hartley, eventually getting home at 11 o'clock at night. I did this once or twice a month.

My marriage to Wendy and the arrival of our three daughters meant that racing had to take a back seat. I was, however, determined to start a small thoroughbred stud. We gradually accumulated a few mares, locally and from South Africa. We usually raced them for a season or two before putting them to stud, sending them out to the better stallions.

My interest and determination to establish a proper commercial stud co-incided with UDI and sanctions. I could never get the best fillies after they had raced in South Africa because their owners kept them for their own studs and so I had to look to Britain, Ireland and France to buy brood mares.

I had some money in my account in London but, after sanctions against Rhodesia came into force, it was illegal for me to have this account. Harold Wilson was in hot pursuit and the money was moved from bank to bank until my banker friends insisted that I get it out of the banking system before somebody was arrested. This gave me the opportunity to buy brood mares, and I gave two bloodstock agents instructions to spend a certain amount of money on up to ten fillies or mares. Our budget was limited but they were able to buy two fillies out of training. These were brought to Rhodesia and continued to race successfully in Salisbury. Eight more in-foal mares came later, bought at the November Newmarket brood-mare sales.

The bloodstock agents knew full well that I was from Rhodesia, that the horses were going to Rhodesia, that sanctions were in existence, and that these prohibited the export of horses (or even racing pigeons) from Britain to Rhodesia. Consequently the mares were consigned to an Irish vet in Cape Town and he was instructed to consign them on to a breeder in Colesberg, a small town in the Karoo.

At this stage, all the transactions had been between the bloodstock agents and my Cape Town veterinary friend and my name never appeared on any shipping documents. The horses were to be consigned from Colesberg to me in Rhodesia. In fact the mares started their rail journey in Cape Town. At Colesberg the steam engine boilers were replenished with water, which took only half an hour, and the re-consigned mares went on their way to Handley Cross.

The mares arrived safely on the farm and they started to acclimatize. Those in foal had been covered in what is called northern hemisphere time, to foal down in the northern hemisphere spring. Our horses in the southern hemisphere foal down in our spring, in September and October, the opposite of what would happen in Britain. So we had what could be described as either very early, or very late, foals from these English mares.

We had built some lovely looseboxes and the mares were a great addition to the stud. Wendy took over all the day-to-day management as I was away so much. In spite of having no experience, she managed the horses superbly and did the record-keeping. Her nursing experience stood her in good stead.

Then we hit a snag. The documents for transfer of ownership were issued in 1966. It was intended that transfer should be made from the English owners to the vet in Colesberg and then after a few months, he would transfer them to us. He did not fully appreciate the sensitivity of the sanctions situation, although it had been explained to him. Without thinking, he had the transfer made directly from the English owner to us, which blew a hole in our cover.

The first I knew of this was when I had a bewildered letter from one of the agents in Newmarket. The racing journalists in the South African press had spotted in the Jockey Club transfer lists that these mares had come from Britain to Rhodesia. Here seemed to be a good story. To make matters worse, one of the fillies they had bought for me, at Tattersalls' brood-mare sales at Newmarket, was bred at the Royal Stud at Sandringham and sold to us by HM the Queen – a cracking good story when Rhodesia was under sanctions.

A local journalist rang up for a story. I told him that there was no story and that I would take a very dim view if he encouraged anyone else to write about it because of the embarrassment it could cause to people who had helped us in the UK. But to no avail, the story was all over the South African Sunday newspapers with headlines like 'Queen sells filly to Rhodesia'. On the Monday after the story was reported in the South African papers, I had just finished a board meeting when I was told that there was a UK call on the line for me. A telephone operator with a cockney accent enquired if I was Mr Tracey and said, 'You must be very famous, Mr Tracey, because when this call is finished please don't go off the line as there are another seven calls waiting for you.' So the game was on.

I parried the questions, ducked and dived, teased the journalists, frustrated them by pretending I couldn't hear their questions on a bad phone line. The *Daily Mirror* asked me where exactly the Queen's mare was.

I said, 'If you people write so much about sex, this story should suit you well. The Queen's mare is currently visiting a boyfriend and they are hopefully having intercourse twice a day. I haven't got time to describe how horses have intercourse but I am sure you can find out.' At that stage the telephone went dead. This incident caused quite a furore in the English horse world.

A week later I got a letter from my very fearful agent to say that the police had called and nearly arrested him for breaking sanctions. This nice chap had tunnel vision, could only think about horses and knew nothing else of what was happening in the world around him. I remember his letter said, 'Dear C.G., I have always vaguely heard about what happens in police states and never really bothered very much until yesterday.'

We assured him we would give whatever help he needed. We got the details of the charges and prepared copies of all the many documents showing the transfers through South Africa. We threw in a few red herrings, some of which were only in Afrikaans. My solicitors kept in touch with his solicitors. The poor man was charged at the Southampton assizes, from where the horses had been shipped.

In advance of the trial day, we had sent him my schedule so that I could be contacted by telephone wherever I was. I took the call in the offices of the Governor of the Reserve Bank; it was a strange place to take an international phone call. My agent's lawyer asked me to clarify one of the key points in the defence, which I did. The case hinged on this and finally the charges against my agent were withdrawn, and, in one of the very few sanctions cases which came to court, he was awarded costs against the government.

Meanwhile our new mares were doing well. Wendy was doing some experiments for Dr Twink Allen – a New Zealander, the brilliant director of the equine fertility research centre at Newmarket – on oestrus control in fertility. She kept immaculate records. Twink Allen was thus able to get two lots of recorded data per year, one in the English spring and one in our spring.

Now we needed a top-class stallion. We found a horse called Princillon, bred and raced in France by the Aga Khan. On the day of the Epsom Derby, he had been the favourite to win the race but had suffered bad interference at Tattenham Corner. This destroyed his chances, although he did eventually finish seventh. He won a number of Group races in France, including the Group 1 Prix de Salamandre at Longchamp (one of the top two-year-old races in France) in a record time which stood for many years. Princillon eventually retired to a stud in Italy for three seasons and topped the list of sires of two-year-olds when his progeny started to race. That is when we bought him.

Princillon

The old Aga Khan had a stud in France and another in Ireland. He had bred winners of all the top races in Europe and the quality of the families in his stud surfaces again and again in new pedigrees. A Polish cavalry officer, Colonel Vuillez, advised him on setting up his stud. In the nineteenth century, when the French aristocracy went into horse racing, they imported, along with the horses, a number of good English jockeys and trainers, which is why today there are still a number of English names in their racing fraternity. Alec Head, who trained Princillon, had been their champion jockey for some years. His principal patron was the Aga Khan. After retiring from the saddle, he became champion trainer on occasions. His daughter, Ghislaine, is currently one of the top French trainers and her brother Freddie Head has been champion jockey.

When I was in France in December 1967, I had introduced myself to Alec. We spent a fascinating lunch with his father, Willy Head, who also had been a jockey and a champion trainer. They had put together enough money to buy Le Haras du Quesnay, a stud in Normandy, from T. M. Sopwith, a rich American who had fled France at the outbreak of the war.

During the occupation it became the headquarters for the German Panzer Division in Normandy, and you can still see, surrounded by shrubs, the enormous concrete pill boxes which were part of their defence lines. It is situated in Arromanches near Deauville, close to the beaches of the Normandy landings.

The Heads were most helpful to Wendy and me, and when we bought mares at the Deauville sales they kindly allowed us to use some of their stallions for out-of-season covering. Through Alec Head and then through Princillon, we met many French, American and Irish racing and breeding people and established a wonderful circle of friends, many of whom came to visit us in Rhodesia.

One August, when I was at the Kentucky sales in Lexington, Alec Head said, 'Are you coming to the Pistol Packer party?' The Pistol Packer party was named after one of Alec's famous fillies. We went to the party and enjoyed a very good and long evening. I don't drink much, but the others did well. Alec's brother, Peter, said he would take me back because I was staying at Le Quesnay. In France the sun gets up very early in August. As we drove along in the dawn light, we saw a strange sight, which was, without doubt, a plantation of pear trees. What worried me was that on the end of their branches they seemed to be growing decanters.

I watched for a bit, but they were definitely decanters. Peter said, 'Don't you know? That is how we make Poire William brandy. When the pear is the size of a walnut, they choose the best fruit on the tree, thread the stalk with the fruit on the end of it through the throat of the bottle, and fasten it. When it is mature, full size, they snip off the stem, pour in the poire brandy and there is a lovely brandy liqueur. Everybody asks how you put the pear in the bottle.'

Just before Easter in 1967, I was leaving London on my way home from a successful trip in the UK. I planned to stop in Milan en route home to look at my new stallion. At passport control I felt a hand on my shoulder and a voice said, 'Are you Mr Tracey?' I had to admit it, and he asked me to 'Step this way.' I stood before three officials, one of whom read out a formal document saying that I was regarded as a friend of Ian Smith, was a sanctions-buster and supporter of the Rhodesian Front government, and that I should not be travelling on a British passport. I was then taken into custody and relieved of my passport. Next I was taken back to my club, told that I would be under surveillance, that I should not leave and that I would be collected the next morning and put on a plane to South Africa. I have never felt so impotent in my life, standing there with three Special

Branch men, two big chaps and one small fellow, absolutely powerless to do anything.

Next day I was taken to Heathrow and no less a person than the manager of Heathrow took me on board and remained with me until we were ready for take-off. I asked the Special Branch people who had confiscated my passport how I would manage to get into South Africa with no documents if I was having a problem entering the UK. One of them made a very sarcastic reply, which showed his lack of enthusiasm for South Africa. I arrived the next day in Johannesburg, where I knew the immigration people well, and managed to get another document and get home.

I was thus unable to visit Newmarket for some time, so we bought a few mares in France through friends of Alec Head's. One of the French agents, using horse transport planes that took thirteen horses at a time, was flying horses regularly back and forth from Deauville in France to Luton. They suggested that I hitch a lift. Everybody at each end knew the horse transport people and there were never any formalities.

They seldom took more than twelve horses at a time because the thirteenth stall would be full of French champagne or the famous old Normandy Calvados. After that had been discharged in Luton, the stall was filled up with English goods, particularly good-quality woollen clothing, which was in great demand in France. And so, on the day after the French sales when everyone was going back to the English sales via Paris – a long journey – I went to the airport at Deauville, dressed in a tweed jacket and cap and Wellingtons to look like a French groom. I was given a mare to hold and twenty minutes later we were in Luton. My friends going to Newmarket had to undertake the long journey from Deauville to Paris, out to Orly, across to Heathrow and then up to Newmarket. This took them five or six hours. By that time, I was safely ensconced in Newmarket. I did this trip a number of times and we even bought a few more mares on these occasions.

One day on the farm, I had a telephone call from Salisbury to say that one of the lesser members of the Royal Family, Lady May Cambridge, was in Rhodesia incognito with her husband and would like to come and have lunch at the stud. Lady May was the last surviving granddaughter of Queen Victoria. They were duly driven down and during lunch one of them said: 'Is it right that you actually bought a mare from the Queen?' Pibroch, as she was called, was in a paddock only a quarter of a mile away, so after coffee and liqueurs we walked down to see her. They used to visit the country from time to time and always enquired about Pibroch. She had been bred by the Queen and was a daughter of Pinza who had won the Derby. Pibroch produced some good foals, one of which won several races in the Cape. Her half-brother was also a very successful racehorse and was sold for stud to Australia.

It was still difficult to bring any horses in from the UK, so we had to buy from Ireland, France or the USA. There again we met a great number of people in the horse world and we also enjoyed visitors from the United States. Breeding horses took us into a world-wide fellowship of people connected with the thoroughbred industry.

I asked Susan Piggott, whose husband was the famous jockey, to try and buy a mare called Exchange at the Newmarket brood mare sales. She was by Mr Jinks and was named Exchange because her owner did not think she was much good and swopped her for another horse. Also because they did not think too much of her, she was never entered for the filly classics, where entries have to be made eighteen months ahead of the race. However, in other Group 1 races she beat top English and Irish fillies who had won the English 2000 Guineas, the English Oaks and the Musidora Stakes. She was in foal to a very good American horse called Jim French, who had run second in the Kentucky Derby. We had hoped for a filly but got an outstanding colt, bought in due course by Tony Taberer. This colt, French Bourse, won eight of his first nine races. Tragically, we lost Exchange from a puff-adder bite, and we never got a filly from her.

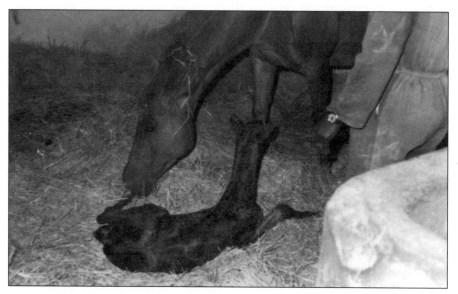

Exchange and her foal, French Bourse, thirty minutes after his birth.

From time to time, I invested in shares in stallions in Ireland. At the time, the system was that, when a stallion went to stud, the owner of the stallion issued forty 'shares'. Each share entitled you to a service each year, either to use for a mare of your own, or to sell to someone else who wanted the service for one of their mares; you could later sell that share itself. For a fairly small amount of capital, I bought a number of shares and, with the rising market, was able, after a couple of years' income from the sale of services, to sell the shares themselves, often at a substantial profit.

We then reinvested that profit in buying a 'leg' or two in top-class mares. Partnerships in mares are usually denominated in legs – four legs equals one mare. This enabled us to buy one or two legs in different mares, which spread the risk, and our investment, over a number of mares.

We had met David and Diane Nagle at the South African yearling sales and became close friends. He was one of the top Irish horse auctioneers and they were starting a small stud in Ireland, called Baronstown Stud, where they had a policy of selling foals rather than yearlings. We used to visit them regularly and often stayed with them while attending the Irish sales.

We met a great number of Irish and overseas breeders. David Nagle was a close friend of John Magnier, who had taken over and was rapidly developing the now famous Coolmore Stud. John Magnier had married Sue, daughter of Vincent O'Brien, a great steeplechase jockey and who trained many Derby and Prix de l'Arc de Triomphe winners. He had also trained horses for Americans such as Charlie Engelhart, the mining tycoon.

The Nagles generously offered us the chance to take one or two legs in mares they had bought. When a particularly well-bred mare, Doff the Derby, came on the market in America we bought a leg in her. She came from a wonderful female line and had already produced one Stakes winner by an unfashionable sire. She went on to breed a couple more Stakes winners and was then bred to one of the Coolmore stallions, Caerleon. The foal was a smasher, and Prince Fahd Salman, a wealthy Saudi who was getting more and more involved in racing, bought him. I think the price he paid was 400,000 guineas. He was so pleased that he had seen off the Dubai Maktoum Team, by

Generous.

far the biggest buyer, that he turned to an aide and said, 'I am delighted to have got this foal. Whatever winnings he makes, I would like the whole sum to go to charity.' The response was, 'That's very generous of you.' His retort was, 'Well, let's call him Generous.'

This foal became the outstanding horse in Europe of his generation. He won two Group 1 two-year-old races and went on to win the English Derby the next season. Across the Irish Sea he won the Irish Derby. Back in the UK he took the Group 1 All Ages race at Ascot, the King George VI and Queen Elizabeth Stakes, and only failed in his last race in the Prix de l'Arc de Triomphe in Paris. It was a wonderful performance. As I could not be at Epsom, we watched his Derby race on television. After his racing career he went to stud, where he was reasonably successful, and his own full sister, Imagine, won the Epsom Oaks. There are very few mares in the world which have produced full brothers or sisters to win both the Derby and the Oaks.

During one of my pilgrimages to New-market for the sales, friends suggested that I might like to join the Jockey Club Rooms.

Membership of the Jockey Club itself is limited to sixty distinguished people, all at the apex of the racing industry, including owners and breeders. They are a fascinating group who, since the early 1800s, have been the guiding influence and dominant force in racing. This is probably the most exclusive club in Britain. Humphrey Cotterell, who had been a successful trainer at Newbury, had retired and had a flat in the Jockey Club Rooms. He used to visit us regularly in Rhodesia.

King George V built a mansion which he used when there was racing at Newmarket. The King later donated his racing lodge to the Jockey Club Rooms, the membership of which, whilst also very limited, was one tier below the Jockey Club itself.

To become a member of the Jockey Club Rooms one had to be proposed by a member of the Jockey Club itself and seconded by a member of the Jockey Club Rooms. Major John de Burgh, who was a member of the Jockey Club and proposed me for membership of the Rooms, ran a stud at Kildangan in Ireland. There was a strong Irish element in the membership. I gladly accepted the invitation for my name to be put forward and was duly elected. I stayed there whenever I was in Newmarket, as the house was within walking distance of the sales complex.

By that time I had made a wide range of acquaintances in the world of racing who all converged from time to time at Newmarket, the centre of English racing and breeding, for the Guineas and other Group 1 races or for the sales. The Heath at Newmarket is a famous training ground, and there are a huge number of horses in training concentrated around Newmarket. It was inspiring to watch the training and to visit the National Stud, where I was able to get them to admit young Rhodesians and South Africans to their twelve-month training course.

In the Rooms there is a feeling of equine history, with lovely old paintings and pictures of horses from bygone years. In the passages and staircases going to the bedrooms is a photograph of every chairman since the club's inception. They have a rule that members or their guests go in to a meal with the most senior person present, who acts as host, and the table fills from his end as people arrive, so you never know with whom you will be sitting – and, of course, during the sales there were visitors from all over the world. I might be sitting next to an American, Indian or South African, but almost always the discussion would be on racing past and present. Until we stopped breeding horses, I enjoyed my visits there enormously. It was a different world and led to many lasting friendships.

Muis Roberts was a leading South African jockey who transferred and rode for some top stables in Britain. Wendy and I were on our way to watch the Derby one year when we noticed Muis in a taxi stuck in a traffic jam. He was due to run in the first race, and the last thing a jockey does is not be on time for the first race of the day at Epsom. He spotted a motorbike and, a man of quick decision, thrust fifty pounds into the taxi driver's hand, ran up to the astonished motor cyclist, said he had eight minutes to get to Epsom, get changed and on to the scales. The last we saw was Muis Roberts riding pillion on a very fast motorbike, weaving his way through the traffic. He got there on time and won the race.

At Newmarket the Nagles bought a mare named Burghclere, bred by the Queen, in which we had a fifteen per cent share. She was very expensive. She was beautifully bred, but the only one of her progeny really to succeed was a filly called Wind In Her Hair, who came second in the Oaks. She was sold later to Japan, where the breeder specifically wanted to breed her to his top American stallion, Sunday Silence. The resulting foal, called Deep Impact, won the top-class races in Japan and was the favourite in the Prix de l'Arc de Triomphe, but suffered interference and came fourth. However, he was near the top of the World Thoroughbred Racehorse Rankings in 2006, and was recognized as one of the best racehorses in the world.

At about that time we decided to take our profit and sold a lot of our shares in the mares. I was getting to Ireland less frequently and it was a rather distant investment, which had nevertheless given us the greatest fun and reward. Ken Mackenzie, who had been with us in our Irish venture, and I reinvested in South Africa, into an Argentinian filly, Ecurie. She was exceptionally well bred, and Terence Millard, who was one of South Africa's top trainers based in Cape Town, selected her. This filly combined the bloodlines of

Ecurie.

some of the top American families with some of the very old Argentinean families, which gave us a complete out-cross. She was a big dark-brown mare with rather a plain head but an immense turn of speed. She won all five of her races as a two-year-old, and then went on to win eight out of her eleven races, including the South African Guineas, against the colts. She was subsequently disqualified for interference with another horse a couple of furlongs from home, a great disappointment.

Wendy, Ken Mackenzie and I attended the gala banquet for the awards for the top horses in South Africa and we were very excited when Ecurie won the top two-year-old filly award. The following year, South Africa was swept with equine influenza. Racing came to standstill and Ecurie was very ill. Although she recovered, it was too late to bring her back into racing and so she went to stud. Top race mares don't always reproduce their own ability and her runners never showed the promise that she had shown. After her fourth foal she died of laminitis. Ecurie was one of our best investments and, because she was racing in South Africa, we were able to see much more of her than we did of our Irish horses.

After the success of Ecurie, Wendy and I decided to go to Argentina to see their studs, and in particular Ecurie's dam. We asked Geoff and Ann Armitage, close friends who had the leading stud in this country, if they would like to come with us. Geoff came from an old-established South African racing and breeding family and was a very knowledgeable horseman. In Argentina, we were well looked after and travelled hundreds of miles through the vast countryside seeing many studs and, of course, Ecurie's dam.

Some seventy years ago, when Argentina was an extremely wealthy country, producing and exporting beef and immense crops of maize and wheat, the rich families invested heavily in top-class bloodstock, and more

English Derby winners were bought and exported to Argentina than to any other country.

We sent some of our mares from Handley Cross down to the Doms brothers in the Western Cape, and added a few mares from Britain as well. We then sold their progeny on the Johannesburg yearling sales. Yet again we found that trying to run a stud investment at long range is not really satisfactory, and we reduced the numbers until eventually that operation came to an end. But we had had an absorbing interest in the equine world in America, France, Britain, Ireland and South Africa.

Back in Rhodesia, we had a modicum of success with the horses we bred, including four or five yearlings that went down to South Africa to Terence Millard for other patrons. That group won fifteen races between them. They were all progeny of Princillon and we also had success with a young stallion, Fairwind, sent to us by Alec Head from their stud, Le Haras du Quesnay, in Normandy. In one season he was the champion sire of two-year-olds in Rhodesia.

> Bill Wakefield, Geoff Armitage and I and others initiated the formation of the Rhodesian Thoroughbred Breeders' Association. I was its first chairman and still have a horse or two in training. Racing and breeding comprise 98 per cent anticipation and two per cent realization.

On one of our trips to Kentucky we took the Armitages with us. An old friend of mine, Barry Ryan, had the lovely Normandy Stud there. His grandfather had invented the Imperial typewriter more than a hundred years earlier and made a fortune. Barry invested his part of the legacy in the stud. He loved his horses and was a reasonably successful trainer, although he did not do this for a living. As he had stayed with us on Handley Cross, he rang up one day to say that he was going to be away for three weeks in the middle of July and if we would like to borrow his house on the stud while he was away, he would be delighted.

It took little persuasion for the four of us to take up this offer and we had a fabulous horse holiday. We drove around Kentucky - the famous bluegrass country - visiting studs with lovely white railings, top stallions and their vets. The industry in America is gigantic, with about 30,000 mares being bred every year.

Wendy did most of the management of our horses at home, and when our daughters started to have babies she was torn between the brood mares and their foals and the grandchildren. Of course, the grandchildren won!

I was away too often to be able to spend the amount of time needed on a stud, so we regretfully held a dispersal sale and now have no horses, although frequently I see horses on the racecourse whose dam or grand-dam came from Handley Cross.

But the stud provided a great upbringing for the grandchildren, who were in and out of the stables. They became acquainted with the mares and knew them by name, and it was lovely to see how a small child, five or six years old, would be looked after by the mares when she wandered into the paddocks. The girls never once had an accident.

Some years earlier, Elizabeth had bought Speedwell, a well-bred South African filly who had not been successful on the racecourse, but she gave Elizabeth a couple of good foals, particularly the bay filly Flounce, who won five or six races.

– 8 –

The UDI Years

Brief history • Rhodesian Front party • Duncan Sandys •
Proposed military intervention • Victoria Falls conference
• Private sector delegation to Britain • Whitney Straight •
Sir Humphrey Gibbs • Bank notes • Joanna V and fuel from South Africa
• Tobacco • Visit to Britain with Vec Hurley • Tiger and Fearless •
Sir Alec Douglas-Home in Parliament • Reggie Paget • Pearce Commission
• Mozambique • South Africa • David Owen's visit
• Sensitive relationships and Boeing aeroplanes
• The US President's prayer breakfast • Lord Carver • The BBC • Awards

Land and its use have always posed a problem in this country, reaching right back to when Cecil John Rhodes obtained concessions from Lobengula, the king of the Matabele, through the Matabele War of 1893/4, the Matabele Rebellion of 1896 and the Shona Rebellion of 1896/7, followed by the granting of the 1889 Royal Charter to the British South Africa Company, led by Rhodes.

In 1922, the year before I was born, a referendum was held for the white population to decide whether they wished to join South Africa or remain as a self-governing colony with allegiance to the Crown. The electorate, in a decisive vote, chose to remain independent, and so the country became self-governing in 1923, with its first small parliament and a premier, known after the first ten years as prime minister. Parliament took over the running of the country from the Chartered Company and had to tackle the problem, among many others, of the allocation of land to the indigenous people and to immigrants.

Under the new constitution, some matters were reserved for approval by the British government. Among them were the control of certain financial matters, foreign affairs and the allocation of land.

In order to enshrine a permanent right for Africans, a Land Apportionment Act was placed on the Statute Book in 1930. This also protected European land, since African land had been protected by a British Order in Council. No white or Asian businesses were allowed to start up and compete in communal land and vice versa. Blacks were not allowed to live in certain parts of the cities. The issue of land was to be dominant from then on.

In 1920 the black population of Rhodesia was 600,000. In 2004 it was 12.7 million, with about another two and a half million citizens living outside the country for economic and political reasons. The success of medical and educational services, which caused the massive increase in population, ultimately put more pressure on the land available in what was called Tribal Trust Land and is now called Communal Land.

The first premier was Sir Charles Coghlan, who was followed by others until Godfrey Huggins, a surgeon, led his United Party to victory. He was knighted and subsequently elevated to the peerage as Lord Malvern. In 1953 he became the first prime minister of the Federation of Rhodesia and Nyasaland.

Internal and external pressures, plus the belief that the three separate territories were too small to be viable entities, led to determined negotiations between the leaders of Southern and Northern Rhodesia and Nyasaland and the British government, resulting in the formation in 1953 of the Federation. Each country maintained its own territorial legislature to deal with domestic affairs, while the federal parliament, based in Salisbury, dealt with broader issues, particularly foreign affairs, finance, agriculture, mining and development.

The Federation came into being without sufficient black African consultation and it therefore clashed with the growing forces of early African nationalism and lasted only a decade. During that period we saw the construction of Kariba Dam, which, at the time, was the largest dam in Africa and the third largest in the world. It led to a great deal of development with particular attention being given to our road systems.

Almost from the start, it appeared that the Federation would not last. The civil servants in Northern Rhodesia and Nyasaland, who had been appointed by the Colonial Office, were largely against surrendering their countries' individuality to a larger entity, and some never really tried to make it a success. Their negative attitude became apparent to the black politicians, and this had a significant bearing on subsequent negotiations on the dismemberment of the Federation and Zambia's full independence. There was always the danger of jealousies surfacing as the two northern territories were convinced that many of the benefits were going to Southern Rhodesia, which was, to some extent, correct.

When Godfrey Huggins became federal prime minister in 1953, he was succeeded in Southern Rhodesia by Garfield Todd, a New Zealander with a missionary background who reached too far ahead of public opinion. In 1958, following a vote of no confidence in the cabinet, Todd was replaced by Sir Edgar Whitehead, who had been our representative in Washington. Sir Edgar had a small farm in the Vumba in Rhodesia but was very much an academic.

Political unrest developed in Northern Rhodesia and Nyasaland, with Kenneth Kaunda and Hastings Banda leading the cry for 'one man, one vote'. Numerous conferences took place to work out a modus operandi for the dissolution of the young Federation. Before Federation, the three countries had been loosely tied together by trade and finance and it seemed likely that they would revert to this position. The British government agreed that their two colonies, Northern Rhodesia and Nyasaland, would be granted their independence upon the dissolution of the Federation.

Southern Rhodesia made similar proposals but, while the granting of independence to the two northern territories was precise and clear, the proposals regarding Southern Rhodesia remained fudged and susceptible to differing interpretations, especially in regard to voting rights for Africans. It was anathema to the Southern Rhodesian government to see the two northern territories, which were far less developed and less likely to manage their own affairs properly, given their full independence, while Rhodesia had to retain her previous status, with the likelihood of interference from Whitehall.

With the dissolution of the Federation on 31 December 1963, politics polarized. Right-wing groups merged and the Rhodesian Front was formed. The Dominion Party, founded in 1956, no longer existed by the time of the 1962 election, nor at the end of Federation.

Alongside Sir Raymond Stockil was Winston Field, an English farmer deeply involved in the tobacco industry. Field was a strong character with good ideas, and clear, forceful arguments, sometimes bordering on dictatorship when overruling his cabinet colleagues. Field, Stockil and Ian Smith had all been on the opposition benches in the Southern Rhodesia Parliament during the Federation.

After the demise of the Federation, Southern Rhodesia had to hold an election, and the central issue was independence. The Rhodesian Front had been formed only in 1962, but the two main parties contesting the election were Sir Edgar Whitehead's United Party, which was in power, and the Rhodesian Front, led at that time by Winston Field.

The Rhodesian Front's objective was to win as many seats as possible, to try and stop the United Party from making too many concessions in their negotiations with Britain. They never thought that they would actually win the election. To their complete astonishment – and that of the country at large – they won a majority of five seats, so the Governor asked Field to form the new government. The Rhodesian Front had no one with cabinet experience, but they set about appointing a cabinet and governing the country.

In 1964 I received a call from London to say that Duncan Sandys, who was likely to become Minister for the Commonwealth, was planning to visit Rhodesia. I was asked to look after him for two days, show him around the country and give him introductions. I pointed out that he was arriving on the first day of the July Rhodes and Founders' holiday, which stretched from Saturday to Tuesday. Many people he wanted to see would be away, but we would be pleased if he would spend the weekend and I would invite a few people to meet him and then help him later with more formal meetings in Harare.

I met him at the airport, we went down to the farm and that afternoon seven or eight people flew in to our landing strip. They were from different sectors of the community but mainly farmers. We had a dinner party for him that night, the ladies withdrew after dinner and we talked about the intractable situation in Rhodesia. This discussion, hardly surprisingly, went on late into the night. I recall my surprise, never before having met anybody who could drink Drambuie not in a liqueur glass but in a tumbler, and he polished off the whole bottle that night.

The next day we drove across country to Sinoia, having arranged on the way to meet groups of farmers, black and white, across both tribal trust and commercial farming areas, for him to see the contrast and to meet some members of Parliament.

It was not generally known that in 1964 the British government, led by Harold Wilson, was contemplating, as one of the options, a military invasion of Rhodesia in the event of a unilateral declaration of independence. The availability of forces and the logistical support required were intensively investigated. They took into account the danger of impairing relations with South Africa, and also, importantly, the reaction of members of the British armed forces who might be fighting kith and kin. The Chief of Defence Staff, Lord Louis Mountbatten, Americans such as Adlai Stevenson, and the former Colonial Secretary, Iain Macleod, said that British military intervention was 'inconceivable' owing to the strength of the armed forces of the Federation. They analysed the reaction of the Rhodesian forces and concluded that the Rhodesian Light Infantry would be the unit to put up the greatest resistance.

An important aspect for British troops would be the supply chain, which would have to grow longer and longer, the availability of aircraft, and how to get into Rhodesia, perhaps through Lusaka. They were concerned about the safety of the Kariba Dam. It was a very thorough investigation. The Governor, Sir Humphrey Gibbs, consulted with Ken Flower, the Head of Secret Intelligence, who told him that the loyalty to the Crown of the Rhodesian chiefs of staff, Major-General 'Sam' Putterill and Air Vice-Marshal Harold Hawkins, was not in doubt, and that many of their senior officers would follow their lead, but that there could be no guarantee that that would be a universal response. After some time the whole proposal was dropped.

It became clear that Great Britain was adamant about not giving Rhodesia her independence, particularly as the country's parliamentary system reserved fifty seats for whites and fourteen, later sixteen, for blacks, eight of whom were elected directly and eight indirectly by the electoral college. This would have resulted in a largely white parliament. (This franchise was changed in 1970.) Anyone with sufficient educational and property qualifications could vote, regardless of colour. Two voters' rolls were established, allowing those not sufficiently educated or well off to qualify for the A voters' roll to be included on a B roll. These B roll voters were nearly all indigenous; five seats were reserved for them. The emerging African nationalists, led initially by Joshua Nkomo (ZAPU) and the Revd Ndabaningi Sithole (ZANU), demanded universal franchise. Numerically, this would have resulted in an almost totally black Parliament, which was the sticking point.

The British Conservative government had given assurances that Rhodesia would be given its independence at the break-up of Federation, but the wording of the texts was not clear. This led the Rhodesian government to mistrust British motives even more, and vice versa.

The Federation was dissolved in 1963 after a conference held for that purpose at Victoria Falls, with all three territories represented. Winston Field refused to participate unless there was a precondition that Rhodesia would be given its independence with no possibility of reverting to the 1961 Southern Rhodesian constitution. Field agreed to attend when R.A. 'Rab' Butler, British Foreign Secretary, said, 'Southern Rhodesia will be given independence on terms no less favourable than the other two territories'.

The British later denied that this meant independence under the existing qualified franchise with continued white rule.

The Labour government was in no position to vary its stance to grant Rhodesia independence because in 1963 Harold Wilson, then the leader of the opposition, had sent the notorious 'Didymus Mutasa letter', saying that a Labour government was opposed to Southern Rhodesia gaining independence on anything less than universal franchise. This tied Labour's hand when it became the ruling party in Britain in 1964.

The long-suspected duplicity of the British government became clear towards the end of the Victoria Falls conference. The final communiqué stated that at the dissolution of the Federation Rhodesia would not automatically be granted its independence. This was unacceptable to Field and his cabinet.

By 1964, the Rhodesian Front cabinet had begun to lose confidence in Winston Field's strength to carry through their policies. They held a caucus meeting on 2 April, with Ian Smith in the chair, and passed a vote of no confidence in the prime minister. Sir Humphrey Gibbs, the Governor, urged him to stay on but accepted his resignation on 13 April. Ian Smith succeeded him. Smith, the son of a Scottish immigrant, had been an RAF Spitfire pilot during the Second World War and had served with distinction. He continued the endless negotiations with Britain, but it became increasingly clear that the impasse could not be broken.

It had become apparent to many of us that the British private sector did not know what was going on in our private sector at this time. I was asked to lead a private-sector group, which would spend three weeks in Britain helping to acquaint British private-sector organizations with the facts about Rhodesia. In my team of eleven were: Jeremy Field, son of Winston and a tobacco grower and banker; Ian Tunmer, a leading cattle auctioneer from Gwelo; the surgeon John Strong from Bulawayo; Charles Allen, a barrister who had been in the Royal Navy; Rolf Henwood, who was involved in vehicle assembly and distribution; and Wickus de Kock, a South African who was farming in Rhodesia. De Kock was a leader of the Afrikaans community and later became a cabinet minister.

Our delegation was warmly welcomed. I spent a week in London organizing the itinerary for each member of the team so that we covered the whole country and met people from industry, commerce, banking, agriculture, education and health.

The national daily newspapers and the BBC were interested, and so, because of our inexperience, we put each of our team through dummy television interviews to see who could handle hostile and difficult questions. We eventually agreed that only three of us should do radio and television appearances or press interviews.

On one occasion I was to speak at the London School of Economics on 'Rhodesia and its Independence'. There were twelve speakers on the platform and we were each given twenty minutes. They kindly gave me the slot after the beer break, by which time the large audience was well steamed up. Patrick Wall MP told me that he had overheard plans at the top table to immobilize the microphone to make me less audible. I gather that out of my twenty minutes they may have heard me speak for ten. The heckling and interruptions were overwhelming. I merely continued with my prepared speech. The Cockney humour and the question-and-answer session afterwards, however, relieved some of the tension. I was also invited to speak to the Oxford Union, but a clash of commitments saved me from another mauling.

On the same trip, the racing driver Whitney Straight invited Ian Tunmer and me to lunch at Bucks Club in London. He was sure oil sanctions would follow any declaration of independence and that the problems which would arise would be substantial. He asked if he could help in some way. Straight had a wide range of contacts in the oil world and asked if we would like to be put in touch with somebody who might be of assistance. Later that afternoon I received a call from Athens from a man in the oil-tanker business, who suggested that we meet to discuss contingency plans.

Whitney Straight was born to wealthy parents in New York, but his father had died in 1919. Six years later his mother married an Englishman and moved the family to Great Britain. As a boy, Straight was driven by two great passions, flying and motor racing. Reportedly he became the youngest licensed pilot in Britain at the age of sixteen. Because Cambridge students were not allowed cars while attending the university, he would ride his bicycle to the local airport, board his own plane and fly to the motor racing event.

In 1933 a victory at Brooklands brought him to the attention of the British motoring press. Then he embarked on the Grand Prix circuit of the Continent. Straight, his personal valet and one or two team drivers would fly to the race. He won the Donnington Grand Prix that year but knew that he would need a more powerful car to compete against the German Silver Arrows. He tried unsuccessfully to buy one of the Auto Unions. The team, impressed by his ability, offered him some rides in

1935 but by then he had promised his wife to quit racing. His swan song was winning the inaugural Grand Prix in South Africa.

When war came, Straight, now a British subject, joined the RAF. He shot down several German fighters, but he himself was downed by ground fire over occupied France. He was captured but escaped a year later and, with the help of the French underground, returned to Britain and resumed flying. By the end of the war he was a much-decorated RAF Group Captain. He would later become managing director of BOAC and serve on the board of directors at Rolls Royce.

On this mission we had great help from the Institute of Directors, the Confederation of British Industries, bankers and many friends. We arrived back in Rhodesia exactly one week before UDI, having met or spoken to people with a wide range of opinion in Britain and, to a limited extent, France. We had established contacts and made friends who stood us in good stead in later years.

The key issue remained complete independence for Southern Rhodesia. As relations with Britain worsened, many attempts were made to broker an agreement, but without success. This was the situation when, in exasperation and believing there was no alternative, Rhodesia made her Unilateral Declaration of Independence on 11 November 1965.

I remember that I lunched with a few friends on that day at the Harare Club. We knew that the prime minister, Ian Smith, would in all likelihood be making a significant statement. We gathered around the radio and listened to his unilateral declaration of independence. It was a sombre moment and our group discussed from different viewpoints the wisdom, or otherwise, of his action. The country had been put in an impossible position following the break-up of the Federation and the granting of independence to Zambia under Kenneth Kaunda in 1964, while the same right had been denied to Rhodesia. The situation had dragged on for too long.

So Rhodesia became independent without international recognition. Its independence was not recognized by the British government who, with the Americans, took the matter to the United Nations. The UN then imposed widespread sanctions, which dominated the affairs of Rhodesia for the next fifteen years. During this period there were some moves to widen their scope and even to impose additional sanctions.

During these difficult political times the Governor, Sir Humphrey Gibbs, had continued at his post, as he would not leave unless asked to do so by Her Majesty the Queen, to whom he owed his allegiance. After

UDI he was virtually a prisoner in Government House, with only a small group of loyal aides to support him. Nevertheless, he remained at his post until the government declared Rhodesia a republic in 1969 and the Union Jack at Government House was lowered. Sir Humphrey returned to his farm at Nyamandhlovu near Bulawayo, having earned the admiration and respect of many people for his fortitude, conduct and principles.

Sir Humphrey Gibbs.

The consequences of UDI are debatable but many of us believed that an alternative course should have been pursued. Clearly a small country such as ours could not defy the rest of the world. We were largely self-sufficient in basic foodstuffs but depended on our foreign-exchange earnings from mining and agriculture, of which chrome, gold, cotton and tobacco were principal. As our country is landlocked, we could not have survived without the help of Mozambique and South Africa.

At UDI, the Germans were developing an increasing interest in what was happening in Rhodesia. When sanctions were applied, our connection with the printers of our banknotes, the established British company, de la Rue, could no longer continue. (Interestingly, a de la Rue descendant was a successful and well-known rancher in the south of Rhodesia.) A German firm was prepared to help. In great secrecy, they printed our banknotes, but the secret leaked, and when the British government discovered what was happening it immediately brought pressure to bear on the German government. A charter plane containing our banknotes was ready for take-off but was intercepted at the airport. Permission to fly was refused because of political pressure.

This developed into a very sensitive diplomatic matter. The Germans were most reluctant to dishonour the contract, especially since the notes had already been printed. We reached a compromise and agreed to release the Germans from the contract in exchange for supplying us with modern printing equipment to print our banknotes ourselves. This allowed us to be completely independent and Fidelity Printers in Msasa was built to print the country's currency. Today (2007), with inflation at such incredible heights, the need for the Reserve Bank to print more and more money is keeping those presses running day and night.

For the Rhodesia National Farmers Union, one of the first consequences of UDI was when our able director, Paul Boenders, advised the presidential group of his resignation. Boenders felt he had no option. He was British and loyal to the Queen and could not continue to work (much as he would have liked to do so) for a national organization in a country now in rebellion to the Crown. It was a great loss; he had served farming well.

Britain applied the first sanctions, blockading the port of Beira to prevent us importing or exporting. Then the UN sanctions came into force with remarkable speed, and very quickly fuel had to be rationed.

Our only oil port at the time was Beira and fuel companies had large oil storage tanks there. After UDI, a deal was very soon set in motion to secure our supplies, by delivering oil to us on a tanker called the *Joanna V*, which would off-load directly into the Beira Feruka pipeline.

The British Navy by that time had instituted the Beira naval patrol and had made it clear that they would prevent the *Joanna V* from entering port, by force if necessary. The naval patrol could only operate outside Mozambican waters. A serious crisis developed in early January and the stand-off continued for some days. The question was whether the *Joanna V* would enter port and off-load, or if she would be prevented from doing so by the Navy. For us it was crucial that she berthed because our supplies were extremely low and, had fuel completely run out, the country would have collapsed in a very short time. In the end, after much diplomatic activity, *Joanna V*, without discharging her cargo, turned round and went elsewhere.

It is less well known that a previous ship,

Joanna V.

the *Manuela* (named after the owner's daughter; the *Joanna* was named after his wife), had unsuccessfully attempted to off-load her cargo of oil in Beira. We never received the oil and both ships eventually returned to Greece.

Besides the Beira–Feruka pipeline, our other source of fuel at that time was the giant oil-from-coal project, SASOL, in South Africa. Its chairman was Dr Etienne Rousseau. I had become acquainted with him and he had visited us on several occasions. He became a very good friend.

In the first few weeks of UDI, South Africa had tried officially to keep out of the sanctions-breaking arena, but when the *Joanna V* was unable to unload they realized that, if Rhodesia were to survive, they had to help. The South African President, Hendrik Verwoerd, was away and the decision whether or not to send fuel to us fell on Rousseau's shoulders. It was a moment of history and the implications for South Africa were immense. His decision was clear and swift and within the day a fleet of road tankers was travelling from SASOL in South Africa to Rhodesia. They arrived when our stocks were down to twelve hours' supply. That incident was the forerunner of many in years to come which enabled the Rhodesian regime to hold out. The pipeline from Beira to Umtali, which had been built by a company in which Lonrho was principal shareholder, remained unused.

Even the export of tobacco on existing contracts was stopped. With Brazil and the United States, Rhodesia was one of the world's three largest producers of Virginia tobacco, making it easily our most important economic crop. The growing season for tobacco starts in August/September, and by 11 November of that year a full crop was in the ground and already growing. Tobacco exports had to cease immediately and stockpiles started to build up. No one knew how long the situation would last and tobacco was placed under strict, secret control.

The Tobacco Corporation, which would handle tobacco sales for the government, was formed under the chairmanship of a good friend of mine, Sam Whaley, senior partner of one of the oldest legal partnerships in the country and director of many companies, who later became a senator. He was followed by Frank Buch, who shared offices with me and was another close friend. He had been deputy chairman of the Roan Selection Trust, a giant copper mining concern in Zambia, and was an astute businessman.

Growers were to finish, cure and grade the crops that were already planted. Public auctions stopped and almost all of the 1966 crop was taken into storage. The Tobacco Board paid the growers for their tobacco, based on weight, quality and classification. That year's crop was 250 million kilogrammes. Simultaneously, growers were allocated production quotas of about a third of their previous annual production, averaged over the past three years. The industry was determined not to lose its growing skills and hoped before long to regain some of its lost markets.

The physical volume of tobacco was enormous. All the tobacco merchants' warehousing quickly filled up. The old Belvedere airfield on the outskirts of Salisbury was commandeered, and acres of storage sheds were constructed, using corrugated-iron roofing, to store the crop. The sheds measured 300 × 100 metres and were built on the old runway. The sheds were clad and air-tight so it was possible to fumigate shed after shed against insect damage and store tobacco for a long time. However, each year we were adding a third of our normal production to the stockpile. By the end of the third year we had two years' tobacco crop in storage.

Sanctions were tightly enforced, although by using alternative certificates of origin a trickle of tobacco was able to leave the country via our neighbours. Only very small quantities of tobacco were sold in the first two or three years after the imposition of sanctions, but the cigarette manufacturers BAT missed our flavourful leaf. All matters to do with tobacco, normally our biggest export, were shrouded in secrecy.

One of the problems was financing the stockpile. But we did succeed in keeping two-thirds of the farmers on the land. It was essential to keep grower skills intact at both management and worker level. We bartered tobacco for textiles, vehicles, fertilizer: you name it, we found a market. Our intelligence people knew their opposite numbers in most countries, and it was their job to develop systems for getting our tobacco to the end user. Special documents certifying a different country of origin were drawn up and tobacco production in Mozambique grew exponentially before the departure of the Portuguese. It is interesting to note that in the first five years of UDI not an ounce of tobacco was lost. Some tobacco was trucked through Namibia to Angola and then on to Europe, with Angolan and other certificates of origin. Once it was blended it was not easy to determine where it had actually originated.

The Tobacco Research Board at Kutsaga did invaluable work. They were able, through changing fertilizing and growing techniques, to adapt cultivars to suit market demand and to change and adapt the actual tobacco leaf so that, with only small time delays, we had what the market wanted from tobacco in storage from our vast stockpile. They also worked on effective pest controls, now that tobacco was being stored for much longer periods.

In 1966, when it became clearer that both sides had under-estimated the effects and timescale of UDI, discussions were reopened. From these, it seemed that a low-calibre, small, non-partisan group might attempt to assess the possibility of another look at the problems. To this end, Vec Hurley and I went to London to see if there was any chink in the door. Neither of us was involved in politics in any partisan way and, if our cover was blown, we were in no way officially accredited. Professor Dick Christie, who had significant legal and constitutional knowledge, was to join us.

Hurley and I had other business to do in France and went ahead whilst arrangements were put in place for us to be received. During this time there was an unfortunate leak relating to Professor Christie's involvement so it was decided that he should not join us.

Before we left we had discussions with Sir Robert Taylor, who had been Secretary of the Zambian Treasury and, in Federation, was Secretary of the Federal Treasury. He was an outstanding man who, after he had left Zambia, was much involved in banking in Britain and became deputy chairman of Standard Chartered Bank and chairman of Costains. He gave me a short memorandum on the lines which he would have taken, had he been negotiating:

> Anyone who has had any experience of lobbying a government knows that it is quite useless going along and saying, 'We don't like such and such'. The chances of success are much greater if you can produce a piece of paper which goes beyond this opening gambit and indicates an alternative which would be more tolerable than whatever it is you are complaining about.
>
> Such a piece of paper cannot be produced by direct negotiation between the British and Rhodesian governments. Indeed, I am even sorry that Selwyn Lloyd has taken a hand in the game because even if he has come back with the right ideas it will be difficult for Wilson to accept a solution proffered on a Conservative platter. This thing cannot be done under the glare of the searchlights of modern publicity.
>
> I think that there must be an intermediate stage between the two governments negotiating again and the present impasse. That period must be used to produce a 'bit of paper' which would define the sort of things that IF they were officially to reopen negotiations they would probably find it possible to reach agreement upon. They must NOT meet to negotiate and break up again without having reached agreement. The two things – Negotiation/Agreement – must go together this time. Therefore they must know what they could jointly agree upon before they start a new round of negotiations. And one of the most important

things on each side would be for the respective parties to consider how they could save the other's face. Strange though it may sound, Smith must think of Wilson; Wilson must think of Smith!

The preparations for this stage probably require a small group of people in London working with a similar group in Salisbury. They must have no official relationship to the governments, but I think the governments must know (secretly and privately) of their existence and tacitly approve of their activities. The governments would in effect say, 'Look, Mr X, Y and Z, don't think you're negotiating for Rhodesia/Britain because you're definitely not: but of course if your studies should result in a substantial measure of agreement we would like to know what it is.'

As I see it there are two new facts to be considered – one on each side.

On the British side it must be accepted as a FACT that sanctions are not going to produce a 'quick kill'.

On the Rhodesian side, it must equally be accepted that, contrary to pre-UDI belief, there are sanctions, they are grievous, and this has been no 'nine-day wonder'.

If both sides will face up realistically to these two facts, we might get somewhere. But it may be that both facts have got to sink in a bit further before effective use can be made of them.

On our visit, we were initially received by the Master of the Rolls, Lord Denning. He gave us lunch at the Law Courts and was positive about what we were trying to do, and he in turn opened more doors. A couple of days later we had a meeting with Elwyn Jones, the Attorney-General. At the beginning of the discussion I complimented him on the quality of Herefords in England; a number of Hereford bulls had been sent to Rhodesia to the Black family at Mguta. Elwyn Jones in turn passed us on to the legal side of the Foreign Office, where we saw Sir William Dale. He had hoped that we would be able to see Michael Stewart, the Foreign Secretary, but, the situation being so sensitive, that meeting never took place.

We met a wide cross-section of people, all committed to try and help in some way with the resolution of the very difficult problem. When we went home, we left behind a small group in Britain who had knowledge of Rhodesia and who had access to the right people to continue what we had started.

Vec Hurley and I were given the opportunity of a useful discussion with Selwyn Lloyd, followed by an invaluable 45 minutes with Sir Alec

Douglas-Home. Selwyn Lloyd had been in Rhodesia and spent a night with us on the farm previously. The opportunity for dialogue and for the expression of different strategies was well worthwhile.

Later that year, further negotiations took place between the Rhodesian and British governments. One of the British team was Sir Denis Greenhill, the Permanent Under Secretary or head of the Foreign Office, who later became deeply involved and who visited Rhodesia several times. His autobiography gives an intriguing account of the negotiations leading up to, during and after the talks on the high seas. The Rhodesian negotiating team included three Smiths - Prime Minister Ian Smith, the Attorney-General E. A. T. (Tony) Smith, and George Smith, before he became a judge of the High Court.

Emotions ran high, and the negotiators from both sides were constantly coming and going between Salisbury and Whitehall, seeking a solution to the problem of Rhodesia's independence. There were strong lobbies in the United Kingdom highly critical of the British government's actions and attitude towards Rhodesia, and some lobbies in Rhodesia strongly repudiated UDI.

Following on from these talks, two attempts to find a solution were made on the high seas, as neither government was enthusiastic about visiting the other country. The first of these was on board HMS *Tiger* in 1966, but the proposals for settlement agreed on the *Tiger* were rejected by the Rhodesian cabinet. The talks on HMS *Fearless* in 1968 did not manage to produce proposals.

Some of the Rhodesian team on the *Tiger* said that relations between Smith and Wilson showed signs of improvement and that, in an informal chat on deck, Wilson said to Ian Smith, 'If you and I can clinch this agreement as it is now - and I think we can - I am going to have a problem with my backbenchers and you are going to have a problem with your extreme right-wingers.'

> Lord Denning told us a story against himself. He had been ribbed by his fellow judges, who asked him how he could have come so much under the influence of Miss Christine Keeler, a call-girl. Her involvement with John Profumo and, at the same time, with a Russian diplomat was sensitive, and Lord Denning was asked to do a report on the security aspects of the case. He denied any such influence until his fellow judges referred him to a certain page in his report. Up to that stage he had been referring to 'Miss Keeler' and thereafter he referred to her as 'Christine'.

Harold Wilson, Sir Humphrey Gibbs and Ian Smith on H.M.S. *Fearless*, October 1968.

By 1971, the small barter deals had accumulated such that the decision was taken to re-open the tobacco auction floors to a limited degree. This was done in complete secrecy but, by 1977, all our tobacco was being sold by auction again. The risks were enormous: anyone found buying Rhodesian tobacco faced a fine of £1,000 and ten years' imprisonment. It all operated on a need-to-know basis and, as chairman of Tobacco Sales, I never went on to the floor, so I could honestly say that I did not know it was happening.

Thus the farming community found itself having to adapt to changes in farming. These imperatives led to an increase in cattle farming, as we were able to export dairy and beef products to the region. The infant cotton industry boomed because cotton grew well in a large part of the country and its origins, once beyond our borders, were easier to mask.

With Rhodesian affairs frequently raised in the House of Commons, the interest of the Parliamentary Correspondents' Association became increasingly focused on us. This group consisted of one or two journalists from each of the main newspapers, whose sole job was to report on Parliament. We invited some of them to visit us and showed them around the country for a week during a British parliamentary recess, to give them a better perception of our country. This visit was of significant value to both sides, and I got to know many of those senior newspaper men. Soon afterwards, I happened to be in London in 1971 when Sir Alec Douglas-Home was in Rhodesia, engaged with crucial talks with Ian Smith. The chairman of the Association, David Thompson of the *Daily Mirror*, rang me up and said that Sir Alec was going to make a statement to Parliament on his return the next day at 3.00 p.m. He invited me to join them to hear what Sir Alec had to say.

When I arrived, I was interested to observe that there were very few Members of Parliament in the chamber for the debate, which was on some very mundane issue. They hardly managed a quorum until about 2.45 p.m. when, like a flood, members entered the chambers from all sides. In a very few minutes the whole of the chamber was full, with some people standing and others sitting on the floor.

The Speaker interrupted the debate and said that he was suspending the current debate because Sir Alec had visited Rhodesia, had held meetings with Mr Smith, and wished to make a statement to Parliament. Sir Alec made a brief initial report, informed the House that the government would make time available for a full debate on Rhodesia, with no time limitation, the following Wednesday, in the light of which he did not propose to go into any detail about his visit at that time.

One of our visitors in previous months had been a fascinating man, Reggie Paget, Labour MP for Northampton, who had a connection with Rhodesia because his cousin, Edward Paget, had been one of the earlier Anglican bishops. Another of his cousins was the well-known war-time general. A wealthy landowner of ten thousand acres in Northampton, who was master of a pack of fox hounds and drove a Rolls Royce, he was hardly the typical Labour MP, but, in spite of that background, he had joined the party. It was a love–hate relationship, his party of course delighted to have such a person in their ranks, despite the fact that he sometimes embarrassed them. (An example of this was his support for the Smith government. He had said in 1965 that he wished there was an African nationalist government in Southern Rhodesia but, as the UK was incapable of imposing one, they had to be practical. This was anathema to the Labour Party.)

When the Speaker told Parliament that they would resume debate on the matter, Paget sprang to his feet and proposed that the House should adjourn on a matter of serious national importance. When that takes place, the Speaker is obliged under parliamentary rules to allow the proposer of the adjournment to make a brief statement as to why an adjournment should be voted on.

Reggie Paget was given the floor and he said he did not wish to lose the opportunity to congratulate Sir Alec on an achievement far greater than anything that his own leader, Harold Wilson, had been able to do. This of course was music to the ears of the Conservatives and infuriated the Labour benches. Bedlam broke out in this august chamber of Members of Parliament and it went on for a few minutes, in spite of repeated calls for order from the Speaker.

I was sitting in the front bench of the Press Gallery, only a few metres above and away from where Paget was standing. He was being hassled by a small group of very young Labour MPs behind him and I was astonished to see him turn on his heel and admonish them, saying, 'Shut up you silly c——s.' I had always thought that there was high decorum in debate in Parliament and turned to my host and asked him if he had heard the same language as I had? He smiled and said I had heard correctly but because words were not spoken with the member facing the Speaker, there would be no record in Hansard and therefore it was not unparliamentary to have said what he did.

Reggie Paget, having made his point, withdrew the proposal to adjourn the house. My friend in the parliamentary lobby invited me to join them on the Wednesday to listen to the full debate on Rhodesia. He suggested that I have a good lunch beforehand and even bring a packet of sandwiches, as they anticipated that the debate would run well into the middle of the night, which it did. It was a fascinating and unforgettable experience.

The late Ted Jeffreys had persistently warned the government of the consequences of its actions in regard to the international tobacco market under sanctions, as had other leaders in this field. The outside world of tobacco buyers had no option but to obey the instructions of their own governments and of the UN. Jeffreys, who was president of the Rhodesia Tobacco Association from 1962 to 1965, wrote, 'at the time, we were poised as second of the world's leading exporters ... In a few years we could have become the world's leading exporter. All this we lost.'

Sandy Fircks, also a former president of the RTA and also a member of the Tobacco Corporation, said in 1971, 'Brazil's tobacco industry would not exist today if it had not been for UDI. This country would be producing 400 million kg per year today.'

The agreement reached on 21 November 1971 between Ian Smith and Sir Alec Douglas-Home, for a settlement between the British and Rhodesian governments, started with the following statement:

> The proposals set out below are conditional upon the British government being satisfied that they are acceptable to the people of Rhodesia as a whole. The British government will therefore appoint a commission to ascertain directly from all sections of the population of Rhodesia whether or not these proposals are acceptable and to report accordingly to the British government. It will consist of a chairman [who was Lord Pearce], deputy chairmen [Lord Harlech and Maurice Dorman] and a number of commissioners. The report will be signed by the chairman and the deputy chairmen. The members of the commission will travel extensively throughout the country visiting in particular all the centres of population, local councils and traditional meeting places in the tribal trust lands.

Lord Pearce later reported that the Smith–Home agreement was unacceptable to the people of Rhodesia as a whole. The Pearce Commission's conclusion was:

> We are satisfied on our evidence that the proposals are acceptable to the great majority of Europeans. We are equally satisfied after considering all our evidence, including that on intimidation, that the majority of Africans rejected the proposals. In our opinion, the people of Rhodesia as a whole do not regard the proposals as a basis for independence.

The sadness, however, for both parties was that the agreement that Sir Alec had reached with Ian Smith was aborted and so the saga of UDI ran on for another nine years.

The Frelimo revolution in Mozambique in 1975 reduced our allies from two to one. Following the Portuguese coup in April 1974 and the granting of independence to Mozambique the following year, that country broke off any form of relationship with us. Rhodesia's Special Branch gathered together in Mozambique dissidents in opposition to Frelimo and helped them in forming Renamo. In fact Frelimo engaged in hostilities along our eastern border as well as providing a launch pad for the ZANU forces.

It was suggested in December 1974 that I should go to Maputo to pay a courtesy visit to the outgoing governor-general and to meet some of the new administration. I took with me Ted Eustace, who was a member of the ZPC, and Terry Leaver, who was in the Rhodesian army. He had to take special leave and dress in civvies. The army had put him through university to read Portuguese because they needed fluent Portuguese linguists to liaise with our Mozambican neighbours.

The governor-general's residence was a magnificent old Portuguese palace. We were well received, and it was interesting that one of the principal members of Machel's staff was the young army office Armando Guebuza. (Now, in 2007, some thirty years later, he is President of Mozambique.) We had worthwhile discussions with Guebuza and his team, stressing the need for inter-dependence for the benefit of both countries, and explained that we were not a political group but were investigating opportunities for linking the transport routes, later to be the Beira Corridor, and for agriculture, tourism and other sectors that could benefit both countries.

It was macabre to drive to the airport from the Polana hotel in Maputo and see half-finished buildings, abandoned when the Portuguese artisans fled the country. There were cranes standing next door to half-finished high-rise blocks of flats, with a concrete bucket dangling from a cable just as it was when they left all those years before.

It has been tragic to see the rich resources of countries such as Zimbabwe, Angola, Zambia and Mozambique being stripped by ethnic divisions, civil war and narrow nationalism. Meaningful development in the fields of minerals, gas and hydro-electricity is, however, now taking place in the region.

International attention began to be directed towards the support that South Africa was giving Rhodesia, which in the world's view was an illegal regime. It had reached the point where Rhodesia was becoming an embarrassment to our southern neighbours. The South Africans had to look seriously at their options, whether to continue propping up Rhodesia in the face of this worldwide criticism or to abandon us in order to take the heat off themselves. They had their own problems with the worldwide opposition to apartheid. It must be remembered that the Iron Curtain still existed, and that South Africa, Angola and Zimbabwe were pawns in the Cold War.

Ian Smith remained obdurate and the South African government's impatience with him increased. Finally, in 1975, when he refused to acknowledge the South African dilemma and to enter into meaningful negotiations, they withdrew the entire support force of their army and police, overnight. It was an evacuation conducted in great secrecy. The order was given one afternoon for every single South African unit, wherever they were, to report to Beitbridge by 0800 hours the following morning and that non-essential equipment could be left behind. Ian Smith told me that, at 7.30 a.m. on that morning, Jack Gaylard, who was the Secretary to the Cabinet, telephoned to give him the news that the South Africans had pulled out. It was a hammer blow and he found it difficult to believe that his friends in South Africa, without giving him any inkling, had deserted him. He had relied on them for too long. The pendulum had swung and the withdrawal of their support meant that our smaller armed forces had to take the full brunt of the nationalist onslaught from all sides.

The South African displeasure sharpened the tensions between the two governments, as was evidenced in a strange way when the South African Rugby Board invited Ian Smith to Ellis Park to watch a test game. He was not seated in his usual place in the front line, but rather pointedly towards the back of the VIP enclosure. The word got around the crowd that he was there and they started to chant 'We want Ian Smith ...', which became the refrain all around the field. Ian Smith rose to his feet, moved to the front and received a standing ovation from the crowd, which went on for some minutes. It had a telling effect on Smith in one way, and on the South African prime minister and ministers in another way, and showed what 'people support' Smith had in South Africa.

It was clear that Rhodesia was getting fuel from somewhere, and not necessarily only from SASOL in South Africa. Accusations were levelled at British Petroleum. The British government established a one-man Royal Commission of Inquiry. The work was entrusted to a distinguished English judge, Lord Bingham. He eventually published 'the Bingham Report', clearing the name of British Petroleum. He had had a difficult task. South Africa was not self-sufficient in fuel despite SASOL and had to import part of its requirements. Once oil had reached South African ports, it was blended and its identity became lost. It was therefore not easy to prove who was selling oil to Rhodesia.

My father had always told me to avoid party politics so as to avoid having to have a blind adherence to party dogma or the discipline of a party whip, and thereby I could retain my independence. Later, this advice proved helpful and effective, as I was frequently asked to undertake work that could not have been done by anybody who had a strong political affiliation. When one of these situations developed, Ken Flower, Director General of the Rhodesian Central Intelligence Organization, would approach me. Ken Flower did an outstanding job in this position. He has been, I believe, unjustifiably criticized, particularly by people who are not aware of the code of conduct between senior intelligence men from different countries. Flower had served three prime ministers, and President Mugabe asked him to continue in his position, an indication of the regard in which he was held.

On one such occasion in 1977, Flower told me that Dr David Owen, the British Labour Foreign Secretary, would be coming to Salisbury for discussions with Ian Smith. Neither was particularly keen to see the other but, because of the political imperatives, they had no alternative. Ken Flower thought it would be worthwhile using the periods between meetings to familiarize Dr Owen with the country and for him to see other groups, and asked me to arrange meetings for him, independent of government.

It was obviously important, in the very limited time available, to get Dr Owen to meet the business community, farmers, especially tobacco and food farmers, miners, the African farmers' unions, and the RNFU and the ZTA and to see something of the country but not too far from Salisbury. So I accepted the task and shortly afterwards a British diplomat, Mike Mansfield, who was at that time British ambassador to The Hague, came out and we spent time together on the plan.

We discussed the various routes we would take both inside and outside Salisbury. Mansfield said he would like to travel along the exact routes with me to be completely familiar with the plan. The main destinations outside Salisbury were Marandellas, fifty miles to the east, and the new, nearby, flourishing Dombotombo township, where we wanted Dr Owen to meet leaders of the African community and of the parties. We also wished to go to the Chihota Tribal Trust area, which at that time was reserved for sole occupation by Africans, so we went to visit Chief Chihota.

The first hurdle was to decide who would receive Dr and Mrs Owen on the tarmac of the airport, and Mansfield asked if I would do that. When they arrived, the plan was that Dr Owen would go straight into political meetings and I would take care of Mrs Owen until that evening.

Mike Mansfield tactfully told me that sensitivity had arisen in their camp. They had found out that my personal car was a sanctions-breaking German-manufactured Mercedes and, as David Owen had a majority of only two hundred in his Plymouth seat in Parliament, undue adverse publicity could jeopardize his prospects of re-election. Mansfield very politely said they would prefer the Owens to travel in a non-sanctions-breaking vehicle. It was understandable and I took the point, but I did advise that the non-sanctions-breaking vehicle in which Mrs Owen would travel would be using sanctions-breaking BP fuel and I wondered if that would be of concern to them – or whether they would bring their own personal supply.

I was then told that one of the British Embassy Jaguars from Pretoria would come up to take David Owen around. I explained to Mansfield that the British Jaguar would be travelling in a Rhodesian police convoy from Beitbridge to Salisbury and would of course be using sanctions-breaking fuel, which might attract attention.

We assembled at the airport. I had been warned that David Owen, one of the youngest foreign secretaries ever to be appointed in the UK, was somewhat arrogant and dismissive, and this proved to be correct. He was said by the foreign service to be one of the most unpopular foreign secretaries for many years.

Lord Bingham's report into suspected sanctions-breaking activities by BP had only recently been released. While waiting for the Owens on the tarmac, I became aware that not far from us was a giant BP tanker waiting to refuel David Owen's VC10. I thought what a sensational photo that would be for the British press. Here was an excellent opportunity for a photographer on the balcony of the airport building to get a photo of the VC10 with the Owens walking across the tarmac and the BP tanker in the background. There seemed no point in being provocative so I arranged with security to have the offending tanker moved to the other side of the airport.

The cars were all lined up to receive the Owens in their Royal Air Force VC10. But, while we waited on the tarmac, we received a message to say that talks with Kenneth Kaunda had been extended and that Dr Owen would be arriving an hour later.

After they landed and after formal and somewhat perfunctory introductions, I explained to David Owen that Mike Mansfield and I, together with the local dignitaries, had planned an itinerary for him, which we hoped he would enjoy. He then went to a meeting with Ian Smith, and we took Mrs Owen to visit Salisbury Central Hospital. As Wendy was away, I had asked a friend of ours, Margaret Strong, if she would accompany me to help look after Mrs Owen, which she did very graciously. We had arranged for nursing staff and a multiracial group of women to meet her at the hospital.

Mrs Owen was delighted with the idea and I asked her who she would like to travel with. The Jaguar had gone with David Owen and she said that she preferred to travel with me, as she would like me to explain the city to her as we passed. I warned her that I had been told that neither she nor her husband was to be seen in my Mercedes for reasons already explained. She was most amused and said, 'What rubbish! I don't mind what vehicle I travel in. I like the look of yours and I shall come in yours.'

For that I received more than a rebuke from the Foreign Secretary the next day. Mrs Owen had an excellent tour of the hospital, met many people, and in the evening we delivered her safely back to Mirimba House, the British government residence.

The next day we took them to Marandellas to see the housing schemes and community halls in Dombotombo township. On our arrival there, and after being told what had been arranged for him, David Owen's immediate response was, 'I know your sort of people and I am sure you have selected a route just to show me the best and to miss out what you don't want me to see!' Stuffing his itinerary into his pocket, he set off at speed in a different direction. He got hooked up on a fence, negotiated a hedge and knocked on the door of an astonished woman who came face to face unexpectedly with the British Foreign Secretary. This 'threw' his security officials completely, panting to keep up and trying to steer the youthful and energetic Foreign Secretary. After he had seen that house, he went on to other homes, chosen at random, and eventually had a long walk back to the community hall, where he met a wider cross-section than the house-wives he had seen. The municipality, mayor and council were justly proud of Dombotombo township.

Then we set off for Chihota. I explained to the British party that the roads in the area had not been designed or maintained to the standard that befitted Jaguars and that it would be extremely dusty. The roads had not been tarred and were very sandy. Would it not be better, we asked, if he travelled in a Land-Rover or a more suitable vehicle? David Owen, however, was determined to fly the Jaguar flag and off they set. Having such a low clearance, the Jaguar played a double role as passenger trans-port and road-grader. All that could be seen was a large cloud of dust, moving steadily across the landscape. Nevertheless, we reached the head-quarters of Chief Chihota, who gave our visitors a great welcome and invited Dr Owen in for a drink of Shona beer, which he, his officials and the journalists bravely drank. For those who know it, it is a delicious drink but it is an acquired taste.

That visit completed, they headed off on the return journey to Salisbury. David Owen preferred to be independent and took a route other than that suggested. Fine dust got the better of the unfortunate Jaguar, with all its filters clogged, and its engine seized, and you could not help but feel sorry for the brave and determined Foreign Secretary. The next vehicle to pass was a sanctions-breaking Rhodesian Police Peugeot one-ton truck, and he was obliged to get a lift with them back to Mirimba House. Having taken a better route, I had arrived there about 45 minutes before David

Owen, who had the grace and humour to thank the Rhodesian police who had rescued him.

After a quick clean up to get the dust out of his mouth, eyes and ears, and in a clean shirt, he set off for another meeting with Ian Smith. On television that night, he did rather wryly acknowledge the escapade.

Mrs Owen was able to meet many more people than if the Owens been hosted by government, and David Owen asked me to call on him when I was next in London, which I did in the wonderful, historic Foreign Secretary's room with paintings by old masters on the walls, but I found him to be a most determined person, not easily persuaded to recognize the existence of an alternative view.

Mrs Owen had bravely travelled with her husband while one of their children was seriously ill with leukaemia. When we corresponded, I was glad to hear of the child's gradual recovery. She did say that I was one of the few people who took the trouble to enquire about their child's progress.

At this time the House of Representatives and Senate of the USA displayed great interest in us and they were continually sending 'look-see' groups. In this regard, we received much help from Ken Towsey and John Hooper.

Of course, because of the proximity to South Africa, there was also a continuous stream of South African visitors. South African business was able to take advantage of our economic isolation, since in many instances our only source of manufactured goods was from that country. There were, however, strong feelings about some aspects of South Africa's exploitation of our situation.

Relationships were sensitive and on a couple of occasions a colleague and I were asked to be messengers directly to the South African Foreign Minister, Pik Botha, in Cape Town, which we did through the good offices of the governor of our Reserve Bank, Desmond Krogh. It was interesting to see a sudden change in attitude from government to government. We got to know some of the South African ministers, which in later years proved most helpful.

> The continued existence of Rhodesia depended totally and utterly on the support of its neighbours for our transit routes to the sea, on their ports for exporting into a sanctioned market, and for the country's financial survival. UDI lasted for fifteen years.

Because tobacco sanctions had been 95 per cent effective, tobacco could not be sold to its traditional markets. Sam Whaley's deputy in the

Tobacco Corporation was Frank Buch, with whom I shared an office, though we were engaged in different operations, which we never discussed between ourselves.

Our small Air Rhodesia fleet of planes was getting older, inadequate and seriously in need of replacement, but to buy aircraft from the manufacturers was out of the question. In what was probably the most closely guarded secret of the time, Buch and his team bought three young second-hand Boeing 720s in Europe. Nobody in Europe knew we had bought them and, critically, we had to send over three or four crews to become familiar with the aircraft and to qualify to fly them. The mission succeeded.

I recall clearly a chat just before lunch one day, when Buch told me he would not be in his office that afternoon. In fact he was at the airport, where, at ten-minute intervals, our three Boeing aircraft flew into Salisbury. They had had to refuel en route in West Africa and apparently absolutely nobody knew where they were flying to when they left Switzerland. Those three aircraft lasted the country until independence. This incident proved that in business a willing seller and a willing buyer can be more effective than politicians.

But the uncertain future started to have an effect in Rhodesia. Opinion hardened and emigration increased. In 1978, when incursions of dissidents from the north had increased across Kariba, an Air Zimbabwe Viscount passenger aircraft was shot down in the Tengwe area by a heat-seeking ground-to-air missile not long after take-off from Kariba. The few survivors were butchered. This was a new escalation in violence. Shortly afterwards,

The three Boeing 720s at Salisbury airport.

a second Viscount was shot down in the same area, all on board dying in the crash, and Joshua Nkomo was seen on British television laughing and boasting.

An interdenominational religious group called the Christian Fellowship exists throughout the world. Wherever they work, small groups in many parts of the world meet once a week before work for a few minutes of Christian fellowship. There is a Christian Fellowship Group in the White House and every year the President of the United States hosts a prayer breakfast given by the Christian Fellowship Group within the White House. In January 1976, I was invited to attend the President's prayer breakfast, held in the Carlton Hotel ballroom in Washington and attended by 2,800 people from all over the world. David Lewis was also invited, together with a few South Africans.

Guy van der Jagt was one of the organizers of the prayer breakfast. There were to be 2,000 people present that year and, because of a mix up with passports, the State Department were aware of David Lewis's and my presence. The Department had been having strong internal differences of opinions about the Rhodesian issue with the administration, and we were told most apologetically that it would not be possible for President Ford to sit down to breakfast with a group which included two Rhodesians. Van der Jagt came to see us, very considerably embarrassed, and said that if we were going to be present then, on the advice of the State Department, President Ford would not be able to attend.

David and I immediately said we did not wish to disturb their arrangements, especially as they had suggested that we have breakfast in the cafeteria and then join the other participants later. That is what happened and it went off without a hitch, but later that day President Ford was told of the incident and was furious. In a letter to me he said that had he known of the issue he would have over-ruled his officials. They were all most embarrassed and grateful that we had not made an issue of the matter. I have interesting letters between various congressmen, Guy van der Jagt and the White House.

In the week after the breakfast, we chose which particular groups we would wish to join, to relate to people of many nationalities. One of the opportunities I took was to look at the American penal system in their prisons, and we were taken through the Bronx – a ghastly experience. I spent a fascinating week meeting people from all over the world, studying and discussing the problems that existed in their countries as well.

On the same occasion, I visited the lovely Bronx zoo, where visitors are taken by a mono-rail trail through the park. The director took me around personally and it was such a contrast after having travelled through what was probably the worst slum area in New York, with burnt-out multi-storeyed tenement buildings being rebuilt, in many cases only to be destroyed again.

It had been intended that Lord Carver would be the interim Governor, and he came to Rhodesia only to find that political problems prevented him from taking up the position. There was a strong group of ministers, led by P.K. van der Byl and including Peter Walls, who did their best to prevent him from seeing the people he should have seen. He asked me for some help – the problem was that we did not have a secure line and my conversation with him might have been tapped. So I went down to where I thought there was a chance that they wouldn't have telephone recorders, to the railway station at Gatooma, and we had a guarded conversation. He left soon afterwards. Many years later, a visitor to our house, Rocklands, at St James at the Cape, came to see us one day and thought that I might like to listen to the conversation I had had with Lord Carver that day. So they did have it on record.

In 1978 or 1979 the BBC were extremely hostile and biased against Rhodesia, and programmes like Panorama put over a very slanted view. I got in touch with the Director-General of the BBC, Sir Ian Trethowan, to complain. He suggested that a meeting between his senior news editors, himself and me would be worth while, to help them achieve a better balance.

Dr Dexter Chavunduka was a member of the Rhodesia Promotion Council. A Shona, he had a good degree from Edinburgh's famous veterinary college, the Royal (Dick) School of Veterinary Studies. Chavunduka and I were in London so we had a couple of hours with the BBC team and were able to point out many distortions and inaccuracies. We said that we accepted that there were different views on the Rhodesian situation, but we hoped that a national body like the BBC would be more balanced. Unfortunately the Director-General could not be with us, but our visit was

In due course, Dexter Chavunduka became the Permanent Secretary in the Ministry of Agriculture. On his retirement, he worked very closely with the Rhodesia (and later the Zimbabwe) Promotion Council. While in Scotland, he had married a Zimbabwean undergraduate who was undergoing nursing training. Their son, Mark, became editor of the *Standard* newspaper and was arrested (for 'publishing false news') and tortured by the Zimbabwe National Army in January 1999.

partially successful, judging by the BBC's comments over the next few months, which did become more objective.

In 1975 I received a letter from the Secretary to the Cabinet telling me that my name had been proposed as a recipient of the honour of the Independence Commemorative Decoration. These were given to mark ten years of Rhodesia's 'independence' after UDI, but mainly to politicians, serving soldiers and officials. I did not wish to cause any embarrassment, but I was reluctant to accept the honour unless it could be made clear on the citation that the award was for economic achievement and work done for the good of the country as a whole. I was telephoned soon afterwards by Bill Margolis, who found himself in the same predicament. We had a discussion with the Secretary to the Cabinet, who understood our position and arranged for the citation to be worded, 'For services rendered in the economic sector of Rhodesia'. Clifford Dupont, who had just become president of Rhodesia, presented the award.

Shortly before Zimbabwe's independence, I was again honoured by being given the Order of the Legion of Merit, for work done internally but also for external promotion of the country around the world. This award was presented by Jim Baker, permanent secretary in the Ministry of Commerce and Industry, because at that time Clifford Dupont was no longer president.

Towards the end of the UDI period I received a letter from an old friend in Ireland, Colonel Sydney Watson, who had visited us several times. He said, 'I am afraid that Kipling's "Ulster", written in 1912, could be re-published as Kipling's "Rhodesia" in 1976.'

From Ulster 1912, by Rudyard Kipling

The dark eleventh hour
Draws on and sees us sold
To every evil power
We fought against of old –
Rebellion, rapine, hate,
Oppression, wrong and greed
Are loosed to rule our fate
By England's art and deed.

The faith in which we stand,
The laws we made and guard,
Our honour, lives, and land
Are given for reward
To murder done by night
To treason taught by day,
To folly, sloth, and spite,
And we are thrust away.

– 9 –

Cotton

Union Carbide • Agricultural Research Council
• Commercial Cotton Growers Association and Cotton Training Centre
• First black board members • Gin equipment
• Ken Mackenzie and the Rhodesian Cotton Company
• Revolutionary grading procedure • Visits to Europe and South America
• Senator James Eastland and a visit to USA
• Monsanto and Delta Pine, Donje and the Bt gene

Over the decades farmers had attempted to grow cotton in Rhodesia but it had not survived attacks from insects such as jassids, red and American bollworm and aphids. In the 1960s, however, the Union Carbide Corporation in America developed a chemical called carbaryl, also sold under the brand name of Sevin, which proved effective against boll-worms. This was the start of an association between this giant American corporation and our cotton industry, which lasted for many years.

The Union Carbide Company had an appalling disaster with their plant at Bhopal in India when a poisonous gas escaped and hundreds of people died. In the consequent litigation, the company was obliged to pay out such huge compensation that it was very nearly destroyed. But initially this great company was at the base of our cotton expansion.

In the mid-1950s, the Agricultural Research Council of Central Africa (ARC), covering the Federation of Rhodesia and Nyasaland, was formed. It was a well-funded and well-staffed research organization. David Worthington and I were the first two from this country to be appointed to the council. Professor Frank Engeldow from Rothamsted in England, the chief of Veterinary Services from South Africa, and representatives from Kenya, Australia and New Zealand were council members.

The ARC's initial brief was to undertake certain fundamental, as opposed to applied, research, which at that time was not being tackled in our region. We filled the gaps in many fields, including the fascinating sex-attractant pheromone work with the tsetse fly in the Zambezi valley. Researchers established fly-traps with the pheromone, a synthetic female sex attractant. Male tsetse flocked to the sites, were caught in the traps and consequently died. The resulting sex imbalance reduced the population drastically and we were able to develop tsetse-free areas from previously tsetse-ridden parts of the country, safe for people and cattle. The ARC also undertook research into cotton pests, eucalyptus tree breeding and a host of other projects.

The ARC had an interesting working relationship with the International Atomic Agency in Vienna on identifying the origins of underground water – where it came from and how 'old' it was. The identification was done by inserting tritium into an underground water source. The water was probed at intervals downstream, still underground, until it appeared either by being pumped from an intercepting borehole or from another stream.

There was an excellent aquifer in the Nyamandhlovu area, with high yielding boreholes which were obviously sourcing their water from some very prolific area. We were able to trace back the source of that water for eighty-five miles. Scientists were also able to determine when that water had fallen from the heavens and thus got into the underground water system. This was of great value, because the Nyamandhlovu aquifer measurements showed that the water being pumped was 'younger' year after year, which showed that the pumps were taking out more water than was being normally replenished; without care, the source would be exhausted.

The team that specialized in cotton research was led by two leading scientists, Dr John Tunstall, an entomologist, and Dr Graham Matthews, a plant breeder, both from the UK. They undertook revolutionary work at the time, with systematic scouting to get early warning of impending outbreaks of insects.

Chemicals such as Sevin, as well as spraying techniques, provided the springboard for a rapid increase in production. The Commercial Cotton Growers Association (CCGA) satisfactorily concluded an arrangement with the British Hunting Group to develop aerial spraying both by helicopter and by fixed-wing aircraft. This proved highly effective, with a plane spraying several hundred hectares a day if the land was in reasonably sized blocks. The joint company was called Agricair and lasted for a long time.

From a marketing perspective, it was important to have beautifully clean, hand-reaped cotton, which fetched a premium on world markets. Machine-reaped cotton inevitably had contaminants, and ginners had difficulty removing them. Some fibres were damaged in that process and machine-reaped cotton could never compete with our hand-reaped cotton.

When I assumed the presidency of the CCGA, I told the council that, if we were to be a force in the land, we could only be so if we were adequately funded. The RTA was a good example of this, and we agreed to set a levy slightly greater than the tobacco levy. That gave us the funding to involve ourselves on the international scene with chemicals in Europe and South Africa, plant breeding and genetic research with Monsanto (see below) and others. To my mind, it was important that, when we decided to do something, we did not have to put out our beggar's bowl. If we had decided to do it and could afford it, then we did it. I think this policy brought together commercial cotton growers, who had made a levy investment, saw that it was transparent and productive, and continued to support it year after year.

With the accelerating collapse of commercial agriculture, fewer and fewer commercial cotton growers remained in production. To safeguard our capital from levy accumulations in the hands of the Commercial Cotton Growers Association, we transferred it to an independent entity, safe from greedy eyes.

I think one of the most important things that we did with that levy was to establish the Cotton Training Centre at Gatooma on a farm owned by the association. Cotton was an ideal communal grower crop. Next to no training was being done by the ministry and there was a big gap which we decided to fill. Our small team worked with our marketeer, Ken Mackenzie, who funded the buildings of the Training Centre, and we funded the other capital requirement and operating expenditure, so that yet again it was being run as an independent entity.

In addition to Mackenzie, our team included Duncan Kennaird, who was responsible for the actual training, collecting growers from all over the country and bringing them to Gatooma in buses, where they were accommodated overnight or for a week in the buildings erected by Kaymac.

Communal growers made no levy contribution and, as the number of commercial growers dwindled, so did each year's annual levy income. But with the Staple Trust board of leading cotton growers, always led by an experienced chartered accountant, we were able to invest the accumulation and offset to some extent the decline in annual levy income.

As time went on, the balance between commercial and communal growers reached the stage when there were only a handful of commercial growers and we were under pressure from some quarters to abandon the training scheme. Because the funds had all come from commercial growers and there were hardly any left, we were making a goodwill payment for the industry and helping people who were enthusiastic about receiving the training but never made any contribution of their own. In the interests of the industry, Staple still (in 2007) magnanimously continues to fund the operation of the training centre.

Doug Dryden was the chairman of Staple Trust, with his team of Duncan Kennaird, three former CCGA presidents, and myself. Duncan and his father, Norman, had been among the most successful mixed livestock and arable farmers in the country, with 2,000 acres of land that they had cleared and then irrigated by the Wengi dam, whose construction they had helped to fund. They grew excellent crops of cotton, grain, maize for livestock, and were producing 3,000 baconers a year. The Kennairds were evicted after the farm invasions of the 2000s. Production now is just an annual crop of weeds. A lot of the Wengi dam water remains unused while the country is starving.

At the time of UDI, I was the senior vice-president of the Rhodesia National Farmers Union. I was at the same time president of the CCGA. My vice-president at Cotton was Mike Butler, who was a good friend for forty years before he died, and he served on a number of boards with me, not only cotton. David Spain, a future CFU president who died tragically in a road accident shortly after independence, was also on the CCGA council.

We took on the challenge of rapidly increasing cotton production to offset the damage done by sanctions. It was vitally important to replace tobacco's foreign earning potential to some extent, which we did with cotton. Cotton production expanded at such a rate that we had difficulty in building new ginneries fast enough to process the crop.

African producers were steadily increasing their production. They had the same problems as any commercial producer and

One of our four-stand cotton gins.

yet government had declined to allow us to bring blacks on to the Cotton Marketing Board, of which I was chairman from 1969 to 1983. Eventually I was able to get them to appreciate the importance of this, and we were delighted to be the first statutory board with black African representation. These first black members of the board were Robson Gapare, president of the African Farmers Union, A. R. Gumbo, Robert Katsande, Matthew Madzimbamoto and Edward Padya.

A key architect of the country's cotton crop was Mike Burgess, an entomologist. He was very practical and a great help to new cotton growers who instead of tobacco were now growing cotton. The CCGA bought Burgess a small aircraft and he flew from area to area.

Rhodesia had only one small Murray saw gin, at Gatooma. Any new gin equipment had to come from the United States, the only significant manufacturer of ginning equipment in the world. We were building a larger gin every twelve to eighteen months, and each of these had to be imported from the USA. At the end of UDI, when the American manufacturers visited us, they had had no idea of the number of ginneries we had bought from them during that time. Many were the sagas of how the equipment was bought, and how it travelled in different directions before reaching its destination. By the end of UDI, we had the skills to build our own gins, except for the saws, and our largest ginnery was almost entirely locally built.

This achievement was largely due to Sam Weller, who had worked with the United Africa Company in West Africa and who joined us as general manager of the Cotton Marketing Board. He was an outstanding administrator and marketeer.

My great friend Ken Mackenzie helped us to establish a pioneering strategy for marketing cotton; he was heavily involved in cotton textiles. Mackenzie's father was a senior banker in Durban and at the outbreak of war Ken had joined the South African Air Force as a fighter pilot. He served in the Western Desert until he was shot down and suffered serious wounds to his leg. This handicapped him for the rest of his life.

At the end of the war, his father gave him a couple of hundred pounds to start a business career and he joined a textile firm, Noel P. Hunt, who were involved in many aspects of the textile trade, including the procurement of textile equipment, and in marketing the equipment and cotton. He successfully ran their Kenya operation for a while and, soon after his return to Durban, he bought out the shareholders, which was the starting point of a remarkably successful business career.

The first board of the Cotton Marketing Board that included Communal growers (left to right): standing, Maxwell Gandiwa, unknown, unknown, Peter Dove, Matthew Madzimbamoto; seated, Edward Padya, Rob Dorman, Robert Katsande, Alistair Davies, Robson Gapare, C. G. Tracey (chairman), Sam Weller, A. R. Gumbo, Tony Goodwin, Henry Muradzikwa, Peter Flanagan.

The cotton industry was thriving and we needed to sell our lint to best advantage. The CCGA commissioned Derry and Lewis, a firm of chartered accountants who later became part of KPMG, to report on marketing possibilities, one of which was to form a cotton growers' co-operative. At the same time we had discussions with Ken Mackenzie. His cotton company, Kaymac, offered to establish the Rhodesian Cotton Company, which would provide technical services and advice for grading and receiving cotton at the gins, and thereafter its sale into world markets.

Traditionally, in the major cotton producing countries, a grower delivered cotton to the gin, which would gin it for him for a fee. The lint and seed remained the grower's property to market where he wished. The crop was almost always machine-reaped, which meant waiting to reap until almost all the bolls were open. The quality of the cotton from the top bolls is not as good as that from the lower bolls, and all the bolls became mixed at the time of harvest; this reduced the average quality of a bale. The cotton was normally graded after ginning. Ken Mackenzie and his young assistant, Graham Elliot, developed a revolutionary procedure to take advantage of the fact that in Rhodesia we hand-picked our cotton. The labour was available and it was possible to reap the crop so that the lower, middle and top bolls were all kept separate, and the resultant bale of lint was much more uniform. This development was watched with interest by the outside cotton world.

After grading, the bales of cotton were stacked according to grade and quality. We constructed huge areas on which cotton bales were stored and stacked up to six bales high with front-end loaders, which meant that any particular quality of cotton could be ginned separately.

In world markets we now had an edge over machine-picked cotton. The spinners looked for uniformity of lint and our uniformity and quality – free of fragments of leaf and stem which would get in with machine-picking – meant that the lint did not have to go through pre-cleaners. The higher price received for our cotton compensated for expenses connected with avoiding sanctions. The quality of our cotton was so good that demand increased and sanctions were more easily overcome.

The partnership between the Cotton Marketing Board and the Rhodesian Cotton Company became stronger and stronger. I was the first chairman of the Cotton Marketing Board and we worked closely with marketeers, who knew the demand for any particular grade of Rhodesian cotton and had authority to control the ginneries. If they suddenly received a good order for a particular style, they asked the ginnery to switch to a stack to provide exactly the required lint. The Micronair measurement indicated the fineness or coarseness of the fibre and the Pressley measured the strength of the fibre. The spinners in our export markets loved our clean, white, uniform lint.

Mackenzie developed wide interests in South African industry. With a partner, he started and developed the GUD Company, which still manufactures all kinds of filters for the automobile plants. Later, he

> Every year I took a small group of growers and men from the ginning operation, and a couple of government officials, to one or two major cotton countries in the world, so that we could look at their operations, compare their techniques, their quality, their marketing, and measure ourselves against them. Most important was to have one-on-one contact with our customers. Members of these groups developed a deep understanding of the industry.

acquired the British Gilbeys wine farm, Hartenberg, near Stellenbosch in the Cape. Gilbeys wanted to disinvest from South Africa under apartheid. He bought Hartenberg and set about modernizing the cellars and improving the cultivars, and it has become one of the foremost wine farms in South Africa. It was his great love and joy in life. He piloted his own Queen Air, flying between Salisbury, Johannesburg, Durban and Cape Town. He and I had a mutual interest in breeding race horses.

A most successful businessman, Ken Mackenzie was a generous philanthropist who enjoyed making money, much of which went to worthy projects. He funded the building of Mackenzie house at Michaelhouse, one of the foremost private schools in South Africa. He was quiet and unassuming in his philanthropy and few people knew the extent of his generosity.

Ken Mackenzie.

Early in his marriage to Megan, Ken had bought the lovely Gombera Estate on the banks of the Hunyani River in the north of the country, where he had his own landing strip and facilities and developed a prosperous and efficient farm and ranch, with irrigated cotton, wheat, soya beans and a herd of beef cattle with about a thousand breeding cows. He flew his own microlight on the farm. Tragically, Megan choked to death. She was at home with her two daughters aged six and ten and no help nearby.

Gombera was listed for acquisition by a former minister with no knowledge of farming. Ken's application to be allowed to keep part of the farm fell on deaf ears. There is hardly any production now on that farm and ranch.

Many hundred mourners attended Ken Mackenzie's funeral, so widely was he respected and admired. I was honoured to deliver a eulogy on the Rhodesian and Zimbabwean part of his life.

Sam Weller quickly got to know our main customers, learned the particular styles each one of them wanted and the people involved, and worked hand-in-hand with the brokers and graders. With his acute market intelligence, we were able to switch our ginning from one style to another in twelve hours, depending on what the market needed.

Ken and Megan Mackenzie had a long-serving faithful worker who had two sons, and Ken felt that these boys had potential. He built a small cottage for the youngsters at his house in Harare, and put them into St George's College. One of them is now studying engineering at Cape Town University. Ken paid all the two boys' expenses, and his family are now paying for their university education. Ken's daughter, Tania, said that he would have felt so rewarded that these youngsters had responded to the help they had been given. In spite of all that Ken had done, his farms were still taken.

Another innovation were the gigantic hard-standing holding areas we cast to stack the bales before ginning, so that we could take the crop in faster than we could gin it and store the balance under tarpaulins on the hard stands for later ginning. The crop was off the farms and we could gin well into the rainy season, giving us a far longer ginning period than in other countries where the cotton had to be ginned immediately after delivery.

In America, cotton was all machine-reaped and blown into a trailer which delivered the cotton to the gin. The trailer had to get back quickly so as not to keep the cotton picker standing. This meant that the period

Cotton bales stacked grade by grade, awaiting ginning later in the season.

for ginning only extended as long as picking continued, and sometimes a gin might operate for only six or eight weeks in a year.

The remarkable growth in cotton production was one of the most rewarding periods of my life. The international competition had become more difficult because of our political isolation. Nevertheless, we did manage to get into many markets and, because of the quality and the size of our crop, we were able to by-pass the merchant system, save their margin and sell directly through our marketing link to the spinner. This improved our return and helped us establish relationships and a good reputation.

We visited spinners in countries such as Switzerland, Germany and France who have to import all their lint. We also travelled to our cotton-producing competitors who process much of their own lint: Israel, Turkey, Italy and South Africa. We visited Brazil, a vast country with enormous resources. They were very proud of their capital city, Brazilia, then in the early stages of its development. Its buildings seemed hard and formal with few trees and parks, but the city will have matured now. The distances in Brazil are great and their rail system was limited. The road system, however, had been superbly developed and trucks carried much of the freight.

After our Brazilian visit, Mike Butler, Wendy and I spent a couple of days in Peru, another cotton-producing nation. One of the main varieties they grew was Pima, a beautiful long-staple cotton akin to Sea Island quality, which is the best in the world. Butler returned home and Wendy and I went on to the United States to look at new developments in cotton ginning.

We were travelling on Pan Am from São Paulo. At that time, relations between Chile and the USA were strained and the Americans had been denied access to Chilean airspace. Our Pan Am pilot decided to ignore the ban and flew over part of Chile. While we were in the air, he received a warning from the Chilean air traffic control to leave their air space immediately, which he ignored. Ten minutes later he received another warning that we were to be escorted to the nearest airport. We soon found a couple of jet fighters flying on either side of us. The captain informed us what had happened and said he had no alternative but to land in Santiago. On arrival the plane was surrounded by armed guards and we were told to keep calm, much to the trepidation of the passengers. The military boarded the aircraft and departed with the captain and all the crew. We were told that our stay might be long and that they had been in touch with the US embassy and Washington.

Some of the passengers took over the role of the air hostesses and, to give people something to do, we decided to dispense the drinks and snacks which we discovered in the galley. Six of us became cabin attendants and managed to calm the situation. We were on the ground for ten hours, and only at the end of that time were we were allowed off the aircraft to stretch our legs – but we were not allowed to go into the airport building.

Eventually the captain and crew returned and said we would be leaving for Los Angeles. We had by that time consumed all the food and drink on board and the crew were not allowed to bring fresh supplies. We had a long, hungry and thirsty flight to Los Angeles. News of a different kind of hijack had reached the media and we were besieged by television reporters and photographers on arrival.

America was the only cotton-producing country that our team had been unable to visit. When Watergate was at its height, I determined to get there. Our team had Rhodesian passports and we were told that there was no chance of getting into the USA where immigration sanctions were fierce.

As chairman of the Rhodesia Promotion Council, mentioned later, I had on a couple of occasions entertained an American Southern Democrat, Senator James Eastland. The Southern Democrats were probably the most right wing in American politics. Senator Eastland had displayed a keen interest in events in this part of Africa. On two occasions I had looked after him and taken him around the country in a small aircraft. At the end of one of these visits, Senator Eastland had said, 'C.G., your hospitality has been such that I do not know how to repay you. If there is anything I can do in the States, I will do so and do not hesitate to use this offer.'

At the next Cotton Board meeting, I told my directors that their next overseas visit was to America. They laughed, knowing that travel to the USA was forbidden. I said, 'Where there's a will, there's a way.'

I telephoned James Eastland in Washington. He said that if I was on the phone there must be something I wanted. I reminded him of his promise and said that pay-back time had come. He had witnessed the expansion of our cotton industry and now I wanted to bring a team to look at American cotton. 'Well,' he said, 'why don't you come?'

I said that his Department of State had refused to give us visas. There were several southern snorts and expletives down the phone and I heard him speak to an aide. Returning to the phone he said, 'I'll sort out the State Department this afternoon and we will make a plan.' He apparently instructed his office to deal with his opposite number in the Department of State, and the next day he sent a message asking me to visit the US consul in Durban to arrange the visas.

When I arrived in Durban, I was received somewhat coldly. On being asked what I wanted, I told the consul that I represented the Rhodesian cotton growers' association and that we wished to visit the cotton-growing areas in the United States. I was promptly told that Rhodesian passport holders were not issued with visas and, in any event, whom would I hope to see?

I said I had a number of friends in America and the consul asked me to name a few. So I said, 'Well, let's start with Senator James Eastland.' Eastland was well known and was at that time chairman of the Judicial Committee of the Senate. The consul suddenly recollected that he had seen some relevant document on his desk a few days earlier. In a second, his attitude changed. He excused himself and on his return advised me that, indeed, it would be possible to arrange visas. As it was 11.30 a.m., however, he doubted if the preparation of these could be done before lunch. He also hoped that it was not too inconvenient for me to come back at 3.30 p.m. the same day? I said that actually it would be most inconvenient, but that I would nevertheless return. The consul called me 'Sir'.

At our next Cotton Board meeting, I advised the team members concerned to make appropriate plans, as we would be leaving in a fortnight's time. Nobody believed me until I handed out the visas. I think that for a long while we were the only Rhodesians with Rhodesian passports who were officially issued with American visas.

Efficient arrangements were made for us to go through immigration in Washington and we had no problems with officialdom. After spending some time at the huge agricultural research centre at Beltsville, near Washington, we had a session with congressmen and staffers at a luncheon in the Senate. During lunch, Senator Eastland presented me with a lovely cut-glass cigar ashtray with the seal of the US Senate in the centre.

While flying across the country on his two visits to Rhodesia, James Eastland had noticed the proliferation of ginneries and wondered how we had acquired the equipment. I told him, and he fully understood, that there were some questions that he might ask to which we would have to decline to give answers. But he knew we were still building ginneries as he had seen these from photographs taken by US satellites as they passed over Rhodesia. After lunch he took Mike Butler and me into his office, and, through the optical equipment, we were able to see on the photos how far the construction of the ginnery we had left two weeks before had progressed.

James Eastland said that he wanted to give a barbecue in our honour at the end of our trip in his state of Mississippi. He intended bringing cotton growers from all over the state. This, however, was in August 1974 and the Watergate crisis culminated in President Richard Nixon's resignation. Under the American constitution, the vacant post of vice-president is automatically filled *pro tempore* by the chairman of the Senate or, if he is unable to do so, by the chairman of the Judicial Committee of the Senate, a senator drawn from government ranks, and, in this instance, our good friend became vice-president.

We were in the plane travelling to Mississippi when the pilot announced the news of Nixon's resignation. 'And so there goes our barbecue,' I thought. On arrival at Greenville, I was met by a government official who conveyed the acting vice-president's compliments, together with a message that, although his inauguration was to be the same afternoon as our barbecue, he would use his vice-presidential jet, fly down to Greenville and be only half an hour late for the party.

Once before, when Vice-President Spiro Agnew had got himself into trouble and been forced to resign, James Eastland had stepped pro tem into the vice-presidency. He had then dismissed the offer of the use of the vice-president's plane and other special facilities. But on this occasion, because of the clash between the inauguration and the Rhodesian barbecue, he decided to use his VP plane and fly down specially for the barbecue. What a great compliment it was.

We had a splendid barbecue, with cotton growers from across the state. During the evening, one of James Eastland's grandsons started playing the piano. David Spain, president of the CCGA, had a superb tenor voice. He walked over to the grandson and, after a short chat, they started a duet. So we were entertained by a Rhodesian and the vice-president's grandson to American and other folk songs. It was such an enjoyable and lighthearted experience. We were most grateful to Senator Eastland.

The whole visit was a remarkable experience, particularly as we saw the huge areas of cotton grown, its mechanization and marketing. We visited the Chicago Board of Exchange and left satisfied that our systems and costs could compete, though our workers handled the crop differently.

We saw the vast areas of cotton in the Texas high plains, as mechanized as any crop could be. One farmer was growing over a thousand acres with his son and one worker. They employed a contractor to do the land preparation. Another contractor did all the herbicide and pesticide spraying, and yet another was contracted to harvest the whole crop by mechanical cotton picker.

We then went to Fresno in California where we saw enormous irrigation schemes, with water coming down from northern California, particularly into the San Joachim Valley. Apart from huge areas of cotton, there were immense orchards of different fruit and grapes and field after field of the special tomatoes used by the processing factories. Think of a tomato plant and you will understand how surprised we were to see this crop being mechanically harvested with a combine. The plant breeders had ingeniously bred a cultivar whose fruit ripened simultaneously from top to bottom.

This was one of the best trips our cotton team undertook.

During the 1990s the Commercial Cotton Growers Association became interested in research on the genetics of cotton in the USA. The biggest problem in the production of cotton was the damage caused by the American and red bollworms, which necessitated frequent spraying with chemicals to achieve control. These chemicals were toxic and expensive.

The Delta Pine Seed Cotton Company at Greenville, Mississippi, had done exciting genetic work on the introduction of a heritable gene (Bt), which would protect the plant from the ravages of bollworms, a giant step forward. When a bollworm touched a leaf from a 'protected' plant, it promptly died. This toxin affected only bollworms and had no effect on other insect life.

The CCGA contacted the Delta Pine Company, an old-established cotton seed breeding company who had patented their Bt gene. Discussions followed on the possibility of establishing a joint company to benefit from that Bt gene. We named the Zimbabwean company Donje, the Shona word for cotton. At that time, the giant Monsanto Company, having seen the potential of the gene, acquired the Delta Pine Company. Monsanto proposed that we should form a joint venture company, which they planned would become their main regional base for all Africa, except for South Africa and the Mediterranean countries, for the supply and production of the Bt gene seed. Under the proposed agreement, we would acquire land for the new Donje Cotton Breeding Centre. Monsanto generously offered to cover all the capital costs for housing, laboratories, greenhouses, scientific equipment and irrigation systems. They would initially staff the station with highly qualified scientists in the disciplines of plant genetics, entomology, chemistry, agronomy and others and would be refunded by the venture itself, as a first charge against revenue.

It was an incredible offer and soon we were in double harness, seeking suitable land, irrigation systems and dealing with a myriad urgent matters.

The Cotton Company were aware of the possible joint venture between Monsanto/Delta Pine and Donje. They saw themselves with no role to play other than ginning the seed cotton, and approached us to share in the Zimbabwe investment of Donje. Again, constructive talks took place with the Cotton Company's chief executive. He had the benefit of having undertaken a Harvard summer course. Full support was given from all the other directors of the Cotton Company, except one who wanted the joint venture to be between him, the Cotton Company and Monsanto/Delta Pine, which would have excluded the CCGA.

This one director went to America and proposed to Monsanto the formation of a company similar to Donje, with a shareholding of 51 per cent for the Zimbabwean entity and 49 per cent for Monsanto/Delta Pine. He had not grasped the fact that the Americans would never allow their genetic breeding material to pass into the hands of any joint venture in which they did not have control. The meeting ended on a sour, aggressive note. The Zimbabwean is reported as saying that if Monsanto/Delta Pine refused to accept the 51%–49% share split, he could and would ensure that no permits for the importation of the genetic material would be issued. However, negotiations continued between Donje and Monsanto/ Delta Pine. They were impressed with Donje as successful cotton achievers and proposed that our joint venture company continue as planned.

The interest from the Cotton Company continued at executive level and we were happy to have them with us. After extensive negotiation, the principal agreements were drafted, and a group from Donje, including Sylvester Nguni, chief executive of the Cotton Marketing Board, travelled to Greenville, Mississippi, where over four or five days the final and complicated agreement was reached between Monsanto/Delta Pine, Donje and now the Cotton Marketing Board as well.

The question of the necessary permits soon became a problem. From the beginning, the Director of Research and Specialist Services in the Ministry of Agriculture strenuously opposed the concept on the grounds that extensive testing in Zimbabwe would have to take place before they would agree to the proposal. It was pointed out that testing and commercial production had been going on in South Africa for five or six years, with no negative consequences. We asked what benefits could result from Zimbabwe testing a variety again, when a few miles over the Limpopo the plant was performing superbly. In addition, there were major strides in development in the USA and Australia. Nevertheless, they insisted that the variety be tested again in Zimbabwe. They were impervious to logic and refused to grant permits for the parent seed and breeding material to be imported. Naturally, Monsanto would not release their genetics for the trials without adequate protection.

As negotiations were advanced, we pressed the Cotton Company either to join us or withdraw. Their response was unanimous agreement to participate with Donje.

The Americans were informed and were delighted at the outcome. They had already signed their copies of the agreement and sent them out for our signature. However, a few days later, I received a three-line letter from the Minister of Agriculture informing me that, unless the agreement gave a 51 per cent Zimbabwe stake, he would refuse import permits for the genetic material.

Monsanto and Delta Pine were understandably furious at the bad faith of the Cotton Company and the Ministry and immediately withdrew their entire team. Our agreement was dead and any communication could be conducted only between me and Delta Pine.

Some ten years later, there is some thawing of relationships from the Cotton Company, which is now floated on the Zimbabwe Stock Exchange, but Zimbabwe is now six or seven years behind our southern neighbours and the rest of the cotton world. We have been deprived of the benefits, which we could have had for many years, of further research, and we lost a wonderful investment opportunity which would have placed Zimbabwe as the main breeding centre of the Bt cotton gene in Africa.

In 2007, ministry officials responsible for influencing the decision about our cotton and denying us permits, and people throughout the industry, were asking why we do not have the Bt cotton gene in this country.

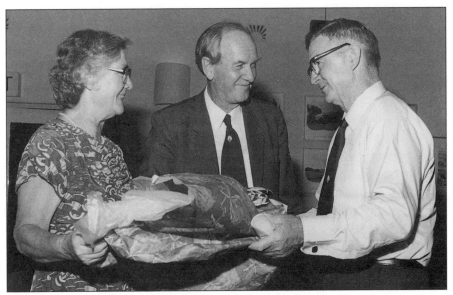

Presentation of a silver tray to Wendy and me by Peter Flanagan, president of the Commercial Cotton Growers Association, for what I had done over forty years.

Rhodesia Promotion Council

Formation of the RPC • Lowveld sugar estates
• Tobacco auction floors, CORESTA • Non-political stance
• Afrika Verein • Salary and Pensions Commission • David Lewis
• Aborigine Embassy • Private sector visit to Europe
• Supplement in the *International Herald Tribune* • Lord George Brown
• Familiarization for black political parties • South Africa Foundation

In 1962 I realized that Rhodesia and our activities were not well known around the world. In discussion with a group of friends, we recognized that the country as a whole was not being marketed adequately. For instance, a steel industry representative might visit us from Japan but he would be quite unaware of the extent of our tobacco industry, or a tobacco trade representative visiting from Germany would have no idea of our chrome industry.

The group included Jim Samuels, head of Rhodesian Breweries, Sir Keith Acutt of the Anglo American Corporation, and Jack Quinton, Irish born and one of the most far-thinking and dynamic men I have ever met. Quinton was chairman of the Sabi Limpopo Authority, which was responsible for the development of the Lowveld, and at one stage was the biggest tobacco grower in the world. He had also been a Member of Parliament and a government minister.

At one of our lunches, I said, 'In South Africa, they have the South African Foundation. There is the Cotton Promotion Council in Liverpool and other promotional bodies around the world. Why don't we form the Rhodesia Promotion Council?' We concluded that with the help of a suitable organization we could persuade visitors to spend an extra day or two here, take them under our wing, and introduce them to other sectors within our country and its economy.

We put down our aims and objectives, with a feasibility study of what the private sector could do to promote the country. Sir Richard Powell, of the Institute of Directors in Britain, gave me a lot of good ideas. We set about drafting a constitution and arranging funding for what became the Rhodesia Promotion Council.

We called a meeting and over fifty people came to the auditorium at Shell House. We asked Humphrey Gibbs, as he was then, to be our patron; George Rudland, Minister of Commerce and Industry, attended and was fully supportive of our

> Many years later, Sir Richard felt it would be a good thing for me to meet Margaret Thatcher, and duly arranged this soon after she became prime minister. She was widening her knowledge of foreign affairs, on which she was less well informed since her principal interest had until then been in economic and financial matters.

ideas. There was an excellent response and it was unanimously agreed to go ahead with the formation of an organization to develop knowledge of the country's economic resources. It would be known as the Rhodesia Promotion Council (RPC). Our mission statement read:

> The Rhodesia Promotion Council is an independent non-political and non-profit-making organization which aims to promote knowledge of Rhodesia's economic development and potential. It will be financed entirely by subscriptions and donations from corporate and individual members. The Council will show visiting businessmen, industrialists, agriculturalists, newspapermen, politicians and other opinion-formers significant farming, industrial and mining activities throughout Rhodesia. It will also arrange for them to meet ministers, senior civil servants and leading personalities in the private sector.

Our mission was simple – to develop a better knowledge throughout the world of Rhodesia and the strengths and diversity of its economy. The RPC lasted for nearly a quarter of a century, and its success reflected the private sector's confidence that the tasks it had set itself and its objectives were worthwhile. Its achievements ensured the continued support of and financing by the private sector.

We had to establish the Council. Ted Eustace, a talented, well-travelled South African diplomat who had retired in Rhodesia, was my staunchest ally. He remained with RPC almost to the end of the organization in 1983. He suggested that a young Rhodesian, Paddy Brown, should be appointed as our director. She had a background of public relations in Britain and gave us a wonderful start. A couple of years after the RPC was formed, Paddy decided to leave us to start her own public relations company. As a replacement, we found David Brewer, ex-navy, who was working for one of the big international tobacco companies in the country, which was affected by sanctions. He knew little of public relations but soon became accustomed to the drive and energy of the group. He stayed with us for nearly twenty years and was highly competent.

Stan O'Donnell, an Australian by birth, Permanent Secretary in our Ministry of Foreign Affairs, joined us on his retirement. He was innovative and indefatigable, and I could always call on him at short notice to do a job. He was also very involved in Rotary for the whole of southern Africa.

I told the steering committee that, if we were to achieve our goals, we would need adequate funding and, of course, all those funds would have to come from the private sector. In order to maintain our independence we should not seek any financial support from government. John Baines, who was chairman of the Rhodesian Institute of Directors, gave us £5,000 straight away, and Anglo American and the Rhodesian Breweries donated and others followed. That gave us a start and we formed a management committee.

Sir Richard Powell told us that there was no substitute for shoe leather and advised us to go and talk to the people who we hoped would support the RPC. We canvassed the private sector and in a matter of weeks we had secured adequate membership and funding. While the RPC was entirely funded by private-sector contributions, David Young, Permanent Secretary at the Treasury, recognized the value of the Council and it was one of very few organizations whose donors could set off their contributions against tax.

I was elected the first chairman of the Council, which was a great compliment. The job eventually lasted for 23 years. Throughout, I had the support of an extremely able and well-connected friend, David Lewis, as vice-chairman. He was a double Oxford blue and a leading lawyer.

Almost immediately we started entertaining senior people who came on business to the country. The Rhodesia Promotion Council demonstrated its value in looking after such people, opinion-formers in their own sector, who came from many different countries. When they went home, they were able to share their new knowledge of Rhodesia with a wide circle of their own contacts. The benefits of these visits were appreciated in the private sector, so fund-raising and financing became a little easier.

We would take visitors by air if necessary. We used to charter a couple of Beechcraft to go and see the immense development taking place at Hippo Valley and Triangle. The huge sugar estates there resulted from the inspiration of Murray MacDougall, who had spent many years tunnelling through a range of hills to divert the water from the Mtirikwe river to the rich, dry, undeveloped plains on the other side of the hills. So great was the potential that government established the Sabi Limpopo Authority covering that area. The Authority worked closely with the Hulett sugar group in South Africa and Anglo American. I've done a bit of development in my time but I was awed by the speed of that one. Where there was bush, thirty days later you had cane growing. Two huge tractors with a 100-metre anchor chain between them drove through the bush pulling out everything. Because of the oil content in the mopane trees, after a week you could burn them. After burning, huge tractors came and ripped the soil, and ploughs and disc harrows followed to do the land preparation for planting.

At the same time Murray and Roberts, the South African engineering contracting company, were constructing the canals, huge concrete-lined waterways. It was like building a railway line: they had several hundred people working behind the machine that dug the canal, trimming it, and after that came the concrete people. Thirty days later the water began to arrive from Kyle Dam, the largest in the country, and three smaller dams sixty miles upstream, eventually to irrigate some thirty thousand acres of sugar.

This remarkable development was comparable in vision to the Kariba Dam. It was driven by amazing people like Jack Quinton, the benefactor of Hippo Valley Estates. They didn't go to meetings, they said, 'Just do it!' and it happened. Along with the sugar project in the Lowveld came the expansion of roads and electricity in the area. Some of the electricity was produced on site by burning bagasse, the residue of the cane after the sugar juice had been extracted. It was burnt in huge furnaces, which provided the heat in tube boilers to produce steam, which was used to generate a substantial proportion of their electricity requirement.

A later development was the erection of an ethanol plant, which converted the molasses by-product of the sugar process into alcohol. The alcohol could be blended with petrol on a four-to-one basis and gave us a considerable saving in foreign exchange.

As the sugar estates grew, cotton was grown as a rotation crop and was also grown by farmers in adjacent areas. As a result of this development, a cotton ginnery was constructed, and many beef cattle grazed on that part of the estate not suitable for irrigation.

Prominent in the team who undertook this development was Sir Raymond Stockil, who was knighted for his achievements in the Lowveld. He was leader of the opposition in the Southern Rhodesia parliament in the 1940s and dropped out of politics in the 1950s after he had opposed the formation of the Federation in 1953. He owned some of the land incorporated into the Hippo Valley estates.

Another member of the team was Nick Cambitzis, the son of a Greek immigrant. His mother was from Poland, with a fearsome reputation as an outstanding and very tough businesswoman. Her son exhibited the same characteristics as chairman of the Industrial Development Corporation. Then there were the directors and management of the two big estates, Hippo Valley and Triangle. This was a dynamic group of achievers who always impressed our visitors. Hippo Valley was an offshoot of Anglo American, while Triangle was a subsidiary of the Tongaat Hulett corporation, probably the biggest sugar producer in Natal.

Back in Harare, our visitors from abroad visited the Tobacco Sales Floor where we auctioned up to twenty thousand bales of tobacco per day.

The man originally behind the concept of auctioning tobacco was Fred Cooksey, who came to this country as a young man to make his fortune. He was a rancher, and one of his achievements was to travel up to the northern part of Tanzania (Tanganyika in those days), where he bought a thousand head of cattle. He proceeded to trek these down to Rhodesia, across rivers, through lion country, across the Zambezi, where they had boats paddling alongside the crossing herd, slapping the water with oars to keep the crocodiles away. Fred said they did not lose very many and, once back home, he sold the cattle, other than those wanted for stocking his own ranches. I think he did this journey two or three times; each took the best part of a year.

Fred went into tobacco production, linking up with Archie Henderson. Fred bought Portelet Estate, a big ranch near Sinoia, and he and Henderson established the first tobacco auction floor in Salisbury. They were joined by a young Scotsman, Neil Gilchrist, a competent businessman who auctioned and sold cattle. Tobacco Auctions, as it was called, was the only auction floor at the time and was occasionally criticized as a monopoly. Consequently, a rival floor was established, an offshoot of the Rhodesia Tobacco Warehouse known as the Tobacco Producers Floor, and much later a third floor was opened called Tobacco Sales, of which I was chairman for 23 years. The rivalry between the floors was intense. It was fascinating to listen to Fred in his old age, when he started reminiscing, as he had many tales to tell about the early days of tobacco sales.

One of the successes achieved by the tobacco industry was hosting the first CORESTA (Centre de Coopération pour les Recherches Scientifiques Relatives au Tabac) congress in 1963. Hundreds of tobacco producers and researchers from all over the world congregated in Salisbury, and discussions ranged over plant breeding, research, agricultural chemicals and residues. The congress was a success and the contacts we made stood us in good stead in future years. The main movers behind it were Evan Campbell, the legendary tobacco grower and past president of the Rhodesia Tobacco Association, and Dr Ian McDonald, Director of Kutsaga Research Station.

The next time CORESTA came to the country was in the mid-1980s. The venue was Elephant Hills Hotel at Victoria Falls, with a golf course designed by Gary Player. Two days before the conference, the thatched-roofed hotel burned to the ground as a result of a fire in the kitchen. Nothing daunted, the organizers booked all the other rooms in the small resort town and brought up a huge tent from Harare. Delegates were delighted to meet in the open, on a manicured golf course surrounded by wild animals, and once again the conference was a triumph.

It should be remembered that the Rhodesia Promotion Council had started in 1963, two years before UDI. It was definitely not a part of government, was independent and entirely financed by the private sector. Sir Humphrey Gibbs, later the governor of Southern Rhodesia, remained our patron through the difficult political years of UDI.

When UDI was declared, we adopted a clear policy of continuing our mission. Some members disagreed with the declaration of independence, which they thought was unwise but, once the decision was taken, the imperative of keeping the country going overtook political reservations. Members of our Council had differing political views but we ensured that the Council's actions could not be regarded in a party-political light. Our objectivity and non-political stance enhanced our position in the eyes of the outside world. One of the people we dealt with regularly was Chester Crocker, Deputy Secretary of State in the US State Department, a man who was particularly interested in the consequences of UDI. He was conservative and a very good friend of Rhodesia; his mother-in-law lived in Bulawayo.

After UDI, the number of visitors interested in seeing for themselves what was happening in this part of Africa increased and Rhodesia became a focus of attention. There were congressmen from America, members of parliament from Britain and the Commonwealth and visitors from many countries in the world.

We developed relationships with organisations such as the American Chamber of Commerce, the Institute of Directors, the Confederation of British Industries in the United Kingdom, a German private sector body Afrika Verein and, very importantly, the South Africa Foundation, which was somewhat comparable to the Rhodesia Promotion Council. The task was time-consuming for me, along with my other activities, and the Rhodesia Promotion Council could not have functioned without willing co-operation and help from my Council members and many throughout the country, all proud to show our visitors what we were doing.

Afrika Verein was a private-sector organization covering all aspects of the private sector in Germany, similar to the Confederation of British Industries. Their director, Dr Max Klaus, visited Rhodesia several times and so we were able to keep interested parties in their group informed. On two occasions we sent a small Rhodesian delegation to Germany. At the conclusion of one visit, I was asked to be a guest of Afrika Verein at a famous festival that takes place once a year, the Matthiae-Mahl (Matthiae Feast), which is the oldest annual feast in the world and the social highlight of Hamburg. There I made valuable contacts, particularly with the foreign editor of the Swiss newspaper *Neuer Züricher Zeitung*. The burghers of Hamburg are immensely proud of their city and its tradition, and the reception and dinner party which followed were magnificent.

This was about 1967, at the time of the construction of the Berlin Wall between East and West Germany. I was driven to Lübeck on the Baltic and was able to see the excavation of the huge dyke, the installation of the electric fencing, the dog patrols and the observation towers with guards and machine guns which were there to prevent people crossing the border illegally. Not far away there was an official border-crossing point for commercial traffic, although individuals were unable to go through there. It was strange to see the contrast of the conditions on either side of the man-made barrier. The Berlin Wall was a highly effective obstacle which for many years prevented East Germans from crossing into the West.

A little later, I was on a mission to buy chemicals for our fledgling but growing cotton industry. I flew into Berlin's Tempelhof airport late one afternoon, and after our negotiations I was driven to the other Berlin airport, Tegel. My host drove me along the Berlin Wall. It was the most moving and heart-wrenching experience. At frequent intervals, a small alcove on the west side had been built to mark where an East German had tried to escape but had been shot and killed and fallen into the western sector. These alcoves were called chapels. I could only ponder the sadness of a nation divided in this way. It was macabre how the wall was built up to the side of a house and then continued from the other side of the house again, with one half of the house on the west and the other half on the east. The evils of communism struck home when I saw that scene.

In 1970, the Rhodesian prime minister Ian Smith established a government commission of three people, of whom I was one, to investigate and advise government on the salary and pension levels paid to ministers and members of parliament.

Ken Wilson, a lawyer of high repute, and Bill Basson, chief executive of the British American Tobacco group, completed the team. It was a novel and interesting experience for me, and the three of us examined our system and similar systems for parliamentarians in countries in the western world, particularly in Europe, America and the Commonwealth.

We found many anomalies in remuneration. In many instances it was clear that a potentially strong candidate for parliament could not afford to spare the time from his own job to devote to his task. We wanted to ensure that poor remuneration was not a reason for the better candidates not to stand. We also wanted to ensure that the level of payment was sufficient for travel and accommodation for those who represented the most remote constituencies.

In 1974, on a visit abroad for the parliamentary salary structure commission, I had been invited to meet Sir Charles Court, who was the dynamic premier of Western Australia. We had been introduced by Sir Richard Powell of the Institute of Directors in London. David Lewis and I flew to Australia via California, where we were able to present Nancy Reagan with a lion-skin cushion, something her husband Ronald, then governor of the state, said she had yearned to own. I had been impressed by the results Reagan had achieved in California, taking over a bankrupt state and turning it around by adopting the principle of small government. I had written to him about this and he asked us to visit him, which led to our second meeting – and Nancy was delighted with her cushion.

Our visit to California was memorable for another reason. David Lewis had had a very primitive cataract operation and had to put a plastic lens in his eye to enable him to see. This gave him lots of problems and the lens irritated his eye. We were staying in a smart hotel in Washington, furnished in 1970s style with deep, shaggy pile carpets. At 7.30 one morning, I received a panic call from David. He had dropped his lens in the deep pile carpet and he did not have a spare. We retraced his steps and started parting the carpet, tuft by tuft. The maid came into the room and David told her there was fifty bucks for whoever could find the lens, so then we had half the hotel staff looking for it and did manage to find it.

David Lewis and I then travelled to Fiji, where we were guests of the Fijian Prime Minister, Sir Kamisese Mara, who had been at Oxford with

David. Unfortunately we missed him, as a cyclone had caused huge damage on one of the islands and he had had to go there at short notice, but we were received by the Protocol Office.

David's lens gave him trouble on that flight, too. For some reason, it slipped up his eyeball under his eyelid and he couldn't extract it. We asked the Qantas air hostess to help and she refused, saying, 'You Americans always sue us at the drop of a hat.' We explained that we were Rhodesians. 'Oh,' she said. 'We like you. Of course I'll help.'

The light in the galley wasn't strong enough for her to see the lens, so they repaired to the toilet, where, after a few minutes, she managed to extract it, much to his relief.

'I've always worked on hunches,' she said. David said he had, too. 'My hunch is that, when we open the door, there will be four men queueing to come in here.'

'Well, whatever you do, don't blush.'

Sure enough, there were four men outside the door and the look of admiration on their faces that a passenger had got an air hostess into the loo thirty minutes after take-off made David's day!

We flew on to Sydney with some trepidation, wondering if we would be turned away at immigration, being Rhodesians. We weren't, and in Canberra were guests of the Shadow Attorney-General, Ivor Greenwood, who had visited Rhodesia shortly before, and we lunched with some of his fellow shadow ministers.

After lunch we were standing on the balcony overlooking the lovely lawns around parliament and noticed a rather insignificant small hut in the middle of the lawn. We were both a bit puzzled until our host said, 'You may be wondering what that small hut is ... well, I can tell you, it is the Aborigine Embassy. It was put up as a protest, consequent on the never-ending problem that Australia has with the Aborigine people, so we just left it there and the Aborigine Embassy staff will tire soon of occupying their premises and will go back home again.'

We were aware that Australia had earlier had a one-man commission with almost the same terms of reference as ours, to investigate and advise on the salary structure of the MPs, ministers, and senators. The one man was Justice Sir John Kerr, who was the Governor-General of Australia. I was unable to see him as arranged on that day, 11 November 1975, as he was dismissing the Australian Prime Minister, Gough Whitlam, an un-precedented act in Australia's history, and was therefore otherwise engaged. We corresponded and I learnt a lot from Kerr's report.

We found the spirit of independence in Western Australia extraordinarily strong. They were irked by the extensive control and intervention exerted by Canberra and sought far greater autonomy to develop their own projects that were more related to Western Australia's plans. Time constraints prevented us going up the west coast of Australia to see the giant iron ore mines and the huge irrigation opportunities on the Orde River, the potential of which has not yet been fully realized.

In 1978 the Rhodesia Promotion Council was invited to bring a group of black and white private-sector Rhodesian leaders to visit France, Belgium, Switzerland and Germany. Our problem was that everyone in the team had Rhodesian passports and it was very difficult to obtain visas.

Our intelligence people had excellent relations with their counterparts in the countries to which we had been invited, and we were assured of a welcome and safe transit across their borders. It was difficult to overcome the disbelief of my team that they would be able to travel unhindered into and through France, Belgium, Switzerland and Germany. Nevertheless, they accepted my assurances and we flew to Johannesburg and thence to Paris. On arrival I sought my contact at the airport. 'Ah yes,' he said, 'we know of the arrangement. Will you please come with me to this room and we will be with you in a few minutes.'

We were shepherded into a room and I could see the apprehension on the faces of my team, who were convinced that we would all be arrested and deported. A little later my security friend emerged and welcomed us to France. He advised us of the arrangements that had been made for us and emphasized the importance of keeping to our schedule and then said: 'We will now give you a *laissez-passer*,' which is a document in place of a visa.

He said he understood that we were moving on to Brussels on Friday and that we were leaving on the 11.40 a.m. train from the Gare du Nord. He emphasized that it was imperative that we travel on that train and no earlier or later train, or the plan would go awry. If we left on the right train at the correct time, twenty minutes later, he told us, there would be a knock on our compartment door. An official, after checking my identity, would greet us and tell us that he had some documents for me. We were to return our French *laissez-passers* and bid him goodbye. Another twenty minutes later, when we had crossed the Belgian border, there would be another knock on the door and we would be greeted by the Belgian officials, who would hand us our Belgian *laissez-passer* documents. We spent a couple of interesting days with the private sector, familiarizing our team with the European Union and other Belgian officials in Brussels, and then travelled to Zurich.

At this stage of the stand-off between Britain and Rhodesia, there was continuous unofficial movement between the two countries, especially by members of their intelligence service, MI6, and some diplomats. A week before our team was due to leave, I bumped into Sir John Graham in Salisbury, a member of the Foreign Office and whom I knew well. Their intelligence was so good that they knew that I was taking this team to Europe and he said with a smile on his face that he hoped that we would have a successful trip. I upbraided him for denying us entry into Britain and said that, as we were going all the way to Europe, why did he not relent and let a decent group of private-sector men, like our team, come into Britain. I asked him to reconsider, as he now knew exactly where we were going in Europe.

He was having great difficulty making contact with the outside world with the telephone in his Meikles hotel bedroom and I offered my help by getting in touch with my contact in the telephone system, where I had priority on international lines. Straight away, I got him his number, which he found impressive, and I then left the room.

When we got to Switzerland we received a call from the British Embassy saying that we would, after all, be allowed entry into Britain. Sir John had done his job well and we were delighted.

An hour later we received a call from Dr Max Klaus at Afrika Verein in Hamburg, who had organized the German visit, to say that the British Embassy had put pressure on the German government to deny us entry into Germany. The Germans said that they were so anxious to see us that they would bring their delegation, which we were to have met in Hamburg, to Zurich. I phoned back and asked them if they would come slightly earlier than suggested because we were, after all, going to Britain and would need to leave Zurich earlier.

Dr Klaus was incredulous that Britain had on the one hand persuaded Germany to deny us entry but at the same time were allowing us to go into Britain. They were extremely annoyed and said they would talk to their own foreign affairs office and they were sure they would now disregard the British request and welcome us into Germany. This is just what happened. We flew to Hamburg and had two productive days with investors and others who were anxious to be better informed about Rhodesia. These meetings were attended by ministry officials and the private sector.

We now had to rearrange our travel schedule to go back through London. I spent some hours hastily putting together guest lists for a couple of lunches and dinners in London and arranging for meetings. This was at very short notice and it was interesting to see how many people were able to adjust their schedules in order to meet the team. We saw the governor of the Bank of England, and again received much help from the Institute of Directors and used their secretarial facilities. Rhodesia was getting closer to a political solution and this had a direct bearing on the interest displayed.

While many sectors of the economy were adversely affected, UDI also led to much development, particularly where import replacements could be manufactured within the country. The Council continued its work of exposing the ever-changing situation in the country, while not necessarily subscribing to some of the political aims of the Rhodesian Front government. After UDI there was effectively a blackout of non-political information from Rhodesia to the outside world. Many developments undertaken by the private sector were, however, of outstanding merit.

We had a succession of prime ministers from Sir Garfield Todd and Sir Edgar Whitehead to Winston Field and Ian Smith, each successive prime minister being progressively more right wing. But the Rhodesia Promotion Council's job, regardless of politics, was to publicize our very real achievements, the development of our chrome and nickel mines and smelters, the expansion of Wankie's coal industry, the rapid increase of cotton production to offset the damaged tobacco industry, and, of course, our ability as the Central African bread basket to feed ourselves and the region.

There were a number of landmarks during those fifteen years of UDI. A stringer came into my office one day to offer his services in the production of non-political supplements that could be included in international newspapers. Because of sanctions, the major newspaper groups were banned from giving any form of publicity or promotion to Rhodesia. He wanted to produce a supplement on Rhodesia for the *International Herald Tribune* and I told him I thought he had only a remote chance of getting it published. He was confident and so, on the basis of the editorial and advertising being written entirely in Rhodesia and paid for only after publication, we agreed to go ahead.

In secrecy, sectors of our economy such as agriculture, mining, commerce, industry, banking and development prepared information about themselves, which we stitched together into a two-page supplement. To our astonishment the stringer came back to say that all was well and that the *International Herald Tribune* were prepared to go ahead.

This stringer hoped to sell the same supplement to the *New York Times*, although we were to hear of a cancellation of that supplement at the last minute. On the Friday I had a telephone conversation with the editor of the *New York Times*. He called me to express his annoyance that we had nearly succeeded in getting them to publish material about Rhodesia in their paper, in contravention of sanctions. The editor told me that they were cancelling the publication. My retort was that I was sorry that he was going to deprive his readers of becoming more informed about Rhodesia and its developments – good and bad. Our supplement in the *International Herald Tribune* was coming out on the Monday when business people all over the world would be able to read it. All hell broke loose as to how this had been achieved and it embarrassed one of the owners of the *International Herald Tribune*, John Whitney, who simultaneously was the American ambassador in London. Whitney and the *New York Times* were jointly the major shareholders in the *International Herald Tribune*, which had published our supplement.

What we had done aroused the interest of other publications and we soon had an approach from the New York *Journal of Commerce*, second only to the *Wall Street Journal* in their field, and they offered to publish a monthly two-page supplement about Rhodesia. Their edition was simultaneously printed in the Far East and European countries. When the first supplement came out, they were attacked in Washington by the Justice Department for breaking sanctions and were told that they would be prosecuted in the courts.

The publisher of the New York *Journal of Commerce* was a dynamic man, Eric Ridder, who among other things was the head of the syndicate that built the America's Cup defender *Constellation* which won the 1964 series. Ridder retorted that he was impatient for the case to be heard, that he would contest it all the way and take on the Justice Department, and furthermore he was confident that under the American Constitution they could not do anything to him. He won the day, the Department of Justice backed off and for about seven years the private-sector team here

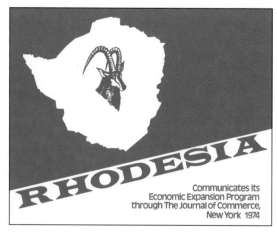

The *Journal of Commerce* published monthly features on what was happening in Rhodesia.

regularly produced a very informative supplement, the only organization to do so.

We soon had the French and the Germans asking themselves why they should not do the same sort of thing. We therefore produced similar supplements for *Paris Match*, *Le Monde* and *Le Figaro* in Paris and the *Neuer Züricher Zeitung* in Switzerland.

George Brown, the Deputy Leader of the Labour Party and Foreign Secretary in the Wilson government, started working for the party at a very early age and came up through the trade union movement. He came from the very roots of the Labour Party. He was said to have quite a difficult personality and on occasion his behaviour had embarrassed officials in the Foreign Office. We found him very quick-minded and pleasant.

At a time when Lord George Brown was out of office, I had a message to say he would like to visit Rhodesia. This was in the transition period when Ian Smith and Abel Muzorewa joined in coalition together. I called Mr Brown on the phone and said we would be delighted to entertain him and was there anything particular that he wished to see? He said the suggestion had been given to him to visit Zimbabwe Rhodesia by other politicians who had come here and he would be happy for us to arrange his programme.

He had one unusual condition and that was that I should fly to Johannesburg to meet him off the London plane and fly with him back to Harare, and at the end of his trip I was to escort him back to Johannesburg. He never said why this was a requirement, but it was easy to meet. By chance, when he was due to come, the Zimbabwe Promotion Council annual general meeting was scheduled. He was our principal guest speaker and made a most amusing speech. It was easier for him, being out of office, to criticize all and sundry.

I discovered on one of his trips that Denis Greenhill, the Permanent Under-Secretary of State for Foreign Affairs, had a great love of avocados, and that afternoon I sent a box of some lovely avocados, to be put on to his plane. He was grateful and it became a standing joke that, whenever he was here, I arranged for a tray to be put on board. In the same way, when I was chairman of the coffee board, I had sent up, by the man in charge of the roasting and the grading, twenty or thirty 2-kilo packets of our very best

> Lord Denis Greenhill's autobiography, *More by Accident*, dwells on the relationship that he had with George Brown. They respected each other but Greenhill had the more difficult task.

Lord George Brown addressing the 1979 AGM of the Rhodesia Promotion Council. In the foreground, members of management, P.W.T. Chipudhla and Stan O'Donnell.

Chipinga coffee, already roasted and with a lovely aroma. Whenever a visitor came into my office, the first thing they met was the aroma of the coffee. Again, it was something that helped start a conversation. As a result, Chipinga coffee found its way into many different parts of the world.

In 1976, when the writing was on the wall for the end of Rhodesia, David Lewis and I hatched a plan. We spoke to Ian Smith, whom we both knew well, expressing the view that it would not be long before the demise of Rhodesia. He had made the famous speech about majority rule and 'never in a thousand years'. We told him we thought that he was wrong and that it would be much nearer to four years. We told him of our admiration for our civil service and the administrative structure in the country. The civil service was based on the British model and, although sometimes a bit stuffy, it was upright, honest and professional. Yet, as the three of us were aware, there had been no training for those people who might form a succeeding administration. If we did nothing until the time came, the hand-over and changes would be much more difficult.

We asked Ian Smith if he would support our proposals, on behalf of the Rhodesia Promotion Council, to approach each minister and parastatal, as the government-owned companies are known in this country. We would ask them if they were prepared in principle to allow their permanent secretary or director to give up four evenings in the week to have supper with us in private, and on each evening to brief the leaders of the four black political parties. Because ZANU were based in Mozambique it was not possible to include them at that stage.

Ian Smith was supportive and said he would consult with his ministers. All but one, 'P.K.' van der Byl, Minister of Foreign Affairs, agreed. We then talked to the leadership of each of the four parties, explaining our plan. We asked if they would be interested in participating, whether they would nominate five or six of their most senior members, and whether they could guarantee, on a week-after-week basis, to bring at least four or five members of their team on their allocated evening.

We told them that we were doing this in the interests of the future of the country and that we had asked all the four parties. Although Robert Mugabe's party was out of the country, we explained that it would be the people of Zimbabwe who would decide which party would form the new government – it was not for us in any way to anticipate or influence that result; and that rather we should help by familiarizing all four parties with the present administration. This would mean that some senior members of the party elected by the people in the first general election would already have a better understanding of the administration they would inherit.

Without exception, the plan was welcomed. We took the top suite in the Monomatapa Hotel and arranged for a simple meal. David and I were the waiters. We had a drink and supper at 6.30 p.m. Afterwards we listened to each permanent secretary or chief executive.

The same secretary spoke for his ministry on each of the four successive evenings, and the following week we went through the same routine with another ministry.

Monday was Abel Muzorewa's evening, Tuesday was for Chief Chirau, Wednesday for Ndabaningi Sithole, and Thursday belonged to Joshua Nkomo, who was out of the country a great deal and whose place was taken by Josiah Chinamano and Cephas Msipa.

As a result of the previous system of segregation, it must be remembered that very few of the people we were targeting had ever been allowed to see inside the operations of the ministries or parastatals and had little idea how they functioned. The parties, almost without exception, brought a worthwhile group of their members to attend on their evening. We covered ministries and also parastatals such as Air Rhodesia, the Rhodesia Railways and the Electricity Supply Commission. We included the agricultural parastatals, covering research and marketing of maize, beef, dairy, oil-seeds, tobacco, wheat and cotton. The whole exercise took six months, and to this day there are some in the Zimbabwean administration who participated and who recall the value they received from that exercise. It is sad that our administration is now not what it could have been, because it has become so political, but at any rate we demonstrated the fundamentals at least three years before the new government took over.

Dr Etienne Rousseau was the chairman of the South Africa Foundation, which was a private-sector operation working within South Africa and, wherever possible, in the surrounding countries and overseas. It changed its name to Business Leadership South Africa in November 2005.

The first of its directors that I met was Peter Souror, who had previously been in their diplomatic service. We struck up a great relationship, and the South Africa Foundation was responsible for bringing a lot of people to visit us and we used to send down some delegations to them. Souror was succeeded as director by a former Secretary of the Ministry of Foreign Affairs, Neil van Heerden.

In the few years prior to and after 1980 I used to go to the annual general meeting of the South Africa Foundation, attended by about 600 of their members from all over the country. The one AGM of the Foundation that I remember particularly well was in April 1980, just after our elections, when Robert Mugabe became prime minister. I had accepted an invitation to speak but no longer had any mandate, and I consulted with Emmerson Mnangagwa to ask what I should do. Mugabe, through him, sent me a message to say he was glad that I was going to speak in South Africa and he asked me to tell the meeting that, although there were serious political differences between the two countries, he recognized the interdependence of each and hoped that economic and financial relations would continue as before. The South Africans were very relieved because of the value of Zimbabwe as a market. Of course, relations between Zimbabwe and South Africa were at times strained until Nelson Mandela came to power.

– 11 –

Mining

John Mack • Small-scale mining • Gold cyaniding on Handley Cross
• Freda Rebecca, Royal Family and Antelope mines • Asbestos

Gold mining was the reason that Rhodesia was opened up in the first place, and agricultural development took place around that thrust. There was very little farming production until after the First World War. Farmers grew a little tobacco, cotton and maize, but gold mining was carried out in many areas. There developed a breed of lonely prospectors, accompanied by a small labour force, who scoured these areas searching for reefs which had been exposed and which, by trial panning, indicated a worthwhile gold content, usually found in a quartz ore body.

In the 1920s, a small-worker prospector sank a shaft north of Gatooma. He ran out of money and abandoned his claim, which was later picked up by another small-worker called John Mack. He had a bit of money to spare and decided to take a chance and go further and he deepened the shaft. Very soon afterwards he struck a reef of very high value: that Golden Valley mine has been producing many thousands of ounces of pure gold every month since then. It could have produced more, but his financial advisers advised him to peg production at that level rather than mine it out quickly. They could not easily have exhausted it, because the mine is still producing at the same rate to this day. If they reach their targets before the end of the month, they either mine a small amount of lower grade, to reach the target, or cease operations until the beginning of the next month.

> Research has shown that from the year 1600 substantial quantities of gold were produced with primitive equipment by the local population.

Ore bodies on other mines varied from 'stringers' only a few inches wide, to those of twelve to fifteen inches. Miners sank shafts that followed the reef, and the shafts had to be supported with square timber trusses positioned to prevent caving in. The trusses were often made of the hardwood mopane trees, which grew well, only had to be cut and transported, and lasted well.

Once past the softer rock, the miners had to use dynamite. Workers with drills and hammers made a hole an inch in diameter and two to three feet deep. They located these with care in order to follow the reef, minimizing the amount of non-gold-bearing 'country rock' shattered in the blast. They put fuses into the dynamite, took the ends to the surface and, from a safe distance, detonated them.

They hoisted the resultant ore-bearing rock to the surface using a windlass and cable attached to a bucket. One man at each end operated the windlass to wind up the bucket with its load of rock. Once the bucket reached the surface, they emptied it and lowered it to the bottom again to bring up a second, third and fourth load until all the loose ore-bearing rock was on the surface. The miner then drilled new holes and repeated the process.

In some areas the water-table was forty and sixty feet from the surface. When these small-workings hit the water-level the miners had to install pumps if they wished to continue mining there. There was no such thing as grid electricity, but producer gas engines were available, which burned charcoal to produce methane gas. They used this methane as the feedstock for the engine, which in turn generated electricity, powering the pumps and the mills. The system was very basic and required charcoal to make the gas. This obviously needed wood, and so the area around a small mine gradually became denuded of timber.

Some of the mines also had small boilers, fired by wood, and these also provided energy to power the pumps. Once a 'daylight miner' got down deep into the water zones he was at serious risk. A pump breakdown meant that the water flooded the shaft back to the original level and the process had to start all over again. In consequence, many men abandoned their mines once they reached the water-table and went in search of new ones.

To provide the charcoal, timber was cut and kilned, encased in mud like a beehive, and charred (but not burnt) right through, which might take a week. When the process was complete, the mud plaster on the outside was taken off and the charcoal was carried on ox wagons to the mines. They used to follow a line along the vleis and valleys and the ruts the wagons made in wet weather badly damaged the environment as they eroded deeper and deeper and turned from gullies into chasms. On Handley Cross we spent a lot of time planting grass in these gullies, which helped to check the flow of water in times of heavy rain and so halted soil erosion.

Reasonable-sized small-workings had their own mill that consisted of either three or five heavy stamps. A steam-powered shaft fitted with cams picked the stamps up one at a time in rotation so that three or five stamps rose and then dropped on to the ore, pulverizing the rock to sludge. The miner shovelled this into an ore box and water was fed into it continuously to wash this very fine sludge through a fine wire mesh on to a table which could be covered either with a copper sheet or, if that was too expensive, with corduroy.

Each morning the miner would plaster the sheet of copper or corduroy with mercury, because gold has an affinity for mercury. The table holding the sheet usually measured three feet by eight feet. As the ore in suspension ran down over the table, the gold attached itself to the mercury and the slime or sand, now largely devoid of gold, washed off at the bottom of the table.

Every evening, the miner would remove the free mercury from the top of the table for re-use. The mixture of gold and mercury, called amalgam, was scraped off the table and accumulated and, when enough had been collected, it would be smelted.

On Handley Cross in 1939 we had a number of mills, ranging between three and five stamps. The itinerant population of small-mine workers was a varied group of people. We had a retired professional footballer from Southampton, an old German bachelor and several alcoholics.

Some of the miners found that at the sixty-foot level the ore body changed from an oxide rock – which, as its name suggests, had been oxidized over the millennia – to sulphide ore. It is easy to extract gold from the oxide zones but the roasting process needed to extract gold from sulphide ore bodies is complicated and expensive. Small-workers usually closed operations when they reached the sulphide zone.

Cyanide was – and is – widely used to extract gold. The spent sand from the mills was carried by barrow to a dump where it accumulated. Over time, the sand oxidized and the small remnant of gold could be extracted by the cyanide process. To do this, the sand was brought back from the dump and put into large circular tanks which had timber poles across the floor, covered by jute bags. Water saturated with cyanide was pumped on to the sand and slowly seeped through to the bottom. The gold dissolved and the solution, pregnant with gold, was drained off at the bottom and, after the solution was topped up with more cyanide, was circulated again.

It took forty-eight hours to extract what gold had been lost in the original pass over the mercury table.

The solution then passed through a concentrator box that was filled regularly with zinc shavings. Gold also has an affinity to zinc and when it amalgamated with the shavings it looked like horrible black treacle. Further zinc shavings were added regularly and in due course the result was smelted to separate the zinc from the gold.

Much gold has been produced by these small-workers over the years. In 1970 we were in the throes of a third successive year of serious drought with small harvests and little or no work for the farm-workers. I decided to provide a job for unemployed workers by trying my hand with cyaniding. There was a large sand dump on the farm from the Juno Mine, originally pegged in about 1915.

A few miles away we had one of the biggest gold mines in Zimbabwe, the Dalny, at Chakari. The metallurgist in charge was Owen Nicolle, whose father had emigrated from the little parish of Longueville in Jersey. He gave me a basic understanding of what to do.

We built ten tanks with a capacity of five hundred tonnes each, made our own concentrator box, and fenced off the area for safety reasons, because cyanide is extremely poisonous. After the solution had left the box, we tested it frequently to check how much cyanide was left. We would top it up to the correct level and this process continued day and night. We took out the treated sand after forty-eight hours and refilled the tank.

As a result, after smelting we had small gold ingots. By law, all gold mined has to be surrendered to the Reserve Bank. There is, however, a clause in the Act that permits the owner of a mining operation to apply to the Permanent Secretary of Mines to keep one troy ounce of refined gold a year for himself and his wife for each mine that they operate. Chris Ushewokunze, Permanent Secretary for the Ministry of Mines, agreed that I was entitled under the Act to keep some gold and we kept our two troy ounces, which we took to 'Daniel the Jeweller', named after a remarkable gold craftsman. With that pure gold reduced to twenty-four carats, there was sufficient to make a signet ring each for Wendy and me, engraved with our family crest, and we also had a ring designed and made for each of our three daughters. I had a set of gold cuff-links made, as did our grandsons.

Chris Ushewokunze was highly regarded and I asked him to join the board of Agricura, where he made a meaningful contribution. He later became Minister of Industry and Commerce and was killed in a car accident in 1994 at the age of 49.

It must be rare to have jewellery made from gold mined by the wearer, and we were very proud of it. Also, our daughter Diana and I designed, with Mr Daniel's help, a lovely brooch for Wendy for our 25th wedding anniversary, using our gold, Zimbabwean platinum, emeralds and rubies with diamonds from South Africa.

A couple of months after we started the cyaniding, we had an approach from a couple who wanted to buy Handley Cross. My father had always said that we should never let sentiment stand in the way of making a good, sound financial decision. We had three daughters, Elizabeth, Diana and Caroline, and at that stage we had no idea who they would marry and whether they would have any interest in Handley Cross, which had been in our hands for over fifty years. So we sold the farm and my short mining career came to an end in 1978.

There is, however, a footnote to this. In the 1980s two geologists, Nick Graham and Phil Dewhurst, were traversing the country to see if they could discover new reefs. On the outskirts of the small town of Bindura, Anglo American owned a gold mine called the Phoenix Prince, but they thought they had explored and exhausted the whole area. Nick Graham, who has a wonderful nose for finding ore bodies, discovered a small reef the other side of the main road from the Phoenix Prince and pegged it. Under this country's mining law, when land is pegged for a mine it is reserved for the man who pegged it, ad infinitum, providing he continues to exploit those reserves. This mining law has caused a lot of near hostility between farmers and miners who are allowed to peg on agricultural land, with certain exceptions such as that they cannot encroach on land under cultivation or within 500 yards of a homestead.

An English entrepreneur, Algy Cluff, was interested in making an investment. He had made a great deal of money in North Sea oil and I believe was the only individual entrepreneur, as opposed to a large company, who had a field for exploration in the North Sea with his own oil rig. He lost his American partner and soon afterwards sold out to one of the big oil companies. He tried his hand again in the Yellow Sea, off China, where he lost a great deal of money. He had a passion for exploration and he joined forces with Nick Graham to participate in this new venture. Together they developed what became the largest gold mine in the country, the Freda Rebecca, named after Algy's mother and Nick's daughter.

Exploration soon showed that there was a huge, low-grade reef of oxide ore close to the surface, which the Anglo American mining engineers had walked over for thirty years without being aware of the potential below

The entrance to the lateral incline tunnel at the bottom of the Freda Rebecca open-cast mine. The open working was over 600 feet deep.

them. The ease of access to the ore compensated for the low grade, and a gigantic open-cast pit developed over a number of years. In 1994, it produced 2,149 kg of gold from a pit that was 200 metres long, 50 metres deep and 100 metres wide.

After the mine had been going for two to three years, Cluff asked to see me when I was in London and offered me a seat on his board. I had never been involved with a mining house so I was interested and accepted his offer. It was an unusual learning experience and very interesting.

Eventually the original ore body petered out and it looked as if the mine was going to come to an end until, by the greatest good luck, they discovered, right at the bottom of the pit, a reef on a steep incline. It was narrow but with a considerably higher gold content, which made it viable and enabled the life of the mine to be extended. The technique changed, open-cast mining was no longer used and the operation changed to underground mining following the reef. The mine continues to be the largest in Zimbabwe. It was bought by AngloGold which has now sold to Mwana Africa.

Algy Cluff also developed a low-grade mine near Filabusi by the name of the Royal Family. The grade was not sufficient to put up a sophisticated plant, but we had a crusher which reduced the ore to large pebbles about half an inch across. These were then spread over a large sheet of very thick plastic. Ordinary farm irrigation sprinklers played continuously on a nine-inch layer of the pebbles, and when this drained off, it was in a state where gold extraction could take place.

Not far from the Royal Family mine was a mine called the Antelope, which was developed quite deep but abandoned. Some time after the Gukurahundi, another mining company was prospecting in the area and needed a water supply. A collar was put around the top of the Antelope shaft to secure it and a pump was lowered. Mining diagrams showed the depth of that shaft, but when the pump tubing reached a particular level, initially it could go no further. It was discovered that the bottom of those tubes were situated on a type of ceiling and, when this was penetrated, it was discovered that the rest of the shaft, right down to the bottom, had been filled with dead people.

The Royal Family mine was in the Filabusi area, at the centre of some of the worst Gukurahundi atrocities. The Gukurahundi has been described in many books, notably in one by the Catholic Commission for Justice and Peace in Zimbabwe and the Legal Resources Foundation called *Breaking the Silence*. It is not necessary for me to enlarge upon that.

In this country we have for many years had a small asbestos production at Zvishavane in the Southern Midlands, which makes some contribution to our foreign-exchange earnings. Asbestos is reviled nowadays as being responsible for lung cancer caused by the asbestos dust. There are, however, two types of asbestos, one of which is far more dangerous than the other. We produce the short-fibre asbestos: although it has a bad name, it is certainly not as damaging as the long-fibre asbestos. It is widely used in insulation, building and roofing.

– 12 –

Chrome

In 1966 I was involved in helping the American steel industry acquire their specialist chrome requirements from Rhodesia, in spite of sanctions.

After UDI, all diplomatic relations between the United States and Rhodesia were terminated, although the US maintained an 'interest office' in Salisbury until 1970. Fortunately, however, Ken Towsey and John Hooper, our two representatives attached to the British Embassy in Washington, had had the foresight to register the Rhodesian Information Office in the United States before UDI. The break in diplomatic relations did not affect its continued existence and it remained open for many years.

Before UDI, the Rhodesian chrome industry had started to expand. At the time, we were an important source of metallurgical chrome, probably the second most important in the world after Russia. Metallurgical Lumpy is the highest of chrome's three grades and is used for high-quality stainless and specialized steels for the armaments industry.

With the development of our ore bodies and the world's demands, it was obvious that it would be better to develop smelters in Rhodesia, rather than exporting bulk ore, and a chrome smelter was built at Que Que by Union Carbide. This was invaluable in that it refined the bulk ore into a smaller volume.

It was not until 16 December 1966, just over a year after UDI, that the United Nations Security Council, by eleven votes to zero, imposed mandatory

Rhodesian high-grade chrome, from Selukwe Peak farm.

sanctions on Rhodesia. This precluded any country that subscribed to the UN charter from importing any of our products, including chrome. Sanctions were supported by the USA and the embargo was broadened two years later. This resulted in our chrome ore (destined for the USA) being stockpiled for want of a customer.

But the mandatory sanctions also affected America. Although the USA had voted for sanctions, they effectively cut its own steel industry off from one of its most important sources of metallurgical chrome. So America was faced with a dilemma, more particularly because they actually owned chrome mines in Rhodesia but were precluded from shipping the chrome they mined back to America.

A clause in the US Constitution, Article VI, states: 'All treaties made or which shall be made under the authority of the United States shall be the supreme law of the land.' In other words, if America made a law that was contrary to a UN resolution, then the American law would be supreme; but, as a member of the UN, America had to support UN sanctions. This dilemma emerged in the court records produced in the Senate proceedings.

With the cessation of exports to the USA, our chrome ore stockpiles continued to grow, and we began selling our chrome secretly to Russia, who saw an opportunity of buying cheap high-grade chrome from a be-leaguered country with no bargaining power. Having bought it from us at a discount of around forty per cent, the Russians then sold it on to the USA at a vast profit. Our chrome was loaded on to a Russian bulk carrier in Lourenço Marques in Mozambique and the Russian captain was told by the ship's agent to sail to a Black Sea port via Gibraltar, but he was to open a second envelope five days out to sea. This directive changed his instructions and told the ship to go instead to a Gulf port in the USA.

It is possible to ascertain the source of chrome ore by the very small variations of its titanium content. No two chrome fields have the same titanium 'fingerprint'. The Americans suspected that the chrome that was supposed to be coming from a new chrome field in Russia was in fact of Rhodesian origin. Scientists at the Crucible organization, on testing the ore, supported the view that it was Rhodesian chrome.

At this time, many senators and congressmen were becoming increasingly concerned with the threat of communism from Russia. Discussions took place as to how the USA could legally get around sanctions and directly import chrome from the Rhodesian mines, which they themselves owned, without compromising their standing at the UN.

The leaders in the American chrome industry were the Union Carbide Corporation, whose principal contact with us was E. F. (Andy) Andrews, a frequent visitor to Rhodesia. Union Carbide was a multinational corporate with a number of alloy and chemical plants in the States, and it also owned Rhodesian Chrome Mines and African Chrome Mines as well as the new Union Carbide Rhomet at Que Que, the first major smelter in Rhodesia. One of its senior executives, James Rawlings, was appointed as United States ambassador to Zimbabwe shortly after independence.

The second group was the Foote mineral company, who were the sole owners of the Rhodesian Vanadium Corporation, which owned and operated chrome mines in the Great Dyke region running across Rhodesia. Both organizations, anticipating funding difficulties if UDI were declared, had deposited very substantial sums of money in their Rhodesian subsidiaries not long before UDI to enable them to continue operations if sanctions made the movement of funds difficult. Together they accounted for more than three-quarters of our chrome industry, the third company being Allegheny Ludlum.

A further complication arose when the Americans appointed Kenneth Rush, who was the president of Union Carbide, to be their ambassador to West Germany. As a representative of America who wished to continue his business enterprises, mines and exports, he found himself in a delicate position, given the American policy at that time of sanctions on Rhodesian chrome, some of which belonged to his company.

America could have vetoed the sanctions resolution when the matter originally came up before the Security Council but had not done so. The issue facing the US government was whether America should import its own chrome, which would be in violation of the UN sanctions, or obey the UN sanctions, which would have clearly been to the country's disadvantage.

The problem was ultimately resolved by the Byrd Amendment. Senator Harry F. Byrd, Jr, from the state of Virginia, the only independent senator, was the author and chief strategist of the legislation that popularly bore his name. It stated that it was in the national interest of the USA to import chrome from Rhodesia in spite of the USA's initial vote in the Security Council.

Senator Harry F. Byrd, Jr.

At the time there was great controversy in both the Senate and House of Representatives, with expressions of outrage on the one hand at the violation of the UN's authority and outrage on the other at the thought that America was importing Rhodesian chrome, a strategic mineral, via the USSR at greatly increased cost.

Shortly before the US election in 1968 I was in the USA with David Lewis. We were asked to talk to the American steelworkers' union led by I.W. Abel, which had significant influence in Washington. They were a tough bunch of people and we were glad to hear afterwards that, as a result of the better understanding that they now had of our situation, they had influenced their senators in the steel states and others to support the Byrd Amendment; many of their jobs would have been at stake if our chrome did not reach them.

We met at the Brackenridge steel plant in Pennsylvania, which is said to be the biggest stainless-steel plant in the world. We were told that they were anxiously awaiting the next shipment of chrome from Russia, which was a vital ingredient in the different blends of steel they used for their inter-continental ballistic missiles, nose cones for their space programme, other strategic armaments and high-quality stainless steel.

> I was kindly given a supply of small core samples from quality control, drawn from one of the smelters blending our chrome with other minerals. I still have one of these on my mantelpiece at home, and we later presented others to our delegates at the Zimbabwe Resources Conference in September 1980.

I was asked to assist Byrd's team with up-to-date background information about the situation in Rhodesia to help in the lobby that developed around the Byrd Amendment. I flew, at their request, to America from Germany ahead of the debate and met a number of people on both sides. The president had difficulty in reconciling his responsibility as head of state with the decision taken by the Security Council. He was under pressure to ensure that the USA did not fall short of this strategic commodity and did not get into the dangerous situation where the supply of Rhodesian chrome shipped by the USSR could have been terminated at a moment's notice.

The whole matter continued to be the subject of much debate, with opposing views in both the Senate and House of Representatives. During March 1971, a Bill, HR5445, which reaffirmed Congress's approval of a strict trade embargo, was brought to Senator Byrd's attention by the steel chrome lobby. His dislike of the United Nations and his abhorrence of all sanctions against Rhodesia were already well known. In the debate on HR 5445, Congressman James Collins said, 'I believe this country should

Pieces of the heat shield from Gemini VI,
which contained Rhodesian chrome from Selukwe (Shurugwi).

never subordinate the position of the US to anyone regarding its foreign commerce matter. It is not a worldwide matter.' Similarly, in his speech to the Senate, Senator Byrd said:

> Now the Congress is being asked by the Administration to release chrome ore from the national stockpile to ease the shortage of this commodity resulting from the Rhodesian embargo. Release of chrome ore from our stockpile is not the appropriate remedy for the present situation in the United States. The current step for this nation to take would be to end its foolish policy against Rhodesia and resume trade with that nation.

Finally, on 29 March 1971, Senator Byrd introduced S 1404 into the Senate. His three co-sponsors were Senators Irvine (Democrat), Goldwater (Republican) and Fanin (Republican).

The Secretary of State, Henry Kissinger, was testifying before the Committee on Amendments to the Federal Trade Act, which would permit the United States to grant 'most favoured nation' status to the Soviet Union. During an open hearing before the Senate Committee on Finance on 7 March, he said, in reply to a question by Senator Byrd, that in his judgement Rhodesia was not a threat to world peace. I quote from the Congressional records:

Senator Byrd: You are to advocate relaxing trade barriers with other nations but you recommend that legislation enacted by the Congress to embargo the purchase of vitally needed strategic material from Rhodesia, which material the United States has none. Now in your testimony before the Foreign Relations Committee, of which the present Chairman [Senator Fulbright] is in the Chair, you are then urging an embargo on trade with another country?

Secretary Kissinger: First of all, Senator, I must say you were very restrained in your first round of questions. (General laughter)

Senator Byrd: Do you think our actions against Rhodesia are just or unjust?

Secretary Kissinger: I think it reflects the decisions of the international community and the general conviction about justice.

Senator Byrd: Well, I am not clear whether you regard it as just or unjust?

Senator Kissinger: Our action? Yes, I regard it as just.

Senator Byrd: You recognize an action in embargoing trade with Rhodesia as being just?

Secretary Kissinger: Yes.

Senator Byrd: Do you regard the Soviet Union as being governed by a tight dictatorship, by a very few persons over a great number of individuals?

Secretary Kissinger: I consider the Soviet Union, yes, as a dictatorship of an oligarchic nature that is as a small number of people in the Politburo.

Senator Byrd: In your judgment is Rhodesia a threat to world peace?

Secretary Kissinger: No.

Senator Byrd: In your judgement is Russia a potential threat to world peace?

Secretary Kissinger: I think the Soviet Union has the military capacity to disturb the peace, yes.

Senator Byrd: In your judgment, does Russia have a more democratic government than Rhodesia?

Secretary Kissinger: No.

Senator Byrd: If it is just to embargo trade on Rhodesia, would it be equally just to embargo trade against South Africa?

Secretary Kissinger: I believe that the embargo of trade on Rhodesia is not based on its internal policies so much as the fact that a minority has established a separate state, and it does not therefore represent exclusively a judgment on the domestic policies of the Rhodesian government, but also a question with respect to the legitimacy of the Rhodesian government.

Senator Byrd: Well, then you say it is because Rhodesia seeks to establish her own government. Is that not what the United States did in 1776?

Secretary Kissinger: In a different international context.

Senator Byrd: Mr Secretary, I am very interested in this Rhodesian matter. I have never been there; I have no connection with it one way or the other. And you have testified that you feel that the action that the United States has taken is a just action and you are entitled to your view, just as I am entitled to my view. I feel that it is a very unprincipled action. Now you have testified, and it is interesting to note that the then foreign secretary of Great Britain, Douglas-Home, in an interview last December, said that while his government supported trade sanctions against Rhodesia because they had been put on by the previous Labour government, he did not feel it was the correct policy. And then he added: 'We disagree with the political system of a number of countries, for example South Africa. But we trade with them. And, by and large, we do not believe in ostracism and boycott.' Would you care to comment on that?

Secretary Kissinger: I agree with the general principle he enunciated.

Senator Byrd: And then you have testified that you do not regard Rhodesia as being a threat to world peace?

Secretary Kissinger: That is correct.

Senator Byrd: And then you know, of course, that under the United Nations Charter action can only be taken against a country in regard to an embargo if that country is judged to be a threat to world peace? And so my question to you is, do you think that the United Nations acted properly?

Secretary Kissinger: I had not thought that the United Nations acted improperly but, in the light of what you have said, I would have to review the particular position of the embargo.

It was a sensational hearing over two days that I was privileged to attend. The amended proposed legislation that would allow America to import Rhodesian chrome legally was part of a Military Finance Procurement Bill, Clause 503. An interesting sidelight to American politics tells us that, while the President of the United States publicly opposed the Byrd Amendment, at no time did he lobby some of the key waverers and request them to vote against the amendment.

The vote was due to take place late in the afternoon and I spent some time at the White House in Richard V. (Dick) Allen's office. He was a member of the National Security Council under Kissinger who was the National Security Advisor. Allen later became the Senior Security Advisor under President Ronald Reagan.

The vote was very close, and it is interesting that a senator called Metcalf, a Democrat, to the surprise of his own office, changed his position on the issue five times in five different votes.

Finally the news arrived – the Byrd Amendment had been adopted and America could now import their own chrome in spite of UN sanctions. Senators had disregarded what the president had said in public and voted according to their own views and so the Byrd Amendment was won by 46 to 36. The amendment was selective in that the only commodity that could be imported was chrome and its allied minerals. Sanctions remained in force in all other respects.

In the intervening years, I visited the United States on a number of occasions specifically to discuss with old and new senators and members of the House of Representatives the changing position within Rhodesia, because there were frequent legislative gymnastics aimed at reversing the Byrd Amendment.

On one occasion in 1970 I was asked by Senator James Eastland from Mississippi to speak at a luncheon he gave for me in the dining room of the Senate. He invited me to talk not only about the chrome issue but about current events in Rhodesia. There were sixty people in the room and I was aware that most of them knew a great deal about us so I had to be particularly careful in marshalling facts and figures. The party was made up of officials, senators and congressmen, the CIA and staffers from the White House, steel men whose particular interest was our chrome and other businessmen.

Senator Eastland thanked me and paid me an unusual honour, presenting me with a cut-glass cigar ashtray bearing the crest of the United States Senate. He had presented a similar one to me during the cotton trip, mentioned previously, when I had also been a guest of the Senate. For many attending the lunch it was the first time that they had heard first hand not only about chrome, but the Rhodesian position in general.

On another occasion, I had a call from David Rockefeller's personal assistant, to say that David Rockefeller was planning to visit Rhodesia as part of a Southern African tour. The chrome people had suggested that he ask me to host him while he was in the country, and I was very pleased to do so.

The saga of chrome exports to the United States makes me think of an earlier story. During World War II, submarines were being built by Bethlehem Steel in the US for Great Britain, who were in urgent need of more submarines. Winston Churchill was a close friend of Bernard Baruch, the American mega-financier. He took Churchill to meet the chairman of Bethlehem Steel, Charles Schwab. Churchill explained the dire necessity for a quicker supply and Schwab agreed to speed up the process and reduce the time it took to make a submarine. With many submarines being constructed simultaneously, a substantial number were coming down the slipway, but because of the American Neutrality Act (the US had not yet joined the war and they could not sell them directly to Britain). They had to build, test, and dismantle the submarines, put them on to trucks and take them across the border to Canada. They were then reassembled and sailed down the St Lawrence Waterway in Canada and on to Britain without problems. In this case the United States were avoiding sanctions. The support of Bethlehem Steel played a major role in the defence of British shipping and, of course, also in attacking German naval forces. During the war Schwab was director-general of the emergency fleet, with authority over all ship-building in the United States.

Under the leadership of Charles Schwab, the Bethlehem Steel Corporation became the second largest steel-maker in the US and one of the most important steel works in the world. He became president of Carnegie Steel and was involved in a merger negotiation regarding that company with a group of New York financiers led by J. P. Morgan, and he became the first president of the United States Steel Corporation. He revolutionized building construction with steel beams and skyscrapers.

One of our hosts in the USA, a leading light in the Christian Fellowship, enabled me to meet two amazing people. The first was Walter Schirra, the second American astronaut. Schirra had served in South Korea and became a test pilot after the war, testing systems like the sidewinder missile and the F7U-3 Cutlass jet fighter. In April 1959, he was chosen as one of the original seven American astronauts. He was also the only man to fly in America's first three space programmes, Mercury, Gemini and Apollo. In 1962 he piloted the Mercury 8 in a capsule travelling at over 17,000 miles an hour. Remarkably, after orbiting the earth, he was able to land it within four miles of the Pacific Ocean recovery ship. Three years later, he flew into space a second time in the Gemini 6A with Tom Stafford (I think that was the first rendezvous operation, when he joined up with Frank Borman and James Lovell Jr). In 1968 he flew a final time as commander of Apollo 7.

When Schirra was flying with Stafford, Borman and Lovell, they had improved facilities in the capsule which enabled them, after having 'spent a penny', to eject the by-products. On the first occasion at sunset they were astonished to see that the urine broke up into its molecular structure once released at those temperatures and at that pressure. A stream of what looked like fireflies spread out from the capsule and made what seemed to be an enormous constellation, stretching about fifty miles long and twenty-five miles wide at the far base. They were all intrigued and the three of them used to choose their time in the loo carefully so that they could have further shows.
After they had returned to earth, in a de-briefing a lady physicist professor said that she could not understand how Walter had been able to photograph this new constellation, which could not be seen from the earth. She said it was making solar history and thought it should be called after him.
'No, no,' Walter replied. 'I think it should be called the constellation Urian.'

Thereafter, Walter Schirra and I saw quite a bit of each other. As he had flown over Rhodesia a number of times circuiting the globe, he was interested in visiting Rhodesia, and he and his wife accepted our invitation. His stories about his trips to outer space were fascinating and he addressed several groups while he was here. He had courage and presence of mind, but he found himself quite unable to aim at a lion when he was taken on a hunting safari in the Wankie area – it was an easy shot of two hundred yards, but he shook when he took aim and missed by eight yards.

Our host from the Christian Fellowship also introduced us to Washington Okumu, a Kenyan who had been imprisoned by Jomo Kenyatta and was working for the United Nations in Vienna. He held balanced views and was now politically acceptable again in Kenya.

Because he was anxious to see what help he could give towards the solution of our intractable Rhodesian problems, we invited him to visit us informally. Inevitably, there were problems to overcome in order to get a person of his position into the country. Clearly, he too was a little apprehensive about his own safety, so effective had been the propaganda about Rhodesia. The South African Ministry of Foreign Affairs became aware of our plan and was anxious to arrange for Okumu to go to Pretoria.

To this end, I paid a couple of visits to Vienna, at two to three week intervals, leaving my office on a Friday morning, supposedly going home for a weekend's rest, but instead travelling to Johannesburg, switching to Olympic Airways to fly to Athens and then on to Vienna, where I was able to brief Okumu and discuss details of the plans. After my third visit, David Lewis accompanied me to the final planning session. We met with a senior Foreign Affairs official from Pretoria and lunched with Washington Okumu and his wife in Vienna to put the final touches to the programme.

We had arranged for Okumu's visit to Rhodesia to be totally informal and private. He met a cross-section of business people, black and white, and became better acquainted with the reality in this country in the three days he spent with us, as well as having a good discussion with Ian Smith. He continued incognito to Pretoria, where he met Prime Minister John Vorster and other Nationalist politicians, and he visited Soweto.

Many years later, these contacts stood Okumu in good stead when the negotiations for the new constitution and democracy in South Africa were in their crucial final stages. A critical stumbling block had developed between Nelson Mandela and Mangosuthu Buthelezi, who broke off the talks and was driven out to Lanseria Airport to return to KwaZulu-Natal.

Washington Okumu was present and volunteered to follow Buthelezi out to the airport to point out the heavy responsibility he would bear if he allowed the talks to fail. And so Washington Okumu was driven at high speed to catch Buthelezi before he left. As they drove into the airport, they saw Buthelezi's plane climbing into the sky and Okumu told me he feared that all was lost. He is a very devout Christian and he told me that he prayed for help.

Back in the terminal building, a message came in to say that the plane had developed a problem and was returning to Lanseria. Okumu went out to the plane and talked to Buthelezi, persuaded him to come back into the negotiations and together they returned to Pretoria. Washington Okumu always maintained that the mishap to the plane was a direct act of God – and the talks ultimately succeeded.

The Byrd Amendment was repealed in 1977 after Andrew Young had become Secretary of State under President Jimmy Carter, who was elected late in 1976. Almost immediately, the American multi-entry visa in my passport was cancelled. He knew exactly who I was and, when we met afterwards, he paid me an oblique compliment by telling me that they 'had been waiting for the day when they would take me out of the equation'. I said I was surprised he would wish to do so when we were trying to ensure the safety of the USA in the face of the Soviet threat to his country.

When it was all over, one of the chrome lobbyists who had done much work on the Hill suggested that the dozen people who had been involved in different ways with the Byrd Amendment should become an informal club. This club would have no constitution, could never be enlarged, and its members were the people mentioned in this chapter and Ken Towsey, who ran the Rhodesian Information Office in Washington with John Hooper. The club was called the 503 Club, after the clause number in the Military Procurement Bill. We were all given a gold lapel badge simply engraved '503'. Few people know of its existence and, although I have worn it on occasion at industrial functions, only on three occasions has anyone commented, 'I see you are a member of the 503 Club ... What part did you play?'

My 503 Club badge.

– 13 –

African Farming Development

Communal and commercial farmers • The company established
• Success on the ground • A model for others

Vec Hurley and Tom Stanning had the foresight to recognize the symptoms of land hunger and low productivity in the communal areas. Some of the commercial farms bordered communal land, yet the difference between the crops produced by a small-scale farmer and those of his commercial farming neighbour was enormous. The climate was the same. The rains were the same. The soil was the same. During the winter, communal farmers would come to the commercial farmers to look for work on contract: cutting firewood for tobacco furnaces, grading tobacco or reaping maize.

In many areas an excellent relationship developed, with many commercial farmers lending the communal farmers a tractor on a Saturday afternoon, or helping with a bit of spare fertilizer, or passing on some burley tobacco seedlings. Centenary farmers came to me and said that they were happy to help their neighbours, but so successful was the scheme that they were being overwhelmed with requests for assistance and, of course, they were very busy on their own farms. Did I have any ideas on how the communal farmers could be further helped?

African Farming Development (AFD) was born: Tom Stanning, Vec Hurley, Humphrey Downs and I established a non-profit-making company. This was properly funded, planned and organized and brought together the resources of skill and capital on the one side, and people and land on the other. We got an excellent response in sponsorship and investment from big companies. The scheme operated in the Tribal Trust Lands (later known as Communal Lands) and demonstrated that the problem of land use was not only a political one.

Several people who shared our views agreed to help, notably Sir Henry McDowell, who had been Permanent Secretary to the Federal Treasury, chairman of the University Council, and after 1970 became the Chancellor of the University. Ted Eustace, who chose to live in Harare on his retirement from a distinguished career in the South African diplomatic service, helped greatly with his diplomatic contacts. Others were the current president of the Associated Chambers of Commerce of Rhodesia (ACCOR) and the current president of the Association of Rhodesia and Nyasaland Industries (ARNI), and John Cameron, who had many international contacts.

They asked me for ideas and I canvassed the situation with suppliers of inputs in the field of commerce and with the banks. The scheme we put in place had guarantees, and communal farmers were able to access their requirements under the advice and supervision of Piet Jordaan, our excellent agronomist.

Under the Rhodesian constitution, we were unable to operate and compete within a communal land without specific approval. This had been inserted in order to prevent large companies with huge resources – for example, the supermarket chains – from selling goods at a far lower price than the small, locally owned, grocery stores in the area, which were often the hub for micro development. However, we were granted this permission, so we could get on with our plans.

Our first centre was in the north of Chiweshe against the Centenary and Sipolilo commercial areas. This was followed shortly by other centres in Sipolilo, Umvukwes, Mashayamombe and Mrewa. At one time 1,650 individual farmers participated, with each district having its own agricultural equipment and an agronomist and, importantly, working with the help and advice of their neighbouring commercial farmers. AFD was poised for rapid expansion into other districts.

The company prospered beyond our expectations. The number of participants grew to such an extent that we had to employ further agronomists and arrange the funding. In all instances, after retention for family use, the surplus crop was sold and the participants for the first time were able to enter the cash economy. With advice from Jordaan, they paid their debts, improved their farming skills, and had surplus cash at the end of each season. It was successful from the start, and the AFD farmers' crops were good.

The team we put in had a big tractor for deep ploughing. All the lands were soil-sampled to ascertain the alkalinity and the appropriate fertilizer. The farmers were growing maize, burley tobacco, groundnuts and small areas of vegetables. Neighbouring commercial farmers allowed the communal farmers in AFD to cut gum poles and to put up a couple of curing barns for burley tobacco. AFD's financial resources were used for tractors and trucks, fertilizer, chemicals and plastic roofing sheets for the burley tobacco barns.

Every Saturday morning all participants met with Piet Jordaan to discuss what had happened during the week, to plan operations for the next week and the remainder of the season. Jordaan was a good agronomist and a good leader who got on very well with the small-scale farmers he worked with.

Even more important was the excellent relationship that developed between the commercial farmers and their neighbours. African Farming Development provided the catalyst for change.

The AFD scheme attracted widespread interest from other countries, as a pathfinder for wider application in communal farming here and elsewhere. In 1964 the British Lord Chancellor, Lord Gardiner, and the Colonial Secretary, Mr Arthur Bottomley, were visiting Rhodesia and asked to see the scheme. They were accompanied by Sir Arthur Snelling, the British Ambassador in South Africa. We took them by light aircraft to Centenary to meet the participating farmers, black and white, to see what was being done.

A normal small-scale farmer's crop against that of one of our AFD participants.

The crops grown by AFD farmers were in stark contrast to those of neighbouring communal farmers. Other farmers used inputs supplied by government, mostly without individual attention, but our farmers' inputs were calculated on a scientific basis. African Farming Development was so successful that the Rhodesian Front government was embarrassed by the contrast in performance between AFD farmers and other farmers in the communal lands.

After seven years they absorbed the scheme into Conex, the government agricultural advisory service at that time. However, the politicians wanted early results from which they could make political mileage. They attempted too much too soon, which resulted in newly settled farmers not having adequate advice and planning for tillage, inputs of seed and fertilizer. The land question, always political, became more and more so.

The rationale of African Farming Development is perhaps best understood from a brochure produced at the time, the text of which follows.

Creating a National Market in Rhodesia
African Farming Development

'The central problem of development on the world scene is not the gap between rich nations and poor nations: it is the gap between the rich and poor parts of the developing nations themselves.'

From an address by the Hon. W.W. Rostow, Counsellor and Chairman of the Policy Planning Council, Department of State, Washington.

Introduction

In Rhodesia, as in most underdeveloped areas of the world, the basic problem is how to bridge the gap between the haves and the have-nots.

The vast majority of the country's African inhabitants live by subsistence agriculture and make little or no contribution to the money economy. Without financial and technical assistance they cannot break the cycle of ignorance and poverty which for centuries has inhibited economic and social progress in Africa, and there is clearly a limit to the technical and other resources which governments can provide.

African Farming Development was registered in Rhodesia early in 1965 as a private, non-profit-making company having two prime objectives:

(1) To increase as rapidly as possible the agricultural productivity of African farmers so as to stimulate economic and social development in the rural areas.

(2) To create a truly national market in Rhodesia, a development which will enable local industry to supply agricultural machinery, fertilizers, insecticides, transport, fuel and consumer goods to a mass market instead of merely to a small, relatively wealthy middle class as at present.

The company grew out of the success of a voluntary scheme initiated by a group of European farmers in the Centenary district to assist African farmers in the adjacent Chiweshe Tribal Trust Area by providing mechanized deep ploughing, credit facilities for the purchase of seeds, fertilizers and insecticides, and technical advice and supervision.

Pilot project

African Farming Development has taken over this scheme at Chiweshe and is developing it into a self-help pilot project for between 100 and 200 African farmers, which it is hoped will set a pattern for the development of rural communities throughout Rhodesia.

Under the close supervision of the Company's agronomist, African farmers in the scheme are growing profitable cash crops such as cotton and burley tobacco with great success, and are getting yields of between 20 and 35 bags of maize to the acre where previously they averaged four. This has been achieved by good land preparation (using early mechanized deep ploughing for the first time), correct seed, fertilizer and insecticide application and sound crop programme advice.

The results speak for themselves and a dramatic contrast can be seen between the crops of Africans farming by traditional subsistence methods and those of neighbouring plotholders operating under African Farming Development's pilot project. Equally dramatic is the human story attaching to families who, for the first time, have been able to lift themselves out of the depressing cycle of subsistence agriculture into the mainstream of economic progress.

Potential

It is estimated on a very conservative basis that, with the aid of mechanized land preparation, adequate credit facilities and technical and management services provided by African Farming Development, 100 farmers can achieve a cash return of approximately £30,000 in one season. This figure is greater than the total value of crops sold annually by the 5,500 African farmers in the whole of the Chiweshe Tribal Trust Area.

Throughout Rhodesia there are something like half a million African farmers. The national economic and social significance of bringing their productive capacity into the money economy is obvious.

Future development

African Farming Development aims to assist as many farmers in Rhodesia as possible – and through them, their respective rural communities – to achieve what has been called the take-off into self-sustained growth. At that point they will be able not only to secure independently the finance they require for their own agricultural activities, but also to make an increasing contribution to the cost of better roads and communications, conservation works, schools, clinics and other community services that will be demanded as a result of greater economic activity in the rural areas. In the process of development such communities will become part of an important new market for the products of Rhodesian industry.

Opportunity for industry and commerce

Industry and commerce clearly have a vested interest in the creation of a truly national market in Rhodesia leading to greatly increased industrial production, and have a key role to play in the programme planned by African Farming Development.

By comparison with an approximate annual output of £65 million by European agriculture, African agricultural sales at present total a mere £3 million a year. To take just one example, the opportunity for expanded markets offered to manufacturers by the development of African farming is illustrated by the fact that only about £150,000 of the nearly £6 million worth of fertilizers and insecticides sold annually in Rhodesia is accounted for by African farmers.

Finance

The sum required to finance one African farmer is approximately £350 a year: a substantial amount of loan capital is therefore required for the Chiweshe pilot project alone.

The marketing of crops through the co-operative system and the registration by African Farming Development of stop orders against these crops will enable the Company to recover the cost of services supplied and to provide the security required by lenders.

Conclusion

African Farming Development has been described as 'community development by private enterprise'. Its sponsors believe the scheme offers the private sector not only an opportunity to make an important contribution to Rhodesia's economic development, but also an attractive incentive in the form of increased profits from a greatly expanded market.

Its success and wide application could bring about an agricultural revolution in this part of Africa, with far-reaching economic and social consequences.

African Farming Development
P.O. Box 592, Salisbury, Rhodesia. Telephone 28515

Directors:
C.G. Tracey (Chairman); The Lord Acton, C.M.G., M.B.E., T.D.;
Sir Henry McDowell, K.B.E.; T.H. Eustace; T.R. Stanning

– 14 –

Industrial and Business Projects

Sable nitrogenous fertilizer factory • David Chigodora
• Cabora Bassa • Lomagundi–Mashonaland East railway • Frogs
• *Property and Finance* newspaper • A Name at Lloyds • Harare airport

One Sunday in 1963 we had three unexpected visitors to Handley Cross. Dr Penny Grant, one of Rhodesia's best soil chemists, brought with her two South African entrepreneurs. They wanted to set up a group to build a nitrogenous fertilizer plant, something we did not have, so that the country would no longer need to rely on imported ammonium nitrate.

Initially, Vec Hurley, president of the Rhodesia Tobacco Association, the industrialist Frank Newton and I, together with the South Africans and Americans, put together a bid to government to build our nitrogenous fertilizer factory. We were aware that, if we were to undertake such a project, we would be up against the two large fertilizer producers, Windmill and the Zimbabwe Fertilizer Company, who were unlikely to welcome a competitor. Also we would need to raise a substantial amount of capital.

We also considered the possibility that the Rhodesian government seemed likely to make a unilateral declaration of independence, which could have serious consequences, such as economic sanctions from the international community that would seriously prejudice the Rhodesian agricultural sector. The local fertilizer companies at that time were importing the country's total requirement of nitrogenous fertilizer. Apart from the drain on foreign exchange to South Africa and elsewhere, this would obviously be a target for sanctions. If the nitrogenous fertilizer were to be produced locally, our supply would be independent.

I was asked to chair the new group, which we called Sable Chemicals, and to select the Rhodesian board members, who were Frank Buch, formerly deputy chairman of Roan Selection Trust, Vec Hurley, who represented the important tobacco production sector, Frank Newton, who was in industry and was then the mayor of Que Que where it was likely we would build the project, and Phil Parkinson, who was the Rhodesian general manager of the American Union Carbide Corporation, which had built the first ferrochrome smelter at Que Que. Later, Trevor Thompson, an experienced practising lawyer, joined the board.

We submitted a formal proposal to the Ministry of Commerce and Industry, demonstrating our serious intent, but it was a long haul to convince them of the need for such a plant. Of course, we had to counter the expected opposition from the other fertilizer companies, who did all they could to persuade the government of the inadvisability of such a project.

In due course, government decided to call for bids for the construction of a plant to produce ammonium nitrate. They had stipulated in this document that the plant would use coke-oven gas, coal or crude oil and naptha as its feedstock. We were not given much time to put together our bid but we met the deadline and complied with their requirements using those different feedstocks, competing with organizations such as African Explosives and Chemical Industries (a South African subsidiary of the British ICI), the Dutch Windmill group, and Fisons Chemicals.

We were very aware that the new plant, Sable Chemicals, would have to close down if sanctions resulted in a ban on imports of fuel oil or the export of steel. In this case there would be no point in producing coke for the steel mills; and if there was no requirement for coke, there would be no coke-oven gas and the plant would come to a standstill. In a caveat to our proposal, we suggested that, in the case of sanctions, Sable should use a home-grown feedstock – electrolytic hydrogen, produced by passing electricity throughwater – as it would be largely immune from sanctions.

At that time, Kariba's generating capacity was vastly underutilized and any incremental sales of energy, even at a low price, would help its viability. Consequently, our negotiations switched from government to the Rhodesia Electricity Supply Commission. One issue was that electricity consumption fluctuated hourly, depending on demand, so we offered to install extra cells at our plant which would give us the flexibility to make use of surplus power whenever it became available at any time, day or night. This would enable Kariba to operate at all times at near its maximum output, so it could sell electricity to us at a much lower price because of the benefits of scale. This lowered the cost of our electricity considerably and this solution assured the success of Sable.

Government recognized the validity of our argument and called for fresh bids using hydroelectricity as a feedstock. We put in our proposals and were astonished to find that our competitors had declined to bid on the grounds that they believed it was impractical to use electricity, which left us the only runner in the field. We were awarded the contract.

The only countries who had substantial experience of the electrolytic process to produce ammonium nitrate were Norway and Brazil. In most other countries the cost of the electricity made fertilizer production from hydroelectricity uneconomic.

We used a linear programme to locate the optimum site for the plant, taking into account such variables as proximity to the 440,000-volt Kariba power line – the plant used more electricity than the whole of greater Harare – availability of water, good rail and road communications and, most importantly, proximity to our main markets.

A site ten miles east of Que Que complied with all the parameters. We bought the land, which bordered the Ngezi River from which our water supplies were drawn. We only required a very small area, fifty hectares, but unfortunately the best site happened to be on land owned by Tiny Rowland of Lonrho. We were aware that he was strongly opposed to the granting of the project to us, because he wished to use the Beira pipeline to bring up oil feedstock and to produce ammonium nitrate from a different system. He certainly would never have sold us the land. However, we overcame this problem through a willing intermediary who bought the land on our behalf. All the land beyond our requirements was donated to the nation and we established the Sable–Ngezi wildlife park. Sable then entered into a contract with the South African construction firm, Murray and Roberts.

By this time, UDI had indeed been declared and all the problems of United Nations sanctions were upon us. The electrolytic cells were made in Germany by Lurgi and the air-separation plant came from Air Liquide in France. The purchasing of the plant and equipment became very tricky as a result of sanctions, but we somehow managed.

The first stage of the plant was completed in fifteen months. Initially, while it was being brought to full operating capacity, we had to import some ammonia through Lourenço Marques (Maputo). This was taken into the port from bulk carriers to their newly constructed ammonia terminal and came on to us in large rail ammonia tankers, similar to those used for fuel.

At Sable we had two high-pressure plants. The first, Section 1, was commissioned in 1969 and used imported ammonia until the Section 2 plant came into operation in 1972. The plants were of American design and were identical. The capacity of each is 300 tonnes per day of acid, which is largely produced as nitric acid 57.5 per cent.

The technical process started with a centrifugal compressor set to take 8-9 bars of pressure, compressing air. Electric power to Sable came in at 88,000 volts, was then stepped down to 33,000 volts, went into the electrolysis plant where it was further stepped down and rectified into direct current before going to the electrolytors. At this stage, it passed through the electrolytic cells where it broke down the water molecules.

Once the plant was fully operational, we used the nitrogen and hydrogen in the separated air, but had no use for the oxygen. The country now had a substantial excess of oxygen, so we had to find additional markets for our by-product in the fields of industry and medicine. We constructed a pipeline seventeen miles long to carry oxygen to RISCO at Redcliff, supplying the Nobel explosive plant en route. RISCO used two old batch smelters to process their steel, which were outdated and uneconomical. They filled the batch smelters with iron ore and, when it had smelted, the hot metal was drawn off, it was refilled with ore and the smelting operation began all over again. With the possibility of using Sable's oxygen, RISCO promptly replaced this old-fashioned process, importing some modern LD converters from Austria, which allowed a continuous process because oxygen from Sable could be lanced directly and continuously into the furnace.

What we achieved was to ensure Rhodesia's supply of ammonium nitrate from Sable Chemicals during a period when sanctions would have seriously damaged our agricultural industry. Sable was a Rhodesian private-sector initiative of which we were proud, and it demonstrated that we could ourselves undertake major engineering operations in the country. Without our realization of the consequences of UDI to our fertilizer industry, which we had foreseen several years previously, there would have been no local source of nitrogenous fertilizer, which would have had disastrous consequences for agriculture and the whole economy.

Later, after serious disagreements between the original shareholders, the company was taken over. My connection with Sable has come to an end, although Vec Hurley and I still have a few shares and I recently attended their AGM.

Today, forty years later, the unit price of electricity has been renegotiated, bringing it up to uncompetitive levels for Sable. Kariba's output is no longer sufficient for the country's needs following the expansion of mining and industry. As a result, a quantity of ammonia has to be imported to augment local production to satisfy the demand for fertilizer. Nevertheless, Sable still helps the country save a large amount of foreign exchange and fulfils most of our requirements for nitrogenous fertilizer. Unfortunately, shortages of foreign currency have almost stopped ammonia imports, and our ammonia tanker fleet has been dispersed. The ammonia terminal in Maputo is in a state of disintegration and disrepair and can no longer be used.

After the 2002 general election, in which Emmerson Mnangagwa was heavily defeated in the Kwe Kwe constituency, his supporters were criticized for inadequate canvassing. They said the blame lay with the senior management at Sable, alleging that this group had supported the opposition. A mob went to the chemical plant and threatened that, if the five senior managers were not dismissed, they would take violent action.

David Chigodora, the general manager of Sable, bore the brunt of the crisis. Two top executives from Harare went down to attempt to deal with the matter. They were unsuccessful and returned to Harare that night. I believe they had a special meeting of directors in the early hours of the morning, and then immediately returned to Sable, where they were faced with the same demand.

An impasse was reached and retributive violence seemed likely, and this could damage the plant. They explained to Chigodora that they believed he had done nothing wrong, and that they had full confidence in him, but they were faced with no alternative but to suspend or dismiss him, although they would ensure that he would receive adequate recompense.

> I was never much good at chemistry at school and had to re-learn the complications of producing ammonium nitrate from water and air. I was pleased with myself when I showed David Chigodora what I had written about Sable for this book, to ask him to check whether I was on target, and he told me my memory had served me well and there were only minor mistakes. This also applied to the production of the heavy water.

And so David Chigodora left Sable and shortly afterwards left the country. He was a highly skilled chemical engineer and his departure was yet another loss to Zimbabwe.

Subsequently, Sable's South African and American shareholders fell out. The South Africans made excessive demands on the Americans to reduce their percentage of equity from 50-50 to a figure that would give the former majority control. When the Americans resisted, the South Africans indicated that they were ready to pass on to the UN and USA all the vital technical information about the plant, imports from which had indeed contravened American sanctions. This they did, which was highly unprincipled. The Americans stood their ground but paid the price by being prosecuted in the United States. Two executives were found guilty and were fined US$150,000.

Planning started in the late 1960s for the giant Cabora Bassa dam, a development between the Portuguese and South African governments, on the Zambezi river below Kariba dam.

I first visited the site out of curiosity, when the early surveying was nearly complete and the engineers were living in makeshift accommodation. I recognized the potential and the opportunity for major electricity generation that could flow into other parts of Mozambique, Malawi, Zambia, South Africa, and perhaps even the southern Congo, through a regional grid.

The dam site has a wall over 150 metres high while its crest width is only 250 metres. The inflow consists of all the water coming through Kariba from the Zambezi, and from the Kafue, Luangwa and Hunyani rivers. There is therefore a much greater volume of water passing through Cabora Bassa than through Kariba. The extra height of the dam wall, plus the extra water, gives much more generating capacity.

I witnessed the drilling of the diversion tunnel to take the water out of the river bed and bypass the wall site, which was enclosed in its coffer dam. This enabled the constructors to build the wall in a dry area within the coffer dam and finally to build the abutments into each bank.

While that was in process, they were blasting the intake tunnels, which take the water through the 'surge chamber' down into the turbines. These tunnels could take a couple of London double-decker buses on top of each other, and the actual generating chamber could accommodate London's St Paul's Cathedral. We were told that staff down in the bowels of the earth manning the turbines some 500 feet below ground level sometimes developed symptoms of claustrophobia, so the walls had been painted with a blend of colours to diminish the problem.

Simultaneously, the high-voltage direct current (DC) transmission line to South Africa was being constructed. When electrical energy is transmitted over a long distance, voltage is lost when using an ordinary alternating current (AC) line, whereas voltage loss with a DC line is minimal. The line from Cabora Bassa to South Africa is over 1,000 kilometres long. The DC system is used in the USA where power is brought down from the big rivers of Washington state to southern California around Los Angeles.

I last visited Cabora Bassa when the last and fifth French generating set was being installed. This coincided with hostilities between Rhodesia and Mozambique, after the latter had been granted independence from Portugal. In all, I and others visited that site many times over four years and were able to show people from many parts of the world how a gigantic civil-engineering project could link three countries for the mutual benefit of the sub-region.

Tragically, the Mozambique Resistance Movement (Renamo), the forces fighting a civil war against Front for the Liberation of Mozambique (Frelimo), who formed the government of Mozambique, set about systematically destroying the power pylons. A company had been formed to operate the transmission of energy from Cabora Bassa to South Africa. This company re-erected the whole line, which was again destroyed by Renamo. It was only after peace between Renamo and Frelimo had been established in 1992 that the transmission company replaced the line for the third, and hopefully the last, time. Cabora Bassa started selling substantial volumes of power to South Africa only many years after its construction. Some of that electrical energy also flows into Zimbabwe's regional grid.

> It was proposed to build what would be the largest single dam in Rhodesia, after Kariba, at the confluence of the Tokwe and Makorsi rivers. Below it was a huge stretch of highly fertile land which had minimal rainfall, and surveys showed that up to 250 000 acres could be provided with water from that dam. Italian contractors were engaged, but government defaulted on payment and they stopped in 1999. Government paid some more and the work started again, but after further default on payment the scheme remained dormant for many years and only now (2008) is the construction work continuing.

The Lomagundi–Mashonaland East railway development was another project that did not get off the ground, but for different reasons. Our railway system terminated at Lion's Den, about 50 kilometres north of Sinoia. Goods destined for Zambia by rail had to go via Bulawayo and Livingstone to Lusaka, or go as far as Lion's Den and then be transported by road across the Chirundu bridge over the Zambezi River and up the escarpment.

By 1967, owing to sanctions, we had a build-up of tobacco and beef supplies. Vec Hurley and I proposed a plan whereby we would do a barter deal with the French for beef and tobacco and they would supply us with the right size of line, the heavy earthmoving machinery and civil engineering equipment for the construction of a new railway line.

The new line was to start from the Zawi siding at Lion's Den, go north-east towards Chirundu and through the Concession and Chiweshe areas and finally link up with the Bindura–Harare line. Such a route would have opened up a big agricultural area that was completely reliant on road transport.

We did our budgets and calculations and were able to demonstrate that it was far better to exchange or barter tobacco and beef, of which we had substantial unsold stocks, for the supply of equipment and construction of the railway line than to buy them for cash under the constraint of sanctions. We negotiated with a group of French entrepreneurs led by Jacques Blumenthal and we talked to the Rhodesian Ministry of Transport.

We found the ministry officials negative and not prepared to permit an exciting private-sector development on the grounds that the existing road transport system served the area well enough. They maintained that there wasn't a great deal of tonnage going through to Zambia and that, if the sanctions and UDI were short-lived, as they believed, then this railway line would become a white elephant.

Their reaction was both perplexing and astonishing, but it showed the negative and over-conservative attitude sometimes taken by senior civil servants. Cecil Rhodes took only two years to build the two-hundred-mile railway line from the northern Cape into Rhodesia, and said that, if a railway line was built, development would follow, but not in the reverse order.

There is a footnote to this story. About the same time, the motor vehicle assembly plant at Umtali had come to a standstill because of sanctions. When we were talking to Blumenthal about the possibility of trading beef, steel and equipment for a railway, we discussed the possibility of the French car manufacturers, Peugeot, sending vehicle kits for assembly at the plant which existed at Umtali. Everything was going swimmingly and we were at the point of discussing the financial implications and transport routes when the ultra cautious staff of the Department of Industry effectively killed the project.

I am by nature an entrepreneur and often find new ideas irresistible. I remember that once, when flying home to Rhodesia on an Air France plane after meetings in France where we had been discussing these barter deals, I enjoyed my hors d'œuvre of frogs' legs. So the thought entered my mind that I might perpetrate a major leg-pull on some of our more gullible ministers and I dreamt up the plan of starting a frog production unit on the dam on our farm. I took the lid off my imagination and let it run.

On my return, I wrote a letter in a serious vein to the Minister of Agriculture saying that we were planning to establish a pilot frog farm. This would, when in full swing, satisfy the tastes of many of our tourists – of course, we did not have very many anyway – and we could export these frogs' legs to South Africa where sanctions did not exist. Would his ministry please, therefore, sanction an import permit and a small amount of foreign currency to import two bull frogs and 48 heifer frogs 'in tadpole', from France? I sat back to await the result.

To my astonishment, I received a warm congratulatory reply, emphasizing how good it was to have innovative people in the country and saying that shortly I would receive both the permit for the frogs and the foreign exchange. The permit arrived soon thereafter, accompanied by a veterinary certificate with various stipulations. The young man who had to write out the veterinary certificate had thumbed through many previous permits, but nowhere could he find a permit for frogs. He did not want to confess his ignorance and resort to asking a superior, so he decided to use the same veterinary import regulations for frogs as were used for cattle. Our permit stated that the frogs at the time of dispatch must come from an area that had not had foot-and-mouth disease for six months, and must be fit and healthy and 'free of ticks'! The game was on and I was not quite sure what to do next.

I had a call a few days later from George Nicholas, agricultural editor of the *Rhodesia Herald*, a little diffident and concerned that he might be treading on dangerous sanctions ground, but he said that there was a matter about which he would like to chat privately. Nicholas was an experienced journalist and a friend, so as we walked together across Cecil Square I said to him, 'What is worrying you? Can I help?'

'C. G.,' he replied, 'I don't know how secret this is and whether I should even talk to you about it, but I was at a dinner party last night when the Permanent Secretary for the Ministry of Agriculture was telling the guests how wonderful it was that, under such adversity, we still had people with an innovative mind determined to widen the base of our agriculture'. Apparently the PS had then gone on to tell the story of my application for frogs.

Nicholas thought that this was absolutely wonderful, and he wanted to know whether there was any chance at all of him writing a story about the venture. I thought quickly and, on the basis of 'in for a penny, in for a pound', decided that I could also tease the head of the British Residual Mission in Salisbury. 'Of course, George,' I replied. 'Go ahead with that if you want to, because, if sanctions were applied to my frogs, the damage to the country would be minimal, but it would be a good thing to show that our people are doing all sorts of new things despite the circumstances.'

So I told him the whole story and suggested that I should have a look at the copy before it was published to make sure that all the facts were accurate. Throughout the interview I maintained the conversation at a serious level with a poker face.

Fifteen minutes later, I got a telephone call from him. 'It just crossed my mind, and I hope you don't mind me saying so, but were you possibly pulling my leg?' I paused to collect my thoughts and said, 'George, why on earth should you have such a thought?'

'Well,' he replied, 'last night all the frogs in my swimming pool made such a noise that there must have been hundreds of them. Why do we need to import them if we already have them by the hundreds?'

Mustering as much pomp as I could at the end of the phone, I replied: 'George, I have always thought you were an intelligent journalist! How do you think we could develop an export market or supply our tourists with local frogs' legs? Don't you know that steak from an Aberdeen Angus or Hereford bullock is far superior to steak from one of our scrawny local cattle? All our beef exports come from those exotic breeds. Perhaps you aren't aware that the conformation of our local frogs' legs is that they are thin, the meat-to-bone proportion is wrong, and they are as tough as can be. Naturally, we looked at this as an alternative, but it would be a long time before we could have a genetic breeding programme to improve our frogs by selection and achieve the kind of export standard required to compete with France. In any event, if you have ever eaten a Rhodesian frog's leg, you will know that the bone is like a thick violin string and when you bite it, your teeth spring apart.'

He was profuse in his apologies and a few days later, in the Rhodesia *Herald* farming section, there appeared a story about the initiative of a Rhodesian farmer who was going into frog production. The same day another journalist picked up the story and began to ask more technical details. I told him that we had dams that were underutilized, that we were able to construct small paddocks out of mesh on the edge of the dam, in the water, because it was important that our imported frogs should not be allowed to waste their procreative ability on local frogs and we must at all costs prevent miscegenation. The Agricultural Marketing Authority had just been started and I told them that this was a matter that they could pursue under their export-promotion sector.

All this occurredat a time when the British government had withdrawn their high commissioner and replaced him with a person with the title 'Head of the Residual Mission', Peter Carter. He was a man with a peg-leg and a very good sense of humour and he had of course read the story. I met him in the lift and he said, 'C.G., I see you are breaking sanctions again. You will have to put a stop to this frog endeavour.' The lift came to a stop and I suggested that, if he would call off the sanctions, I would guarantee him a free supply of frogs' legs for the duration of his stay in the country. With a smile, he said that it was a brilliant idea and the lift went on up.

When I was being questioned a few days later about the progress of the scheme, I was asked whether sanctions could affect the viability of the project and my reply was in the usual format: 'Informal discussions had taken place with the head of the British Residual Mission on the matter and it was hoped that a satisfactory solution could be reached.' When this appeared, the text went humming to the Foreign Office. Peter was curtly told that there should be no discussions about anything connected with sanctions or frogs' legs.

The story – or, rather, the joke – was getting too hot to hold, with lots of people quizzing me after they'd seen the *Herald* story, and so I thought I'd better come clean. I had a chat in the Harare Club with George Nicholas and his editor, and told them that I had indeed been pulling their leg: it rather tested their sense of humour. Thereafter, when I met members of the civil service they were cautious with me in case they were going to be the victims of another tease. It provided us with a lot of fun at a time when tobacco sanctions were really hurting and there was a lot to worry about.

However, I've always been puzzled why people did not realize that I had given the game away when I talked about heifer frogs in tadpole, an expression used in the cattle world when one talks about heifers in calf. The reproductive system of a frog is quite different from that of a cow, who carries her offspring in her womb, whereas frogs lay eggs that are hatched in water. That point was never grasped – if it had been, the story would have stopped then and there.

A year later, a charming young woman telephoned us at the farm from Salisbury. She had been appointed the special features editor on the *Rhodesia Herald* and, to get the feel of the country, she had been reading a couple of years of back issues of the paper. She enquired how our frog project was going and wanted to write a series of follow up articles demonstrating the initiative of farmers. She was so disappointed when I told her that she was even more gullible than the man who had first written the story in the paper.

Rhodesia was well served by daily and weekly newspapers such as the *Rhodesia Herald* and the *Bulawayo Chronicle*, owned by the South African Argus group. There were several weekly or monthly technical publications. In the financial field there was a smart, well-produced weekly paper called *Property and Finance*, owned and capably edited by a man called Gerald Aberman. He wished to retire and the paper was for sale. There existed another financial weekly paper, the *Financial Gazette,* funded by the Afrikaanse Pers for the first two years and chaired by Sam Whaley. An unsuccessful attempt was made to fund it locally, but the corporates who had been approached declined. However, we found finance from individuals, and it still continues to this day.

In the early to mid-1960s a group of us who had together been involved in other enterprises, such as Sable Chemicals, were interested, assembled a number of investors and bought *Property and Finance*. The board was chaired by Frank Buch, and the former assistant editor, an Englishman named Wilfred Brookes (he had been Garfield Todd's private secretary), continued as editor. When Brookes arrived from Britain he was very left wing, but he changed his outlook once he observed that the extreme policies of the left-wingers were unsuccessful, and, jumping ship, he moved over to the extreme right.

When we bought the paper, we told Brookes that he would have editorial freedom in respect of financial and economic content but that he was restricted to non-party-political comment since we did not wish to become associated with either side of the political spectrum. He chose to ignore this and steadily became more and more virulent in his leaders, levelling personal criticism at the politicians, including Ian Smith. We found this embarrassing. In the end we had to call the editor to order, reminded him of his contract and told him that, if he did not adopt a financial rather than a political view, we would have to part company. He ignored the warning and was duly asked to leave.

Our actions were challenged by some of our more right-wing shareholders. One was an English tobacco farmer called Robin James, who came from a well-known political and aristocratic family in the UK. He called for an extraordinary general meeting of shareholders to reverse the decision to dismiss Brookes. His lobby won the day by a small margin, the board resigned and Brookes was reinstated. The original shareholders then sold their shareholdings at a considerable profit. At that time, the press in Rhodesia was becoming increasingly polarized between left and right.

I was invited by David Palmer, who was the worldwide chairman of Willis Corroon, to become a Name at Lloyds. The qualifications and obligations of a Name are serious. The Name signs away his entire wealth in the case of a disaster, and I became a member of four or five syndicates run by the broking arm of Willis Corroon. The rewards could be immense, but the penalty was that a Name could lose every penny he had and every asset. Syndicates varied. There were those that were very aggressive, cut corners but made a lot of money until the crash, when hundreds of people were bankrupted. There were conservative syndicates sensibly and prudently managed, content with smaller returns but with a far greater safety factor. I was interviewed by one of the senior members of Lloyds and my obligations were explained to me. Names signed away guarantees for their entire worth. I accepted the obligations and was intrigued to meet my fellow syndicate members. Our syndicate performed well and provided us with modest returns, without too much risk, whilst our reserves accumulated.

When the crash took place it appeared that Lloyds as an institution might be insolvent and destroyed, but some of the best financial reinsurance brains in the world took on the task of rescuing and then resuscitating it. To save as many Names as possible, a company called Equitas was formed to manage the affairs of Lloyds. Underwriting continued but it became obligatory for Names to have funds deducted from their reserves or to contribute funds to go into Equitas. With skilled management the effort succeeded over a period of some years, and recently those of us who had been solvent and who had had funds paid into Equitas had those funds returned to us relative to the extent of each Name's underwriting. Existing Names were not allowed during the intervening period to resign from Lloyds, and their guarantees and responsibilities remained in place. The combined reserves of underwriting members of Lloyds were quite substantial and Lloyds was saved.

Some years ago, I resigned as a Name and ceased underwriting. In 2006, eight years after Equitas was formed, we received the last of our refunds of payments made into Equitas and no longer have any obligation. It was a sad and salutary story for those who were tempted by the quick profits and the glitter.

I have always had a passion for development, and in Rhodesia there was no shortage of opportunities; the same was true of Zimbabwe. By the late 1990s, I could not help but be aware of the shortcomings of the Harare airport, which, having been built nearly fifty years earlier, was congested and hopelessly inadequate. If we were serious about expanding our tourism industry, it was imperative that we should have a modern, up-to-date airport capable of handling large numbers of people efficiently.

I talked to the First Merchant Bank (FMB), one of our leading merchant banks, to ask if they thought it feasible to establish a private-sector Zimbabwean company which could negotiate with government and financiers and plan, finance, build and operate a new, modern airport. I was delighted that they accepted the concept and we established a company called Airport Development Limited.

I wanted the initiative to be a demonstration of our ability to undertake a really major civil construction project in the same way as our Sable chemical plant project had been such a success. I wanted Zimbabwean industrialists and construction companies to be the main beneficiaries of the opportunities that lay ahead, as they would become the sub-contractors to the main company.

I assembled a small board with Dr Chris Ushewokunze, formerly Permanent Secretary in the Ministry of Mines, Solomon Tawengwa, one-time mayor of Harare and a non-executive director of Tobacco Sales Limited, John Graham, an executive at FMB, and Alwyn Pichanick, the senior partner of Winterton's legal practitioners. We asked Costain Zimbabwe if they would lead the construction consortium on the undertaking that they would subcontract to as many Zimbabwean entities, large or small, as possible. John Graham undertook the complicated financial structuring.

Our offer to government was that we would raise all the funds internally and offshore so that its financial involvement in raising capital was almost nothing. FMB made out a schedule, which, after providing for a normal rate of interest for the financiers we had approached, allowed the government to repay Airport Development over anything from 5 to 45 years.

Alexander Gibb, the international consulting engineers, had done an initial technical appraisal and feasibility study, which was useful as a starting base for us. We held further discussions with organizations in Zimbabwe to ensure that we kept the initiative truly Zimbabwean. At all costs I wanted to avoid commissioning some airport-building organization from the First World to build us an airport. I wanted to demonstrate to the outside world that we could handle a project of this size ourselves, although using appropriate special skills from overseas. We planned to have capacity for five 'jumbos' with air bridges, duty-free shops at both Arrivals and Departures and an adjacent conference centre and hotel.

However at this time, many people were aware of rumours of serious corruption between some of our political leaders and overseas firms looking for development contracts, with obvious financial spin-offs. I wanted to be sure to avoid anything like this. While we knew that some of the more technical equipment, such as air traffic control and radar, would have to be installed by overseas companies, we wanted to keep their involvement to a minimum. In my usual travels, I began looking at the technical side of every airport I visited.

We had contacted British Airport Authorities Limited as possible consultants or even as shareholders. They owned and operated most of the large airports in the UK, including Heathrow. I also visited airports in Tokyo, Paris, Singapore and South Africa, which was beginning to redevelop Johannesburg international airport.

The Minister of Transport at that time, Denis Norman, and his Permanent Secretary had been kept informed of our plans for the construction of the new airport. By our standards, the project was immense, and it presented an opportunity for international entrepreneurs who had their own benefit at heart, rather than Zimbabwe's. Denis Norman arranged for us to make a presentation to the president, Robert Mugabe, who expressed interest. One of his staff had become aware of the plans and was present at the meeting.

On a visit to London, I was in a very long queue at the immigration desks. I looked at the scene and thought I would count the number of people in the queue, see how many immigration desks there were and work out the speed of handing passengers. I paced up one side and then paced down the other to ascertain how many people were travelling, how many queues there were and how long it took for a person to get to the head of the queue. Suddenly I felt a hand on my shoulder and a very polite individual enquired what I was doing. I laughed and said I was sorry if he was concerned about security but we were building a new airport in Zimbabwe and I was going from country to country to get a feel for airport buildings and facilities. I told him I was in London to talk to BAA and Costains. His response was, 'Oh, really!' I assured him that this was indeed the case and he had a look through my briefcase at all the correspondence. He seemed satisfied. We shook hands and I went on. I guess he and his colleagues spoke to both organizations to confirm that I was indeed seeing them later in the week.

Soon afterwards I was told that the project was of such magnitude that another Zimbabwean corporation, controlled by Joshua Nkomo, wanted to be involved, with a 51 per cent shareholding. This would give them majority control and we would have been powerless to prevent any downside implications. In our discussions I was told, 'Mr Tracey, just think how much money we can make out of this project!' From that moment, the pressures were such that realistically we were forced to abandon the project.

The airport was eventually built, almost entirely by offshore companies, led by Air Harbour Technologies, which is based in Cyprus and owned by Hani Yamani, son of the Saudi oil minister, Sheikh Yamani. According to the *Daily News* of 20 November 2000, very high-level Zimbabwean officials were alleged to have been paid a total of the equivalent of three million US dollars (Z$165 million) to ensure that that corporation won the Z$5 billion contract.

There was considerable criticism in Parliament as to why the contractors were given government guarantees, which was unusual and which had to be passed through Parliament. Why had certain companies been brought in? These questions were brushed aside. According to the *Financial Gazette* of 5 January 2001, Zimbabwean taxpayers would have to pay Z$150 million annually for the next decade to finance loan repayments. (This is the figure quoted, but the repayments would be made in hard currency.)

In real terms the project cost the country between three to four times as much as it would have done if a local consortium employing local contractors had been allowed to build it. It also took twice as long, with subsequent legal wrangles between the parties. It is, however, a good, medium-sized international airport, but sadly is vastly under used these days with our seriously reduced tourist trade. Except for South African Airways, no big international airlines fly to Zimbabwe now.

– 15 –

Rhobank and Zimbank

Rhobank • Sale of Nedbank investment to government
• Visit to China • New management • Changes to the board

In 1977 the then chairman of the Rhodesian Banking Corporation (Rhobank), Sir Cornelius Greenfield, asked me to join the board, which was the start of another absorbing chapter in my life. (Rhobank had grown out of the Netherlands Bank of South Africa, Nedbank.) A couple of years later, the vice-chairman retired and I was asked to take up that position. Sadly, Sir Cornelius, who came from a distinguished family of lawyers and had been Permanent Secretary in the federal Ministry of Finance, suffered a heart attack a year later, and I was asked by the share-holders to step into his shoes. I hardly felt ready to take on the responsibility so soon after joining the board, but I had the full support of the joint managing directors and of the board itself.

It was a balanced board, drawn from the legal and accountancy professions, industrialists, and from the farming, tobacco and mining industries, with some members from Matabeleland. It was an interesting team, initially including Sir Roy Welensky, who had been Northern Rhodesia's prime minister and later the federal prime minister. He had been asked to join the board of Rhobank after the dissolution of the Federation in December 1963.

Physically and mentally a large man, Sir Roy came from a working-class background, was a heavyweight professional boxer, and began his career as a fireman in the steam locomotives of Rhodesia Railways that traversed Northern and Southern Rhodesia and Portuguese East Africa. He joined the railways' trade union movement and was elected to the Northern Rhodesia Legislative Assembly, where he became leader of the nominated unofficial opposition members, who were there to contribute to the good running of government. As Northern Rhodesia was still a colony, their parliament consisted, to a large extent, of nominated MPs working alongside a small number of elected members. In due course Welensky became a member of the federal parliament, deputy prime minister and, after the retirement of Sir Godfrey Huggins, prime minister.

Another distinguished board member was Professor Dick Christie, head of the Law faculty at the University of Rhodesia and a lawyer of international repute. His wife, Philippa Berlyn, was a well-known journalist, broadcaster and poet, who did a lot of translations from Shona in addition to being a founder of Two Tone, a poetry magazine which published local poetry from 1964 to 1982. She died tragically in a light-aircraft accident in 1982.

The political situation after UDI caused increasing concern from the overseas banks, which started to look more carefully into the extent of their relationship with us, credit lines and our offshore borrowing facilities.

As tobacco was subject to sanctions, the financing of tobacco was an intricate matter but, with the help of sister offshore banks, we were able to provide almost exactly the same service to the tobacco industry as banks had offered before sanctions.

At the time of my chairmanship of Rhobank, the Standard Chartered Bank was by far the largest bank in the country. We stood second in the inter-bank ratings, slightly ahead of Barclays, which was a matter of great pride, followed by Stanbic and the Commercial Bank of Zimbabwe. Newer and smaller banks followed in their wake.

We were proud of the first two significant international syndicated loans organized by Zimbank (as Rhobank was renamed at independence in 1980) after the lifting of sanctions.

In 1981, as relations between white-ruled South Africa and newly independent Zimbabwe gradually worsened, the South African board of Nedbank became concerned about continuing with their investment in Zimbabwe. They informed me, as chairman, that it was their intention to disinvest and that they had found a potential investor to whom they could dispose of their majority stake. There were no pre-emptive rights to other shareholders.

The suitor was the Bank of America, with headquarters in California, which at that time was said to be the biggest bank in the world. They were banking in neighbouring countries in the region and thought that a branch in Central Africa would fit well into their overall network.

I immediately informed the Minister of Finance, Enos Nkala, suggesting that he should have a meeting with Bank of America officials. This took place and, after the introductory courtesies, the Americans explained their interest in buying the South African equity and sought the government's

The first two international syndicated loans obtained in Zimbabwe after independence, for Air Zimbabwe and the National Railways of Zimbabwe.

view, which was unambiguous. Nobody other than the Zimbabwe government would be allowed to buy the South African shares. The Americans
were somewhat taken aback, the very short meeting drew to a close and
the Americans courteously said that if there was anything they could do,
government should not hesitate to let them know.

To this offer came a swift response from Minister Nkala: 'Mr Bouma,
how kind of you to offer. Perhaps you would be prepared to fund us, to
enable us to buy out the South Africans?' The Americans said that they
were delighted to have had the approach, but that it was a matter beyond
their authority and would have to be referred to senior echelons in the
bank, a long, drawn-out process!

Two days later, I was called to see the Deputy Minister of Finance. He
reminded me in no uncertain terms that I should not discuss the sale, or
the possible sale, of the South African shares with any other party who
might be interested, because the government were going to acquire them.
As an afterthought he said, 'By the way, what is the price?'

I had to think on my feet. It was not for me to negotiate the price
between the two parties. It suddenly dawned on me that what he wanted
to know was the stock exchange price, which he thought would be the
basis for the evaluation of the worth of the bank. I asked him if he had a
copy of that day's paper and I looked up the stock exchange price for the
day and gave him that figure. He asked how many shares were in issue and,
as it happened, with all the negotiations that had been going on, I had the
figure at my fingertips. He reached for a calculator, multiplied the price by
the number of shares and said he thought that it seemed reasonable. There
was no suggestion of any further investigation into the affairs of the bank
and no one suggested that a 'due diligence' be undertaken.

I immediately telephoned Rob Abrahamson, the chief executive of
Nedbank in South Africa, and related the gist of the discussions. He
could hardly believe what I told him and, of course, he asked the obvious
question, 'Have they asked for a due diligence to be done, or any other
aspects of our accounts and balance sheet?' I advised that they had not
and had indicated to me that they thought the price was a fair one. I
told him he should waste no time, charter an aircraft to fly to Zimbabwe
and tie up the deal on a willing-buyer, willing-seller basis, at a price that
was likely to be far greater than what would have been achieved from the
American suitor had more usual negotiations taken place. I had done my
task of bringing the two parties together.

Abrahamson was reluctant to believe me but did fly up. At our meeting
with the deputy minister, he discovered that I was correct. He agreed to

draw up the necessary documentation over the next few days and said he would return for the signing of the agreement.

Two or three nights later I was at our house in Harare when there was a knock at the door at 9.30 p.m. and my guests were three members of staff from the Ministry of Finance. I naturally expressed some surprise at their need to talk bank business at that hour. They said it was most important and that cabinet had been critical of the deputy minister for agreeing to the price without negotiating it downwards. They were now in a predicament where their deputy minister had committed the government to the purchase of the South African shares. They wanted to know if there was anything I could do to help them resolve what could become an embarrassing impasse between the ministry and the cabinet.

I emphasized that our discussions were off the record but, if they wanted to go on the record, I would have some suggestions to make and would need to ask them some questions to relay to the other party.

The bank's year-end was not far away and I knew, more or less, what our final dividend would be. I asked them whether the sale price should be regarded either as ex or cum dividend. They had not considered this aspect. They enquired why I had put the question and I explained that if they were prepared to leave the sellers with the final dividend, this could be reflected in some downward adjustment of the share price. This was greeted with relief and they thought it would satisfy their critics in cabinet.

I received a call after the next morning's cabinet meeting and was told that the arrangement would be acceptable. If Nedbank agreed with the overall compromise, they could keep their final dividend. By accepting a reduction in the share price, they were in fact returning some money in the final dividend, leaving the South Africans better off than in the original deal. I must confess I felt a twinge of disloyalty in having to mediate in the deal, which was manifestly worse for Zimbabwe, but my responsibility was to the shareholders, and public shareholders at that.

Again I telephoned Abrahamson and again he expressed disbelief. I told him that he should fly up pretty quickly and bring his lawyers with him so that the final agreement could be drafted and signed without further delay. He arrived at lunchtime, they went into discussion, the agreement was resolved and signed. Everyone was satisfied. I doubt that anywhere else in the world could negotiations for the purchase of a 64 per cent stake in any reasonably sized bank be carried out without any due diligence or other investigation taking place.

Later, at a further meeting, the deputy minister said that, on their examination of our Memorandum and Articles of Association, the board should comprise no less than seven and no more than twenty directors. As we had eleven directors at that time, a simple calculation told them that with their increased shareholding they could appoint nine new directors without removing any of the existing board. As they did not wish to remove any of the members, government increased the board to twenty. I pointed out that it was cumbersome for a bank to have so large a board, but they were keen to publicize not only that the transaction had taken place but also the names of the new directors.

We found ourselves with nine new government-appointed directors, some of whom had very limited business experience, particularly of banking or finance, let alone banking terminology. I had to take the greatest care to be understanding and help them to acquire some basic knowledge of banking.

The bank went on as normal, and relationships with the new shareholders proceeded reasonably well for a time. Understandably, with some directors who had no banking background whatsoever, problems arose from time to time, which had to be ironed out.

At that time there was no banking relationship between Zimbabwe and China. Negotiations began with the National Bank of China to establish at least initially a correspondent banking relationship and it was suggested we should go over to China. As a non-executive chairman, I usually left such tasks to our senior executives. The Chinese ambassador, however, discreetly pointed out in discussion that they attached great importance to the position of the chairman and that if the chairman of our bank did not participate at this meeting it would be taken as an affront. Therefore, after preliminary discussions, one of the two managing directors and I went to Beijing, where the inter-bank agreements were duly finalized and prepared for signature.

While the bankers were discussing technical matters, I saw a little of the city centre, and observed some youngsters flying kites. Chinese kites are famous. Their design and ability to fly to great altitudes intrigued me. The kites were attached to the end of a ball of string and went so high that sometimes it was difficult to be sure that I was looking at a kite designed as a bird, and not a real bird. They used to insert a small bright stone in the eye, which glinted as the kite moved, and then you could be sure what you were looking at was a kite.

I decided to buy two or three kites, dismantle them and take them home. I was unaware that visitors were unable to deal in Chinese currency, called renminbi, and that it was also illegal for them to take payment in foreign currency. So the deal was off until one of the Chinese bankers saw me, explained the situation, changed some money for me and I bought the kites and brought them home. They attracted a lot of interest when my grandchildren flew them off the coast near Cape Town.

We were taken up to the Great Wall of China, originally constructed as a frontier protection against China's enemies. Although the basic engineering design is simple, it is remarkable that the wall, of varying heights and some 6,700 kilometres long, was built with hand labour. The wall is wide enough to accommodate a platoon of horses and there are guarded checkpoints at frequent intervals. Walter Shirra, the astronaut, told me that, when he was circumnavigating the earth, the Great Wall of China was one of the features that is clearly identifiable from outer space.

We were very well entertained and were able to a degree to observe the Chinese way of living. Their agriculture was highly intensive. Every square inch of land that could be cultivated was cultivated. Draught power was largely provided by mules or horses. I only saw a few tractors in the whole of my visit, and the standard of living of most people in the countryside seemed very low at the time. Theirs was basically an intensive subsistence agriculture using only family labour, with small surpluses reaching the market. But, however small those surpluses, when multiplied by the enormous Chinese population they still had a substantial volume of commodities for export, one of which was cotton. China was the biggest cotton producer in the world, but lack of information about their crops made it difficult to forecast the size of the cotton crop coming on to the world market; its impact often caused serious and rapid fluctuations in the world price.

After the agreement was concluded, we flew to Shanghai and were accommodated at a palatial government guest house. It was comfortable, provided western food and was set in lovely gardens; but when we left the main entrance gate, we were at once in the slums.

I asked the Chinese managing director of their bank whether the refrigerator in his house was manufactured in China. I wanted tactfully to get a measure of the industrial domestic equipment being produced. His response was that they didn't have a refrigerator in his house and they didn't need one, as his wife was able to purchase their food requirements at any one of the thousands of nearby small markets, two or three times a day.

We discovered that, under their communist regime, salary differentials were very narrow, with managing directors earning only slightly more than the doorman. We formed the impression that China was a slumbering giant with enormous potential, which, when more fully harnessed, could prove an enigma when more of its surplus production spilled over into world markets. Subsequent events have proved the point.

It was becoming clear to me that the unspoken policy at the Ministry of Finance was to replace systematically the existing management at Zimbank in line with their policy of affirmative action.

One of our two managing directors had recently retired and the other had resigned. The ministry told me that they had arranged for the deputy governor of the Reserve Bank, Dick Parke, to be seconded to Zimbank as acting managing director until replacement arrangements had been made.

If I had not acquiesced, the majority shareholders could have called an extraordinary general meeting and replaced the whole board, which would have created a crisis situation for both the bank and the country. The wider ramifications had to be taken into account. I offered my resignation to the minister, who firmly refused to accept it. It was most embarrassing for me, for Parke and for the whole board. The board and I had been entirely bypassed and I had an extremely sensitive situation on my hands.

Shortly after my meeting with the minister, Dick Parke called on me, effectively to introduce himself as the government's nominee as interim managing director. To my astonishment, Parke told me that he had been instructed in secrecy to look for a replacement for the previous managing director. He was quite embarrassed about what he had been obliged to do. Unbeknown to me, he had already interviewed a replacement. Parke now told me that the person who was to be appointed by the board was already in the country and was at Meikles Hotel. My board and I were completely unaware of these events as they unfolded.

I was asked to meet the nominee, a Canadian banker, Derek Johnston, but I was told that his name had to be kept secret. After I had met him, I told Parke that I would call the board together to recount these events; in essence that there was a man whom Parke had selected, who had travelled to Harare and whom we were being told by the majority share-holder to appoint. Extraordinarily, he emphasized that I was forbidden to disclose the appointee's name to my directors or to give more than a broad description of his record and background. It was a most incredible example of the usurping of the powers of a chairman and his board in the management of a public company.

In view of these high-handed actions, Jim Back, Dick Christie and I, as a group, looked at the alternatives to offering the government our resignations. In normal circumstances, the government and Reserve Bank action would have created widespread resignation. If we had gone, we believed that the whole of the old board would have resigned too, leaving only the government's new directors, who were largely political appointees - and we still had a responsibility to all the shareholders, including the minorities. The bank's credibility with its overseas correspondent banks would have been severely damaged and we were manoeuvred into a position where we had to assess the potential damage to the bank of a major resignation of our experienced board members and the potential damage to the country.

I called an extraordinary meeting of the board and it was a most remarkable one. I told them of the events of the previous few days and that I had met the new nominee and that I was asking the board to be aware of what I had been instructed to do. The ministry refused permission for me to arrange for the new nominee, who was still in Harare, to meet the board, nor was I allowed to name him.

The board was astonished at what the ministry was instructing us to do. They were sympathetic to the dilemma in which I found myself, and were fully supportive. Either the directors not appointed by the government tendered their resignations as a whole, or we went along with ministry's proposals that Johnston be appointed. After all, the ministry had a majority on the board and in any event they could achieve what they wanted by a simple vote at the boardroom table.

We all knew we were compromising our principles by accepting these instructions and the way in which they had been issued. But after taking everything into account, the board felt they had no alternative but to accept the situation. The outspoken comments and remarks from some of the directors around the table gave an indication of the degree of their anger and dismay. Many of these were senior figures in their professions and in business and were amazed at the crudity of the strategy that had been concocted. But they authorized me to go ahead as we had no satisfactory alternative.

I was glad that the whole board had stood together. Parke was embarrassed because he had been required to travel outside the country without informing me and with no authority from the board to conduct the interview or to offer Johnston the post, which was not in his gift. I knew Dick Parke well in his capacity as deputy governor of the Reserve Bank. His performance in that position was always impeccable. He was widely liked and respected and certainly earned my sympathy for the deeply embarrassing position in which he had been placed.

After further discussions Derek Johnston, our new managing director designate, returned to Canada, and shortly thereafter I was in the United States and signed the contract with him, authority for which had been given to me by the board. He was appointed as group chief executive officer and director on 1 October 1985.

When he took up the position of managing director three months later, Parke withdrew to his normal work as deputy governor in the Reserve Bank. Johnston's performance, once he had learnt the local ropes, was excellent and certainly helped to reassure overseas bankers that, up to that stage at any rate, the bank was in professional hands. He had plenty of international experience and we were fortunate to have him. He worked with me at the bank for three years. He had a good knowledge of Africa and had, in fact, worked in Zambia.

In order to develop closer contact and to get the government nominees more actively involved in the operations of the bank, we formed a small executive committee of the board.

Affirmative action was the order of the day and the government directors told us that Bernard Chidzero, the Minister of Economic Planning and Development, had urged them to push for the appointment of a managing director designate to work under Johnston, with a view to taking over the reins at the conclusion of his contract, which was originally for two years, but was extended to a third year. The government directors gave me the name of a person whom the ministry wished us to appoint to be groomed as deputy managing director designate, and he started to work with Johnston.

A few weeks later, to my astonishment, I was called to see the Minister of Finance and the Permanent Secretary of the ministry to explain why we had appointed this man to this position without reference to the ministry. I explained that we had understood and had complied with the government policy of affirmative action and that government's own nominee directors had told me in an executive committee meeting that this man was the ministry's choice. We had thus proceeded in good faith on the information given to me, although Johnston expressed reservations as to this man's banking ability and experience.

Then, I was told that this was not the case, and that the ministry did not support his appointment, which would have to be reversed, even though this was going to cause very considerable embarrassment all round – and, understandably, great disappointment to the man concerned. I told Dr Chidzero I now had difficulty in being confident that the information contributed to my executive committee meetings by government nominees could be taken as correctly reflecting government's wishes. The board was responsible for the appointment of senior executives.

It became clear that there was political infighting, with several influential groups within the party, each of which wanted their nominee to get the job. Political pressure had been brought to bear on Chidzero, who been 'persuaded' to change his mind. He had then passed the responsibility on to us to sort it out.

The afternoon that I saw the minister coincided with one of my monthly executive meetings, which I had to leave to see the minister. When I came back and told the government nominee directors what had happened at my meeting at the ministry, they were mystified. They all confirmed that the name they had given me was, without question, the nominee of the ministry and now this was being reversed without their knowledge.

I believe this incident shows how difficult it was to accommodate ambitious people from different groups, all of whom wanted simultaneously to get their nominee on to the ladder.

I had the difficult task of telling the man concerned. He became ill, but none of the medical profession was able to diagnose any fundamental problem. We sent him overseas to specialists who again could find nothing wrong. We had to terminate his employment with Zimbank with a hefty golden handshake, although his contribution to the affairs of the bank had been minimal.

A few months after Derek Johnston's appointment, I was called by the minister and permanent secretary to say that they wished to appoint Parke as a successor chairman to me. It was clear to me that this was just the next step in the ministry's plan to reconstruct the bank's board and management team.

My removal as chairman was very pointed, especially as no other non-executive directors were changed at that time. Alwyn Pichanick, Mike Butler and Tikki Hywood stayed on. I was concerned with the possible reaction to this news from our correspondent banks in other countries, most of whose executives I knew well. As I had close contact at that time with the Minister of State Security, Emmerson Mnangagwa, I discussed the matter with him to ascertain his view of outside reaction. He was more than concerned, and took me that afternoon to Chidzero's house, where he explained that cabinet were unaware of this move and that government, as a majority shareholder, might be concerned at the consequences.

We discussed and agreed a strategy whereby I would announce my intention to resign when the mid-year results were published, which would give time for the outside banking world to become aware of the changes that were under way. During that period, the principal shareholders never lost an opportunity to find fault, in spite of the fact that both the board and the executive committee were packed with government nominees.

Following my retirement, Dick Parke assumed the chairmanship. Dr Leonard Tsumba left the Reserve Bank to become the chief executive officer of Zimbank. Elisha Mushayakarara succeeded Leonard Tsumba at Zimbank when the latter was appointed governor of the Reserve Bank in 1993. Albert Nhau took over as chairman from Dick Parke.

– 16 –

Independence and After

Lancaster House • Guerrilla assembly points • Independence ceremony
• *Zimbabwe News* editorial • Michael Shea • Prince Philip • Border Gezi
• A Bill removed from Parliament • Major General Sir Peter de la Billière
• Chrysanthemums at Centre Point, London
• Orientation tours for new MPs • Young people's dinners

Over the years the Rhodesian war had intensified. The agreement reached in 1978 between Ian Smith and Bishop Muzorewa proved short lived; indeed, the war intensified. Mrs Margaret Thatcher, leader of the British Conservative Party, won the general election in the UK in May 1979, and she determined to try and resolve the long-running problem of Rhodesia, now called Zimbabwe-Rhodesia, a country that did not have international recognition.

The Lancaster House negotiations to try and resolve the issue lasted from September 1979 through to the end of the year, and during this period, I remember various events and interventions that enabled me to play a small part in our future.

For example, on one occasion, I learnt that General Prem Chand was to be in transit through London. He was military adviser to the United Nations and had been appointed Resident Commissioner Designate for Zimbabwe-Rhodesia, but had scant knowledge of the country. Ken Flower, head of the Rhodesian secret service, and I thought this presented an opportunity for me to brief the General should the opportunity arise. As it happened we were able to arrange a meeting prior to his arrival though it meant me travelling to London to do so. It was a long way to go for a one-day meeting, which proved very fruitful.

During the Lancaster House conference, it seemed to me that, while much emphasis was put on the land issue, very little thought was being given to economic policies. There was one person who was thinking about these matters, though, and that was David Smith, Minister of Finance in Ian Smith's government.

He took a flat in London during the conference proceedings (which lasted three months) and he asked me, as chairman of the Rhodesia Promotion Council, to arrange meetings with bankers, industrialists and politicians, and branches of the European and American banks in London with a view to looking forward.

I was pleased to be able to do this, and introduced him to bankers, Tate and Lyle, who were deeply involved in the marketing of Zimbabwe's sugar, and other industrial giants, as well as the editors of *The Times*, the *Telegraph*, the *Daily Express*, the *Financial Times* and the *Guardian*, and people at the BBC.

One of the agreements made at Lancaster House was that twelve assembly points for the guerrillas would set up throughout the country each manned by a very small contingent of the British Army. All the ZANLA and ZIPRA guerrillas in any one area were to go to the closest assembly point.

Tension was very high in and outside these assembly points. In addition, there were a number of militants who were hostile to the concept of settlement and who could easily have created an incident, lit the fuse and 'taken out' a couple of assembly points. In a matter of hours, violence would have escalated across the country. Great tribute must be paid to the senior civil servants, the police and the army who kept the lid on the pot and the temperature slowly cooled down. Feelings of elation were mixed with those of pessimism and distress.

A general election was held in February 1980. As the election results started to come in, it became clear that Robert Mugabe's ZANU(PF) would have a huge majority. Until a few days before the election, Christopher Soames, the British interim Governor of Southern Rhodesia, and his British group in Zimbabwe firmly believed that Robert Mugabe would come nowhere near winning the election. They disregarded the opinion of many citizens, black and white, who understood the influence of ethnicity and intimidation in the way people voted and believed Mugabe would romp home. When the results started to come in, they were in a state of shock and panic.

There was also great apprehension in the white community, particularly among the farmers. The lead-up to the election and the accompanying propaganda had centred on repossession of the land, which the politicians said had been 'stolen' by early settlers, which was an emotive issue.

In his first speech after the election, however, President Robert Mugabe, statesmanlike, offered an olive branch to white Rhodesians and tensions gradually eased. He spoke about the need for the whole community to work together. He said he wanted the hand of friendship to be extended both ways, and this had a surprising and calming effect. Nevertheless, large-scale emigration took place, of both whites and skilled blacks.

It is interesting to see how clear and specific Robert Mugabe had been on the subject of land while he was in Mozambique. By chance I have a copy of the September/October 1979 issue of *Zimbabwe News*, the official organ of ZANU(PF). Its editorial is reproduced in full (opposite).

Prince Charles was present at the ceremony to lower the Union Flag and raise the Zimbabwe flag, at midnight on 17/18 April 1980. Wendy and I were seated in Rufaro stadium next to Dr Bernard Chidzero, who was to become the new Minister of Economic Planning and Development.

The evening before, at the celebration banquet at Meikles Hotel, leaders in the private sector, white and black, hosted tables with visitors from many different countries. I saw a man looking lost and clearly unable to find his place at a table. When I asked if I could help him, he introduced himself as Michael Shea and said that he was with the Buckingham Palace party, part of the Queen's private secretariat; somehow he had been overlooked.

I noticed that we had an empty chair at our table, which should have been occupied by someone from one of the West African countries who had not yet arrived. I quickly obtained a new seating card, wrote Michael Shea's name on it and removed the original one. He was the Queen's Press Secretary. This started a very interesting conversation at our table.

Shea asked me to see him when I was next in London. Soon afterwards, we were planning the International Economic Resources Conference and were looking for international leaders to chair each of the sections at the conference. One of the sections was 'Wildlife, Environment and Tourism' and we had in mind to ask Prince Philip, Duke of Edinburgh, if he would honour us by his presence and chair that sector. I took some soundings and it looked promising, so I rang Shea, canvassed the idea. We had a positive response from the Palace and arranged for a preliminary meeting. Dexter Chavunduka accompanied me and was very impressed by the size and extent of the Palace.

We had an excellent reception and it looked as if the dates were compatible with His Royal Highness's programme, and we were advised that he was interested in participating. The Wildlife Society of Zimbabwe, however, was also keen for the Duke to open the first Zimbabwe Wildlife

Editorial

Lancaster House and Beyond

Every member of ZANU has always known that imperialism would try to off-set the conquests of the Zimbabwean masses and their ZAN-LA Forces achieved during 1978 (The Year of the People) and 1979 (The Year of the People's Storm.) Signs were everywhere. The imperialist forces were ganging-up behind the Muzorewa regime, lest it falls under the incessant blows of the people. ZANU would have to be stopped.

We warned in these columns (see Volume XI N.ʳ 2 of 1979 editorial) that the Lancaster House Conference would pose a serious threat to our revolution. It is now clear that the British constitutional proposals, the transitional scheme and the so-called ceasefire arrangements combine to confront our revolution w i t h its greatest challenge. The Party must defeat the threat and survive. To survive the Party must look at the rules of the new game of imperialism. It is by understanding those new rules that we can check-mate the enemy.

The so-called «Free and fair» elections will never and can never be truly free and fair. The purpose of imperialism is to destroy ZANU first and then eat the people. It is therefore important for every member of the Party to carry-out whatever orders the Central Committee will give in order to defeat the enemy in this regard. Our position has been made abundantly clear by the Central Committee during the London Conference:

a) We remain opposed to white representation in parliament on a racial basis.

b) We have vowed to seize the land, without compensation from those who stole it, in order to restore it to the people.

c) We are sworn to dismantle the white power-structure in the public service, the army and the police and reconstruct these around our vanguard Party.

d) We will, at the earliest opportunity tame and transform the present archaic and racist judicial system.

e) We will place the entire economic system in the hands and service of the masses of Zimbabwe.

On these matters we cannot prevaricate. The thousands of the innocent Zimbabweans who have been butchered by the enemy and the comrades in the mass graves at Chimoio; Nyadzonia and Tembue and those buried everywhere throughout Zimbabwe would otherwise have died in vain.

Whatever game imperialism plays, we must beat it at it. There is no doubt that ZANU will win and the revolution will survive.

The editorial in the September/October 1979 issue of *Zimbabwe News.*

Congress later in the year and implored us to stand aside. Prince Philip would, of course, not come to Zimbabwe twice within a short space of time. After a lot of deliberation we reluctantly agreed to give way to the Wildlife Society, but we suspected that their international congress might never get off the ground. We were proved right – it never took place – and the Duke of Edinburgh did not visit us. What an opportunity lost.

Border Gezi was Member of Parliament for a constituency bordering Mozambique near Tete. He sought a meeting in my office one day and said that this was one of the least developed areas in the country. The few administrative buildings and the clinic had collapsed and the schools were run down. He asked if there was anything I could do to help them resuscitate their infrastructure.

I asked him to come back the next week and, when he did, I had had an idea. The essence of it was to involve George Loverdos, the Greek founder and owner of Speciss, a non-residential training college, the largest in Zimbabwe. Students came to Speciss for secondary education and coaching in specific subjects. I asked Loverdos if he would help. He agreed to select six trainees from a group of ten who would be identified in Border Gezi's constituency as potential students on a basic computer training course. These six students would stay in Harare and attend Speciss College. Loverdos also donated four good second-hand computers.

I canvassed the building industry for help in constructing a new administrative centre. PG Timbers donated the building material. Turners, the large UK-based asbestos company, agreed to supply the asbestos sheet roofing and Portland Cement provided the cement. Radar donated steel door and window frames. It was then to be up to Gezi's people on site to dig the foundations, make the bricks and build.

The youngsters were selected and completed their course in Harare successfully. But, after all that had been done for them, the constituency officials failed to raise sufficient funds themselves to meet local costs. Gezi wrote me a grateful and complimentary letter and said he was sad that because of their situation they had been unable to bring the plan to a satisfactory conclusion.

Since his war days, Border Gezi was known to have a fiery personality. He became a junior minister and later Provincial Governor of Mashonaland Central. He established the Border Gezi training unit that later developed into the notorious Youth Brigade, and these young people provided much of the support for farm invasions. Gezi was killed in April 2001 on the way to Masvingo in a car accident.

In early 1989, the medical profession was confronted with legislation brought by the Minister of Health, Dr Felix Muchemwa, who had qualified at Makerere College in Uganda. He proposed that all specialists operating from their own rooms would be obliged to close them and work in government hospitals. The profession were appalled at this proposal, which could only result in an exodus of specialists.

A meeting was called to plan a response. It was chaired by David Smith, Minister of Industry and Commerce in the first Zimbabwe cabinet, and was well attended. Smith suggested that a small committee should gather information for a response document, and the meeting asked if I would chair that group and select its participants.

The minister had already laid the Bill on the Table of the House and there was no time to waste. We quickly collected information, produced a document, took it to Eddison Zvobgo, Minister of State for Political Affairs in the President's Office, and explained the gravity of the position. He arranged a special meeting of the ZANU(PF) caucus, which instructed the Minister of Health to go to the Speaker of Parliament and to crave his indulgence and permission to remove the Bill from the Table. That was done.

Major General Sir Peter de la Billière commanded the British forces in the first Gulf War and, having enjoyed reading his autobiography, I was determined, if the opportunity arose, to meet him. Shortly after he retired, he was offered a seat on the Board of Directors of Robert Fleming, the huge Scottish merchant bank – probably the biggest in the UK at that time. I noted how shrewd the bank was to invite somebody to sit on their board who had such a wide knowledge of the Middle East.

I then noticed in the financial press that Flemings had taken over a company on the Johannesburg Stock Exchange called Martin and Co. Not long afterwards, I saw that they had taken over Edwards and Co., a stockbroking firm in Harare, so now Sir Peter was much closer.

I was part of the official delegation that went to the UK at the time of President Mugabe's state visit in 1994, and at the conclusion I telephoned Sir Peter and introduced myself as the chairman of one of the companies under the umbrella of Flemings. Of course, he was unaware of the chain link until I explained it to him. When he learnt I was from Zimbabwe, he asked if I could come and have a chat, and I spent a very useful hour with him. At the end he enquired whether I would be free on the following Tuesday to join the non-executive directors of the bank for lunch at the bank, which I was delighted to accept.

There were very senior men in the financial and industrial sector and they were most interested in affairs in Zimbabwe. The lunch went on until 3.30 p.m. and then I suggested that they should not just believe what I told them, but that one of them should come to Zimbabwe to see for himself, and I enquired whether one of them would volunteer. Sir Peter immediately put his hand up, and the deal was done.

The plan was for Sir Peter and his wife to fly out four weeks later. As soon as I knew what flight they were coming on, my secretary contacted his secretary and on the quiet we got the details necessary for his immigration entry forms. I then contacted a man on the airport staff and asked if he could get me a tarmac pass so that I could welcome them at the foot of the steps by the aircraft. I also challenged British Airways to guarantee that the de la Billières' bags would be first off the plane and first on to the carousel.

I was at the steps of the plane that morning to greet a surprised couple. Sir Peter asked me how on earth I was on the tarmac, and I said that when we had particularly important guests I liked to welcome them personally. So we walked into the immigration hall, and my airport friend approached them and said, 'Would you please sign these two forms?' Sir Peter scrutinized them, saw that all the information was correct and looked up quizzically and said, 'How the devil did you get this information?' My response was, 'By enterprise. Please sign them,' which they did.

We walked into the baggage-collection hall. There were only two suitcases on the carousel, both were theirs. BA had done well. Sir Peter said, 'If this country can still do this sort of thing, it really is most impressive.'

That evening Sir Peter spoke to a full house of the Farmers' Dining Club, on the Kuwait war. The question-and-answer session was as interesting as the speech itself.

The next day for lunch we had as many former Rhodesian army and air force officers as we could collect. It was good to see that, although Britain and Rhodesia had been on opposite sides during our fifteen years of UDI, the discussions that took place were just between soldiers and soldiers.

The next morning we took our visitors to the tobacco floors for a special breakfast, for which the floors were renowned, and to see the operation and meet staff of the floors.

After the Kuwait War, Sir Peter had been assigned to the military command of the Falkland Islands. When I told him that a group of our friends were going there and on to the World Discoverer on our way to the Antarctic, he contacted his successor and arranged for Wendy and me to tour the islands and to visit the battlefields and the Falklands museum.

At that same state visit of President Mugabe to London, there was a support team from the Zimbabwe government and I was one of four people from the private sector. A gathering organized by the Confederation of British Industries and our government, focusing on the Zimbabwean economy, was to be held at the huge Centre Point hall in London. It was a plain, unattractive hall and I suggested that, if our government would give the transport, I would send 10,000 chrysanthemum blooms on Air Zimbabwe. I insisted on the flowers being handled by a professional florist.

The florist made a lovely show with our flowers. Along the top table, in a bower over the centre, along all the different tables around the room, there were chrysanthemums, and that was only part of what we had sent. The remainder were in plastic sleeves in water, and so on the afternoon of the second day, after lunch, I arranged for all the rest to be put into buckets at the exit, with a little notice, 'Zimbabwe chrysanthemums – please take a bunch'. There was a steady stream of people emerging from the Centre Point with a bunch of chrysanthemums. People still talk about those flowers. Even then there were still quite a lot left over.

The next day I was going on a tour with a car and driver kindly lent by the chairman of Willis Carroon. On my circuit were the Bank of England and the Foreign Office, and we ended up at Number Ten, Downing Street. There had been a major reshuffle of the Cabinet that day. All except one of the new members had been announced. When I arrived with my flowers in front of Number Ten, the horde of photographers thought that I must be the last person joining the Cabinet and crowded round the car. They were disappointed. But the flowers duly went in to friends at Number Ten.

During the state visit, the Lord Mayor of London gave President Mugabe the traditional banquet for such visitors. I was invited to this magnificent occasion. I think only Great Britain could mount such an inspiring and well-organized function. Several members of the royal family were present. I sat next to one of the Queen's ladies-in-waiting, who was intrigued with my gold ring produced on Handley Cross from our own gold. I saw someone on the far side of the banqueting hall and asked if it was Tiny Rowland. She said, 'Yes, it is Mr Rowland,' and, somewhat tartly continued, 'He is your guest, not ours.'

It was at this dinner that a young Zimbabwean concert pianist, Manuel Bagorro, played for the Queen. I was later able to help him in establishing HIFA, the Harare International Festival of the Arts, which has run so successfully for many years and has become well known throughout the world.

In the early 1980s I and others had discussions with the new politicians and with western diplomats who were anxious to help the new young country. I had suggested that it was of the greatest importance to establish quickly a number of training farms across the country. These would give some practical experience during the course of a year and the students would then pass on their practical farming knowledge to new black farmers and extension officers. These teachers would help to get new small-scale farmers established on land already owned by government, which had been bought on a willing-buyer, willing-seller basis. Alas, there was insufficient interest in the scheme.

At the time, I believed that we could develop an expanding economy with government and the private sector hand in hand. Government could help private productive sectors, which had not happened in neighbouring countries that had become independent before Zimbabwe; they had paid the penalty of seeing the swift disintegration of their economies, a situation that we wanted to avoid at all costs.

However, after Zimbabwe's fourth general election in June 2000, which ZANU(PF) won by a narrow, disputed majority from the Movement for Democratic Change, an analysis showed that about two-thirds of the 120 elected MPs were new to Parliament. I then had a lengthy discussion with Nathan Shamuyarira, whom I had known from the days of ZANU's first economic briefing, and suggested that those newly elected MPs would be, through no fault of their own, largely unaware of the systems and extent of our economy.

Shamuyarira agreed to ask the Speaker of Parliament to get the two party whips to select twenty new MPs from each of the two parties. Emmerson Mnangagwa was shortly to be elected the new Speaker and the three of us met to discuss possibilities. I was asked if I was prepared not just to theorize but to run the project myself. This was to become invaluable in developing new relationships. I undertook to organize the funding and the logistics and we planned to take the forty MPs to visit different parts of the country to familiarize them with the economy.

The concept was well received, and there were seldom spare seats on bus or aircraft. These journeys brought together MPs from both parties, who had to sit together and could talk on our way or when we all spent the night in the Sikumi Tree Lodge in Hwange. The private sector supported us with finance, and the UNDP regional director, Victor Angelo, allocated a staff member to help.

Our first visit with the MPs was to the Tobacco Sales floor, described in Chapter 6. Then we visited the Zimbabwe Leaf Tobacco company, owned by Universal Leaf Tobacco, of Virginia, USA. Tobacco was bought on the floors, handled, packed and sold in a form ready for blending to buyers in fifty countries throughout the world. Our tobacco, with its low sugar, nicotine content and lovely flavour, could compete with the best American leaf, and what Zimbabweans call 'the golden leaf' has helped to sustain our economy for close on a hundred years.

We took the MPs by air to the giant open-cast coal fields in Hwange, the Hwange power station and to Victoria Falls – where they could not believe that our hotels were so empty – then on to one of the best game lodges in the Hwange National Park, almost devoid of tourists, and for a game viewing drive in the evening.

On another trip we went to the Trojan nickel mine in Bindura. Here we went three and a half thousand feet down the shaft to the rock face. Back on the surface, they saw the smelters producing the nickel, a valuable export earner. On that same day, they saw cotton from adjacent commercial and communal farming areas being ginned.

We also went to a Grain Marketing Board depot, which was receiving maize, mostly from communal areas. At the GMB they saw many farmers in the queue waiting for payment. This delay had given the GMB a bad reputation and led to 'informal marketing'.

All maize is supposed to be marketed through the GMB, but informal traders were able to buy and amalgamate small growers' crops and bypassed the system. The efficiency of the informal market, where growers did not have to queue to get paid and were paid in cash, usually with a premium, became increasingly attractive, especially during periods of inflation. However, the cost of inputs had been secured on stop order against the delivery of grain to the GMB. When the grain was sold elsewhere, these debts were often not collected and bad debts mounted, so the credit risk of small growers grew worse and worse. As only part of the small-scale crop went into the formal sector, the GMB were short of grain and could not fully supply their customers, the millers and stockfeed companies.

We showed the MPs the huge Mitchell and Mitchell vegetable-packing complex, close to Marondera, where 6,000 workers graded and packed vegetables, long beans and mixed stir-fry vegetables. These vegetables from satellite farms were picked early in the morning and delivered, graded and packed in the afternoon, left by air in the evening, and appeared on supermarket shelves in England the next day, proudly identified as a product of Zimbabwe. The company had its own bus service ferrying workers from the local township. It was a highly efficient operation, although their good name overseas was frequently damaged by inconsistent flight arrivals.

Next we went to Nyanga to see the expanding fruit and export-flower farming and the tourist opportunities in the mountains. A week or two later, we visited two plants near Harare – Fresca, which bought vast quantities of vegetables for dehydration and export, and the Seed Company, which handled ninety per cent of Zimbabwe's hybrid seed maize. Both these projects were situated in an Export Processing Zone, with tax incentives to stimulate exports.

We went on to see a pilot scheme where the Zimbabwe Tobacco Association, with their own grower funds, had established training points where young farmers could work for a year. They learned to plant, grow and grade the crop, and those who succeeded were promoted on to small farms where they could grow initially four, six and then eight hectares of tobacco annually. Groups of these young farmers had the services of a good agronomist. The MPs were impressed with the speed at which the young farmers, using family labour, had become sufficiently viable to afford a tractor and improve their homes. We also visited one of the big high-quality rose-growing projects, for export to Holland, where Zimbabwean roses were making a good name for themselves.

Unfortunately we could not complete the plan to tour with the MPs to the Midlands, Matabeleland and the huge sugar estates in the Lowveld as disruptions to farming activities and political antagonisms had worsened. Morgan Tsvangirai's epic trial for treason had begun and it became impractical to continue.

To this day, when I meet in the street some of the MPs who took part in these visits, they remind me of the pleasure they had in learning more about their own country. Some members from Bulawayo in the west had never visited Mutare in the east. Emmerson Mnangagwa supported us throughout and regularly announced the next visit from the Speaker's chair. I believe the scheme had started to soften relationships and in a small way to begin understanding and friendships; it was sad to see all this potential aborted.

In the early years of the new century, after the farm invasions, the younger generation grew increasingly concerned about their future and sought help and advice from community leaders, black and white, as to what their future held. I organized a number of young people's dinners where we had about 65 people between the ages of 20 and 35, with speakers of wisdom and foresight, such as Nigel Chanakira, chief executive of the Kingdom Bank, and Patrick Rooney, former chief executive of the Delta group.

– 17 –

Zimbabwe Promotion Council

Briefing for ZANU(PF) • Denis Norman •
Permanent Secretaries meet Robert Mugabe • ZPC organizes visits
• Proposed fertilizer plants at Cabora Bassa •
Zimbabwe Economic Resources Conference • Kuwaiti interest
• International dignitaries visit • Fernando Honwana and Mozambique
• Herbert Murerwa, High Commissioner in London
• Admiral Sir Jeremy Black • Dinner on the *Victory* • Jimmy Carter
• Bill Deedes • Lord Balfour • *The Times* • Press comments
• World Economic Forum • Dawie de Villiers

When Zimbabwe became independent, the country boasted something like 3,000 university graduates. When Zambia was granted its independence, it had three graduates, and Malawi had just one. Zimbabwe started off with a strong foundation of well-educated people who were able to participate in the new government.

Robert Mugabe, leader of Zimbabwe African National Union (Patriotic Front), ZANU(PF), returned to Zimbabwe in January 1980 and spoke to a packed and ecstatic audience at the Rufaro Stadium. Early the following morning, I had a call from a man who introduced himself as Emmerson Mnangagwa, a member of ZANU(PF)'s Politburo. He said he was aware that we had been giving seminars, lectures and meetings to the four existing political parties regarding the civil service and the economy but that his party had not been a participant (See Chapter 10). I replied that we would have been pleased to have afforded them the same opportunity but, as they were a party in exile, it was not feasible to travel to Mozambique for this purpose.

He conceded the point but said that nevertheless they wished to catch up. Robert Mugabe asked me to put together the best available team of people to speak about all aspects of the economy, for a full day session two days later. This showed the importance that they attached to the state of the economy.

We grasped the challenge and brought together a dozen of the best-informed men from all sectors. We had representatives of finance, banking and the stock exchange, industry, commerce, farming, tobacco, mining, tourism, transport. The briefing continued throughout the day and finally we had supper with some members of their Central Committee. Mugabe to this day recalls that experience which, for some time, helped to enable and maintain dialogue.

This was the first occasion for Mugabe to hear other views on the current state of affairs in Zimbabwe – the negative and the positive. I asked Denis Norman, then president of the Rhodesia National Farmers' Union (soon to be re-named the Commercial Farmers' Union, CFU), to speak on agriculture. In the question session, he and Mugabe got on well and from that first meeting their acquaintance strengthened.

Soon afterwards, Mugabe asked Norman to become his first Minister of Agriculture. This wise decision gave confidence to the commercial farming community and to the whole country. Norman had been a British farmer and, on arrival in Rhodesia, had learnt the tobacco-growing trade. In due course, he bought his own farm from the McGills at Norton. He became a council member of the RNFU, representing the maize commodity. He subsequently became vice-president, and then CFU president in 1980, before being appointed Minister of Agriculture.

At the second election in 1985, Norman was not reappointed to the cabinet but remained close to Mugabe. He became chairman or director of many companies. Mugabe later asked him to return to politics and he became Minister of Transport and was invaluable in bridging the gap between Zimbabwe and other countries. Importantly, the briefing we had been asked to arrange provided face-to-face contact with members of the Central Committee and the Politburo, some of whom later became ministers, and in particular with Nathan Shamuyarira, who often provided a bridge between government and the private sector. Educated at Oxford and Princeton, USA, he was a courteous person and, although our opinions were often dissimilar, he was prepared to listen.

During the transition period, a vacuum developed, with almost no contact between the Permanent Secretaries and Mugabe's new team. The Zimbabwe Promotion Council (ZPC), as it had become, was asked if we could arrange an informal meeting with some of the Permanent Secretaries to meet Mr and Mrs Mugabe. About a dozen came, and each spoke on his ministry. It was very worthwhile, and we had the co-operation of almost all of them. The meeting was unusual, the private sector introducing members of the administration to a new political entity. David Lewis was helpful at these meetings, and Mrs Sally Mugabe was charming and served all the participants at the tea table. Lewis later wrote of that time:

> At the time of assuming office, Mugabe was an outstanding person who had a complete capacity for statesmanship, reasonable approaches to problems, and was prepared even to follow lines or courses which were a reversal or different to his own courses or suggestions.
>
> One might estimate that this capacity continued to be the case until arguably about 1993. It was believed that his wife Sally played an important role in those early years.
>
> At the meeting of Permanent Secretaries, David Young, Secretary of the Ministry of Finance, showed tremendously good sense and advice to those who sought it, and particularly to his fellow Secretaries of Ministries.

After that introductory meeting, we took members of the ZANU(PF) Central Committee to see aspects of the economy such as tobacco, cotton, mining, secondary industry, the major Lowveld irrigation development for sugar, and other development projects. We believe that this helped them appreciate the jewel they were inheriting. As a non-political organization, the Zimbabwe Promotion Council emphasized the productive and developmental sectors of the country.

Samora Machel had told Mugabe that many of Mozambique's problems stemmed from the loss of confidence by their Portuguese inhabitants, who had left in droves taking their skills with them, and it is said that he told Mugabe, 'In particular, don't lose your farming expertise.'

After independence in 1980, the ZPC continued its role, although the methods we used were quite different now that the country was recognized internationally. In addition to promoting Zimbabwe, we took groups to projects in the region such as Cabora Bassa, which I had last visited in 1973, when the final and fifth French generating set was being installed, as recounted in Chapter 14. On one occasion we flew down in a Dakota full of dignitaries, including Sir Humphrey Gibbs, the Chief Justice Sir Hugh Beadle, heads of ministries from the economic sector, bankers and businessmen. We were the guests of the Governor and stayed in the lovely old Governor's Palace at Tete on the banks of the Zambezi. It gave us an opportunity to see the immense size of the dam, and we drove right down into the intake tunnels, which are now under water.

After Zimbabwe's independence it was clear that significant, and probably surplus, amounts of hydroelectric power would become available from Cabora Bassa. As Chairman of the ZPC, I brought together in London a small group of inter-national engineers from Britain, France, Germany, America and South Africa, including General Electric, Brown Boveri, Air Liquide and other major international construction companies. We discussed the possibility of erecting a plant similar to Sable in the vicinity of the Cabora Bassa dam. If it was placed immediately adjacent to the power station, it would hardly require any transmission lines, which are very expensive.

An added advantage would have been the possible exploitation of phosphate deposits forty kilometres from the site, which could have supplied phosphate ore to the plant. Extremely cheap electricity would have made a phosphate smelter feasible, and the resulting phosphoric acid could then have been blended with Cabora Bassa's own ammonium nitrate to produce ammonium phosphate.

The three elements most needed in African tropical agriculture are phosphate, nitrogen and potash (all Zimbabwe's potash had to be imported). We believed that a viable project could be established, and this ammonium phosphate, distributed into countries in the region, would have had a materially beneficial effect of increasing food production in Mozambique, Zimbabwe, Zambia, Malawi and Tanzania.

In April 1980, Robert Mugabe's first Cabinet was formed. It included a dynamic young man, Simba Makoni, who was Deputy Minister of Agriculture. He later became Minister of Industry and Energy Development. We were unable to convince him to give Zimbabwean support to an international consortium because he would not accept that, because of the high cost of the transmission line, the location of the plant was to be in Mozambique near the Cabora Bassa dam and not in Zimbabwe. To our great regret, the project got no further thanks to Zimbabwe's reluctance. More regional and less exclusively national interests would have benefited us all.

A good example of such regional and international co-operation would be the Pande deposit, which has been developed by a consortium from the United States, Mozambique and South Africa. Gas from Pande goes by pipeline to Richard's Bay in South Africa, where it is used in the aluminium smelter to smelt bauxite ore coming from Australia by sea. The natural gas from Mozambique, the ore from Australia and the smelting process in South Africa tie three different countries together, producing a range of products for their mutual benefit.

There is another major dam site on the Zambezi, forty kilometres down-stream from Cabora Bassa, which could still be developed. With its hydroelectricity and with the giant Pande natural-gas field, many chemical products could be produced there. This region of Africa has some of the key natural resources for significant industrialization and mineral beneficiation projects.

Several people have asked me why the Rhodesia Promotion Council had promoted and so often visited such a project in Mozambique. My answer was that it was my belief that, where major projects such as gas pipelines, energy distribution and communication links existed, they could span boundaries to neighbouring territories and integrate projects for mutual advantage. The country boundaries laid out in Africa by politicians in the 1800s – France, Belgium, Portugal, Britain and Germany – did not necessarily follow ethnic boundaries. An important effect of the inter-linking of projects like Cabora Bassa would be a positive step towards integrating the economies of the neighbouring countries in the region and focusing on combining politics and the economy instead of – as so often happened – concentrating almost entirely on the political aspect of their new-found independence.

At independence, Rhodesia had been largely isolated from the outside world for fifteen years, and it was clear that a concerted effort was needed to get leaders and opinion formers from the overseas and private sector and in some cases, from governments, to see for themselves the developments that had taken place.

Before independence David Lewis and I had an introduction to Dr Bernard Chidzero, who at the time was based in Lausanne, Switzerland, heading the UNCTAD team for the United Nations. He had been groomed to return to Rhodesia as soon as politics permitted and was to become a key member of the new cabinet with his experience of international organizations and finance. On his appointment as Minister of Economic Planning and Development, Chidzero became an important link for us with government and, for example, with senior UN staff. We, at the ZPC, were also able to help him, as some members of government lacked sophistication and had little understanding of First World economic affairs. His assistant at that time was a young man called Kombo Moyana, who later became the first black governor of the Reserve Bank.

Following his ministerial appointment, Dr Chidzero was supportive of our proposal that the ZPC should, as a private-sector organization, set up an economic resources conference. We needed to show as many people as possible, throughout the world, the developments that had been steadily taking place during the fifteen years of UDI and, perhaps more importantly, use the opportunity to build on what had been achieved so far.

We established a small working team and subdivided the economy into the sectors of finance, industry, commerce, agriculture, mining, tourism, transport and banking. Each subsection chairman chose his own working party and was given full responsibility for it. The university very kindly gave us full use of their campus for a week for the conference, which we used for both residential and lecture purposes.

Attracting the right sort of people from all over the world to attend such a conference was a challenge, and I discussed our problem with a leading industrial group in Britain, Davie Ashmore. Their managing director's experience was that, to attract the top people, a telephone call or an invitation letter was no substitute for visiting the person concerned and personally handing him the invitation. His group offered to fund the air-travel costs of a team to do exactly that. This was an extremely generous gesture and I immediately set about dividing our working parties into pairs and they visited Britain, all the main countries in Europe, America, the Middle East, Japan and the Far East region. We did not visit Russia because of the Cold War.

Acceptance of these personal invitations exceeded our highest expectations, almost a hundred per cent of those we approached responded positively. We had 370 visitors from 33 countries. It was essential that we had a top secretariat, and the British American Tobacco Company very kindly lent its second-in-command, Syd Kelly, for four months to lead our organizing team. He had as his assistant Alison Biggs, an experienced and capable young woman who ran her own conference company. They worked with the various companies, parastatals and ministries. Each team developed its own programme for the five-day period. We organized several twin-engine planes and had aircraft available every day so that people who wanted to visit tourist destinations, or the big sugar estates in the Lowveld, or Bulawayo, or steel and chrome smelting in the Midlands, could do so with relative ease.

Before the opening session, we had asked the participants to indicate which sector they wished to attend. Each sector had its own lecture hall; the university's catering was superb, and visitors either stayed on the university campus or in hotels or were entertained in the homes of Zimbabweans.

The opening ceremony was held in the biggest theatre in Salisbury, the 7 Arts. The prime minister, Robert Mugabe, opened the conference. The hall was packed with people of many different nationalities, keen to see what had taken place and what we planned to do in Zimbabwe.

It was a fitting introduction to the newly independent country, one of the major achievements of the ZPC, and it was a great reward for the immense amount of team work and effort that had gone into its planning and implementation. The fruits of this labour were harvested for many years until changing policies brought the country to its knees.

The Kuwaitis, in particular, showed a special interest in agriculture, and we flew them to several areas such as Lomagundi, north of Harare, the fruit orchards

International economic resources conference on Zimbabwe

SALISBURY SEPTEMBER 1st — 5th

The brochure of the 1980 International Economic Resources Conference.

Prime Minister Robert Mugabe opens the 1980 conference, 'Zimbabwe: Land of Opportunity'.

in Nyanga and to the sugar estates. They were considering establishing a Kuwaiti/Zimbabwean private-sector investment group. Inter-country investment would normally have been done on a government-to-government basis through the Kuwaiti Ministry of International Finance, whereas my point of contact was Mr Walid Said, who had led the Kuwaiti group attending our Zimbabwe Economic Resources Conference; but their idea was to establish a private Kuwaiti investment group to work with the private sector in Zimbabwe. The Kuwaitis saw Zimbabwe as a springboard for development into other countries in the region, and I visited Kuwait several times with Dr Dexter Chavunduka.

Plans had reached a fairly advanced stage, with our government responding positively, when suddenly the Kuwaitis went cold. We had no replies to cables, letters, phone calls were not returned, and we were at a loss as to the reason. I called the head of the fund in London and asked what had gone wrong. He diplomatically told me that there was nothing that the Kuwaitis feared and disliked more than communism and, when they heard that our government had asked the North Koreans to train our 5th Brigade, they decided to walk away from the whole project. It would have been a wonderful opportunity to establish a bilateral development operation and it could also have been the pattern for other countries.

Later on, when Zimbabwe hosted the Commonwealth Heads of Government Meeting in 1991, the Singaporean foreign minister was a delegate. We enjoyed entertaining him on our farm and introducing him to a cross-section of Zimbabweans.

At another conference, Dr Mahathir Mohamad, prime minister of Malaysia, brought a delegation to this country, and my wife and I were dinner guests. He was at that stage not well informed about Zimbabwe, but saw an opportunity for far closer relations between the two countries (he has subsequently been one of President Mugabe's closest friends and supporters). Security was very tight, but late one night I received a call to say that the Malaysian prime minister had become bored with the repetitive speeches from delegate after delegate about the sins of apartheid in South Africa. He had heard how much the Singaporean Foreign Minister had enjoyed his day on our farm and could he bring some of his team out the next day? So, unknown to the organizers, he left the conference. There was quite a panic until he was located looking at crops on Mount Lothian.

A year or two later, Dr Mahathir's wife was in Zimbabwe at the same time as Graça Machel, wife of Mozambique's President Samora Machel, and they also asked if they could spend an afternoon with us. We all had a lovely time and I was most impressed with Mrs Machel.She is a talented painter of china and gave us some lovely little bowls which she had painted herself.

In 1980 I was asked to look after Fernando Honwana, who had been sent to Salisbury by President Samora Machel to open a liaison office and then to monitor the elections. He was a graduate of York University and had a wide grasp of the politics between metropolitan countries and their colonies.

The Mozambican government emphasized the marriage between politics and the productive sector. The government was well aware that its economy had been devastated by the civil war between Frelimo and Renamo, which had laid waste so much of the country, and the mass emigration of Portuguese skills had made the situation worse. Honwana was quick to recognize the strength of Zimbabwe's economy and, in particular, our agricultural sector, which had done so well in contrast to the chaotic agriculture in Mozambique, and he warned against taking any steps in Zimbabwe that might lead to a similar situation.

During this period a Swiss lawyer, whom I had known for some time through our mutual relationship with the Zimbank, appeared, unannounced, in my office one morning to tell me that he was seeking the release of three men who had been on routine business in Mozambique and who had been arrested and thrown into jail in Beira. One victim was Bertie Lubner, chairman of a number of industrial companies in South Africa, including the giant Plate Glass, and an active member of the South African Foundation. He was accompanied by another South African and a Portuguese. Their mission was to look at increasing the exports of Mozambican hardwood to South Africa.

My Swiss friend had no idea where to start. Both David Lewis and I spoke to Emmerson Mnangagwa, at that time Minister of State for Security, the political head of the (feared) Central Intelligence Organization. He had been based in Mozambique before 1980 as intelligence chief of ZANLA, the Zimbabwe National Liberation Army. He said he would be happy to give our Swiss friend a personal letter to Fernando Honwana, who worked in President Machel's office. I telephoned Honwana personally to alert him to what was happening.

My friend chartered an aircraft and flew to Maputo, where he met several people who had been waiting for days to see Honwana. He was told that he had no chance and had better resign himself to a holiday at the sea. Mnangagwa's letter of introduction, however, swiftly opened the door, and the following day he was able to fly to Beira to open negotiations with the head of police in the province for the release of the three prisoners.

This he achieved, although one of the South Africans – not Bertie Lubner – had been so severely beaten while being interrogated that he had to stay for a period in hospital. Lubner said he had been quite convinced that they would not come out of prison alive. I met Honwana periodically in later years. He tragically died in the air crash that killed Machel in October 1986. Behind the scenes, he was a person of great influence in Mozambique, and his brother is a dominant figure in their government today.

Herbert Murerwa, Permanent Secretary for Labour in Zimbabwe, was appointed the second Zimbabwean High Commissioner to London. He had no international diplomatic experience, other than being the ZANU representative in the USA, and had very few contacts outside the British civil service. I suggested that he would, as a representative of Mugabe's government, find it difficult to make the contacts he needed to penetrate the system. The ZPC had a wide range of contacts and, if he so wished, I could come over to London and, within a week, arrange a series of small lunches, dinners and meetings with people who were likely to be involved in Zimbabwe's affairs, people who could be helpful, and this way he would get to know them sooner rather than later.

He greeted the idea with enthusiasm and I asked John Laurie, a farmer, a director of the Standard Chartered Bank, former president of the CFU and a friend of Sally Mugabe's, if he would accompany me. A young Zimbabwean woman in London who had often helped me before kindly undertook to do all the leg work of issuing invitations and organizing functions. We were to have a lunch and a dinner every day for a week, never with more than four or five British guests.

A few days before I was due to leave Zimbabwe, I had a call from Murerwa, who had now arrived in London, saying he had run into trouble with the Zimbabwean Permanent Secretary for Foreign Affairs, Stan Mudenge, a history lecturer, who did not like the idea of the white private sector being seen to help Murerwa or, in fact, of acknowledging that any help might be needed.

I explained that all the arrangements and invitations had been put in place and it would be most embarrassing and negative for Zimbabwe if the plan had to be aborted at such short notice. In a subsequent conversation, I told him that I would be going to London in any event and hoped to see Mudenge the following afternoon. I called on him. He declined to see me so I simply remained in his office in Harare until six o'clock. He came out with a smile and said it looked as though there was a sit-down strike. I explained what Murerwa and I had done, and he took refuge in saying that his minister was away and that he was unable to agree to the proposal. I told him that I would be leaving that evening in any case. On arrival in London, I met up with Murerwa, who was becoming increasingly embarrassed.

Then Wendy and I went to Liverpool to watch the Grand National at Aintree, returning on the Sunday. Our arrangements had been excellently set up, and our first lunch appointment was hosted by the Standard Chartered Bank. Murerwa, his councillor, John Laurie and I attended. It was a valuable and informative event, as Standard Chartered is the largest bank in Zimbabwe and had invited to the lunch a lot of clients interested in investment.

During the afternoon, Murerwa called again to say he had now received an instruction from Mudenge forbidding him to attend any more of the arranged functions. It was a very unfortunate decision, and I told Murerwa that there would inevitably be a negative effect when we had to explain to our invited guests, as tactfully as we could, what had happened. John Laurie and I decided to go ahead and host the functions without Murerwa, and we were at any rate able to update our guests on how the country was settling down in the early stages of independence. It could have been a most successful endeavour and it would have given Herbert Murerwa a head start.

This saga seems, in retrospect, a forerunner of the government's intention to eliminate any white involvement at senior level. John Laurie had done an immense amount of work for the country as president of the Commercial Farmers' Union, and by helping Sally Mugabe to establish the Zimbabwe Child Survival and Development Foundation, of which she was patron. It is sad that, when his farm was seized by 'war vets' in 2002 and he appealed to Mugabe (by which time Sally had died), the President turned a blind eye. Laurie and his family were evicted and his farm shuddered to a halt. He had been a significant exporter of roses and a tobacco and cattle farmer. His fate was the same as that of 4,000 other commercial farmers.

In May 1989, I was at a sixtieth birthday party in Mvurwi for Ben Norton, whose adopted son, Larry Norton, is one of Africa's foremost wildlife painters. At that party, I met an interesting man, Jeremy Black, and we sat at the same table. He was out on holiday from Britain and interested in what was going on in the country. During the conversation, I gradually learned that he was actually Admiral Sir Jeremy Black, Commander-in-Chief of the home fleet, based in Portsmouth.

Because of his interest in the affairs of the country, I asked him if he would like, in the few days left of his holiday, to meet some ministers and other leading people in the private sector. He said he would be delighted, but first would have to get approval from 10 Downing Street. Subject to that, he would love to spend a couple of days with me.

The approval came through and he met Emmerson Mnangagwa, Cephas Msipa, and the Minister of Defence. He saw our tobacco floors and met many private-sector leaders. At the end, in thanking me, he said he would find it difficult to return the hospitality we had extended to him, but he did have one idea – when I was next in Britain, he said he would arrange a dinner party for me on HMS Victory, which was in dry dock in Portsmouth. What an invitation!

A month later, I was met at Portsmouth station by two naval ratings, taken to Admiralty House, where I was to stay, and after cocktails, we drove to the dry dock and went on board. He had kindly invited several very senior guests, including Air Chief Marshal Sir Patrick Hine, who was Air Officer Commanding-in-Chief, Strike Command, RAF High Wycombe; Major General (later Field Marshal) Sir Gerald Templer, former Assistant Chief of Defence Staff; David Middleditch, former director of Jardines-Matheson in Hong Kong; Captain Mike Parry of Lloyds of London; and Miles Rivett-Carnac of the ill-fated Baring Brothers bank which was later collapsed by a rogue trader.

It was fascinating, after dinner, to be taken over the Victory by her captain. It was a shore appointment since she was in dry dock. Going from deck to deck was like travelling through a remarkable history book.

The next morning the five of us breakfasted together – one had just come back from Moscow, and one had spent the previous day at the Treasury in London. The Soviet Union had recently disintegrated into its member states. The Cold War was over and Patrick Hine was irate with the view taken by the Treasury officials, who felt that there was no longer any need to keep the armed forces at their current size to counterbalance the communist block, and as a consequence the Treasury would be

One of the invitation and instruction cards for the dinner warned guests that they should make themselves comfortable before going to HMS *Victory* because there were no suitable facilities on board as she was in dry dock.

able to reduce the armed forces budget figure considerably. Hine told them that they were entering a new phase, with a threat far worse than they had experienced in the communist block, and that it would come from the Arab world. How right he was.

In 1983 the Fourth of July, the USA's national day, coincided with a visit from Jimmy Carter, who was travelling in connection with his post-presidency Carter Foundation. Relations between America and Zimbabwe had started to deteriorate. Witness Mangwende, Minister of Foreign Affairs, had been invited to address the US reception to be held in the Stewart Room of Meikles Hotel in Harare to mark the occasion. He was unaccustomed to making extempore speeches and he read from the text, observing it closely.

David Miller was the US ambassador and he and Jimmy Carter were the joint hosts for the day. Mangwende rambled on, criticizing the United States, and the Americans became increasingly uncomfortable. Finally it was more than they could stand, and Jimmy Carter led the way out of the reception room, followed by a good number of the guests. So absorbed was Mangwende in his text that he did not notice and, when he had finished, he raised his glass to propose a toast to the United States, only to find that all its citizens had walked out in disgust. I remember him looking around, disconsolate.

I went up to Jimmy Carter afterwards and apologized, as a Zimbabwean, for the tenor of the speech, which I said was quite beyond the pale of normal diplomatic niceties. But he was a seasoned politician who took such incidents in his stride.

The ZPC established many contacts with the principal British media: *The Times*, the *Daily Telegraph*, the *Daily Express*, the *Guardian* and, of course, the BBC. At *The Times* I became acquainted in particular with the editor, Charles Douglas-Home, who became a close personal friend and we were saddened by his untimely death in 1985.

I also got to know Bill Deedes, later Lord Deedes, the famous editor of the *Daily Telegraph*, who died in 2007 at the age of 93. He was the only man to have been at different times a member of the British Cabinet and the editor of a national newspaper. His contacts were of enormous value to us. On a few occasions, at both *The Times* and the *Telegraph*, David Lewis and I were able to sit in on the evening editorial conference when the format and content of the paper going to bed later that night was discussed and finalized.

Bill Deedes was a regular visitor to South Africa, and he came to Rhodesia from time to time. He was therefore better able to write about the current situation in the country and was clearly fascinated by politics in Southern Africa.

Following Harold Macmillan's famous 'Winds of Change' speech in Cape Town in 1960, countries throughout Africa were being granted their independence. Britain was increasingly aware of the continent's need for people who had an understanding of true parliamentary democracy to form the basis of sound civil service and administration. Deedes visited East Africa to deliver a series of lectures on the ways of Westminster and Whitehall. He said that in retrospect it was a 'frivolous episode', writing in the *Daily Telegraph* that:

> To spend three weeks discussing constitutional problems with members of two new legislatures brings no answer to any local difficulty, but it suggests one or two fundamental issues which will in the longer run count for much. At the head of a long list stands the civil service administration and financial responsibility and they are interrelated. We have laid tremendous stress on the Westminster model throughout Africa's new legislatures and have excited Africans with romantic hazy notions about it.

At that time there were two schools of thought. On the one hand, there were those who believed that the introduction of Westminster-style government overrode centuries of African custom and governance. Many people thought this was patronizing since it assumed that their type of governance was inferior to the Westminster model. In the 1800s, Africa was colonized by Britain, France, Germany and Portugal, all with different ideas on how to run their new colonies.

In 1920 Lord Balfour, former British prime minister (1902-1905) and foreign secretary (1916-1919), wrote an essay on this subject, questioning the policies that should be followed. It is so perceptive that I it feel merits an extensive quotation:

> If we would find the true basis of the long-drawn process which has gradually converted medieval monarchy into a modern democracy, the process by which so much has been changed and so little destroyed, we must study temperament and character rather than intellect and theory. This is a truth which those who recommend the wholesale adoption of the British institutions in strange lands might remember

with advantage. Such an experiment can hardly be without its dangers. Constitutions are easily copied; temperaments are not; and if it should happen that the borrowed constitution and the native temperament fail to correspond, the misfit may have serious results. It matters little what other gifts a people may possess if they are wanting in those which, from this point of view, are of most importance; if, for example, they have no capacity for grading their loyalties as well as for being moved by them; if they have no natural inclination to liberty and no natural respect for law; if they lack good humour and tolerate foul play; if they know not how to compromise or when; if they have not that distrust of extreme conclusions which is sometimes misdescribed as want of logic; if corruption does not repel them; and if their divisions tend to be either too numerous or too profound, the successful working of British Institutions may be difficult or impossible.

Until Rupert Murdoch, an Australian, bought *The Times* in 1981, London newspapers were printed on hot-metal presses, which required many more men than modern, automated equipment. The stand-off in 1986/87 with the unions over the introduction of the latter resulted in *The Times* being unable to replace its outmoded equipment because modernizing would lead to job losses. There were days when they were unable to print a newspaper at all. Indeed the situation became so bad that *The Times* actually ceased publication for a year and dismissed their entire workforce. During that time they acquired a huge warehouse on the Thames at Wapping and, bit by bit, installed a modern automated newspaper-printing press, which gave them the ability to reduce costs and be less subject to the whims, constant work stoppages and wild-cat strikes of the trade unions. It is difficult to imagine how they managed to do this undetected, but they did.

Once the equipment was assembled, the new *Times* team was reassembled and, under the noses of the trade unions, moved into Wapping. The following day *The Times* was printed in Wapping, for the first time in a year, much to the fury of the unions. The area was picketed and there was some violence. But *The Times* was now able to use the latest technology, without interference from the shop stewards.

I was in London shortly after the move and had a meeting scheduled with Peter Stothard of *The Times*. He explained that my taxi would drop me outside the picket line and that I should simply walk straight through the line to the security officer inside where I would be received and taken into the building. On arrival, I set off on my journey through the picket line, a new experience. There was plenty of abuse and a lot of four-letter words, which I acknowledged with a cheerful wave, but I was not molested, went inside and had my meetings.

One of these meetings was with a journalist who was investigating Tiny Rowland and Lonrho, which at that time was highly relevant. The British government had investigated Rowland and his activities and issued a report about his business behaviour. Tiny Rowland was interned (with Krishna Menon) on the Isle of Man during the war because of his part-German parentage. On his release he began developing his empire in Africa, concentrating it in Rhodesia, where he started farming at Hartley. He bought out a group of farmers near Norton who were the Mercedes agents and took over the franchise himself. (The story of the Rowland empire is well documented by Tom Bower, who wrote Rowland's unauthorized biography.*)

I was amused to read how the press saw me. In London, Frederick Cleary of *The Times* wrote a Business Diary profile on 18 February, 1980:

C. G. Tracey, Rhodesian ubiquitous

.... Of Tracey, Dr Isaac Samuriwo, a Salisbury black businessman and senator in the last parliament, said, 'Through his efforts, many whites have learned that there were blacks of the highest calibre in any field. We need people like C. G. Tracey in the new state of Zimbabwe ... people who are dedicated to the cause of unity and who know no colour bar.'

... Although firmly apolitical, Tracey was drawn unofficially more into the shadowy world of diplomacy as successive Rhodesian governments struggled vainly to reach a political settlement.

Regarded as a man who could be trusted implicitly, and with his vast network of contacts, he was soon to be seen in Whitehall, in Washington, in Paris. His lean, angular figure flitted from continent to continent and like some restless shadow he popped up in the homes and offices of some of the most important and famous people in the western world.

The travel restrictions imposed on Rhodesians after UDI seemed rarely to hinder this subtropical Kissinger. Last year he

*Tom Bower, *Tiny Rowland: A Rebel Tycoon* (London: Heinemann, 1993).

visited Britain and Europe seven times as well as making side trips to America and the far East.

'It was tragic when in 1965 UDI came and sanctions were imposed,' Tracey said. 'I never agreed with UDI but equally I considered sanctions to be immoral. Once UDI had taken place, I felt that it was imperative that all of us should defend our country to the best of our ability, regardless of our political beliefs.'

I was delighted to read the following, from an article in the Harare *Sunday Mail* of 27 November 1983, by Tendayi Kumbula:

Tracey: A human dynamo with flair for innovation
Mr Edward Padya, one of the first two blacks ever appointed to the Cotton Marketing Board in 1978 at Mr Tracey's insistence, said the other day, 'He is a very good person. He battled the colonial regime to get black representation on the Cotton Marketing Board. Although it was opposed for a long time he finally succeeded and so Mr Axon Gumbo and I were appointed.

In the early meetings he helped us a lot, even translating the proceedings into Shona for us so we could keep up with the discussions. In short I can say we have lost a man [on retirement] who has a great love for Africans. He did a lot for us and for other African farmers, including taking some of us outside Zimbabwe so we could see what other people did with the cotton they bought from us.

The greatest compliment paid to me was by someone who said I was a true patriot. So my love of my country is the right way, I suppose, of describing overall what motivates me. I happen to think that this is the best country there is, and I am determined to try and keep it this way for all people, black and white.

If the Zimbabwe Promotion Council enabled me to travel and promote the country at various forums, so did my visits to the World Economic Forum (WEF) in Davos, Switzerland. The WEF, is a non-profit, private-sector organization founded in 1971 by Dr Klaus Schwab in Zurich. Its members include businessmen, industrialists, political leaders and journalists from most industrial and industrializing countries of the world, but generally not those with strong communist leanings, though in 2006 the

WEF opened offices in Beijing. Their annual general meeting is held in the first week of January in the mountain resort of Davos and provides a remarkable forum for businessmen and -women to meet and exchange ideas. Over the years of my attendance, I made valuable contacts, some of whom we persuaded to visit Zimbabwe. For example, the outstanding young WEF operations director, Fred Sicre, visited the country in 1989. He asked if I could act as an informal link between our private sector and the WEF in order to interest people in attending their AGM, so Zimbabwe's participation at the forum grew.

The Forum attracted such world leaders as Henry Kissinger, Prince Sadruddin Aga Khan, who was the director of the United Nations High Commission for Refugees from 1966 to 1978, Nelson Mandela, F.W. de Klerk, and, within a month of the break-up of the Soviet Union, the newly elected presidents of the five new Russian republics.

I attended these meetings for seven or eight years. It was appreciated that I could generate further involvement and interest, not only in Zimbabwe but also in South Africa, once it was under majority rule. On one occasion a speaker had let them down and at the last moment they asked me to chair one of the food and agriculture sessions.

The WEF often provided a place where leaders of different persuasions could meet on neutral territory in a relaxed manner. After Nelson Mandela's release from prison, the WEF convened a special session at their annual 1992 meeting between Mandela, the future president of South Africa, Dr F.W. de Klerk, then president of South Africa, and Mangosuthu Buthelezi, head of the Inkatha Freedom Party. This session was chaired by Dr Schwab himself. He drew lots as to which of the three statesmen should speak first. All three speakers received a very good response with much applause and many questions. It was at that meeting that I first met Nelson Mandela, as well as Tito Mboweni, who was to become the first governor of the Reserve Bank in independent South Africa, and Trevor Manuel, who became Minister of Finance.

On one occasion, just before Nelson Mandela became president of South Africa, our WEF team from Zimbabwe arranged an informal party in Johannesburg and persuaded, among others, very right-wing members of the South African Nationalist Party to meet Buthelezi, the Zimbabweans and others. Our team of black and white helped to break down long-standing barriers and the party went on until late that night. The next day an ultra-right-wing MP from the SASOL constituency breakfasted with one of the ANC leaders. They had never met before and the discussion was cordial.

When South Africa had once more received international recognition, the WEF held a Southern African regional conference every year, with the venue in Harare on one occasion.

At the final dinner of a WEF South African regional meeting I was seated next to Dr Dawie de Villiers, then Minister of Information in the South African government. I asked him if the following story was true and he confirmed that it was.

Dawie de Villiers was a predikant or preacher in the Dutch Reformed Church, but he was also a brilliant rugby player and in 1969 he captained the last Springbok side to tour Great Britain before those tours were banned for political reasons. The president of the English Rugby Board then was Lord Wakefield, an immensely rich businessman, one of whose primary interests was the Castrol oil group. The South Africans were due to play a match at York, not far from Lord Wakefield's estate, so he invited the entire squad to visit Wakefield Castle, tour the stately home and lunch with him.

After a tour of the castle and pre-lunch cocktails, a butler appeared at the great doors to announce that luncheon was served. De Villiers and Lord Wakefield headed the procession. They were seated at a long refectory table able to accommodate all the guests. When de Villiers's saw the beautiful family silver with the cut glass and napery at each place, he sincerely hoped that a member of the squad might not slip a bit of Wakefield silver into his pocket as a memento, as some of his players were better versed in rugby than in social etiquette. Lord Wakefield welcomed the gathering and said that as Dawie de Villiers was a man of the cloth he would ask him to say the grace.

De Villiers was a quick fly-half and had learnt to think fast on his feet. He put his hands together and gave the grace in Afrikaans, part of which when translated read, 'If any member of our squad is discovered lifting valuables from the table, he will be sent home tomorrow.' Then with a loud amen they all sat down. But there was one Englishman present, who was fluent in Afrikaans, and he enjoyed the benediction as much as anyone.

– 18 –

Our Family

Our three daughters • More travels and Wendy's balloon trip •
A Midsummer Night's Dream • Martin and Jill • Bridget • Wendy's death

Our first daughter, Elizabeth Bridget, was born in 1948 on the night of an enormous storm. The roads and rivers were flooded and we only just got to the hospital in Gatooma on time. She was a very pretty little girl and showed early promise of being bright and studious. At the age of three and a half I fitted her out in jodhpurs and a minute hard riding hat, and she would ride out with me around the farm. On her fourth birthday we gave her a Jersey heifer and from then on she took great interest in the dairy and loved the cows, learning all their pedigrees and familiarizing herself with their milk production. When her cousins, the twins, who were a year older, started their correspondence course at the age of six, Liza was very envious and wanted to start learning as well. She badgered Wendy to teach her, with the result that when Liza did eventually start at Highlands Junior School she was immediately promoted to the class above her age group. She also loved the horses and later on when we developed the stud took a very active interest in racing.

Diana Alice was born three years later in 1951. My mother, Eve, soon nicknamed her Dido, a name which has stuck to this day. Initially she was much quieter and more reserved. She loved nature, plants, flowers and animals, and was always rescuing small orphan animals that she collected from around the farmyard and then hand-reared. We had a succession of wild baby rabbits, orphan kittens, baby birds and lizards in the house. At one stage Wendy had to put up with a clutch of ducklings in her best spare room. Dido even collected a large number of the big land snails, painting numbers on their shells for identification purposes. She loved to dance and sing and dress up, a passion which later developed into her involvement with theatre and music. She started having very definite ideas about her clothes and appearance when very young and started to make her own clothes.

246

Our youngest daughter, Caroline Margaret, was born in 1955. She was a quaint little girl with enormous eyes, a snub nose covered in freckles and brown curly hair. Caroline was very like Wendy, always kind and patient, with a good sense of humour. She followed in her mother's footsteps and studied nursing at Addenbrooke's hospital in Cambridge.

Caroline was more interested in sheep and was always rescuing and rearing orphan lambs. She had piano lessons up to Grade 8 and then went on to study the organ at the Salisbury cathedral. There she discovered a litter of starving abandoned kittens which she rescued and brought back to Handley Cross. One of the kittens was decidedly odd with squint eyes and couldn't walk in a straight line. She named this peculiar kitten after her organ teacher, an eminent and well- respected musician.

Caroline and Liza shared their love of riding and would ride out on the farm together, much to Dido's envy. Dido was scared of horses after experiencing a bad riding accident when she was only four; she never really regained her confidence after that. Liza and Caroline both took riding lessons at school and went on pony camps in the holidays.

The three girls ran wild round the farm, always barefoot and rather scruffy but having a wonderful time helping at the dairy with the cream and cheese making, feeding the calves, preparing the animals for the Salisbury Agricultural Show, collecting the eggs, riding on the tractors, and swimming in the reservoirs. It was hard work getting their feet clean and respectable for school. Wendy never dressed them in white or pale colours because their clothes became irreparably stained with the red Chakari mud.

We encouraged the girls to take a string of their animals to the agricultural shows, and they spent happy afternoons preparing the animals for the show ring. They trained the cattle to walk properly on halters and show themselves to advantage. The cows and pigs were scrubbed with a special mixture of blue soap and Reckitt's blue, boiled up in an enormous pot on the old wood stove. Hooves and horns were polished with linseed oil, and tails washed, plaited and tied up in plastic bags which would be removed minutes before they went into the show ring. We all camped at the showgrounds in the cattle truck next to the cattle lines for Show Week.

Wendy would make each of the girls a new dress for the Opening and cattle parade. Dido remembers with particular affection a white dress with pink spots that she wanted repeated year after year. This was a highlight of the year, and the girls would get wildly excited about the prospects of candy floss, ice cream and Luna Park. As they grew older this anticipation included all the young men they might meet from Gwebi agricultural college or the mounted police display.

Liza grew up to be fairly academic. She studied at the University of Zimbabwe and later became a literature teacher. At the age of sixty she has just embarked on a doctoral thesis. She and her husband moved away to Johannesburg in the early 1980s.

Caroline continued her nursing and music and often played in church. She also left the country in the 1980s and moved to Australia.

Dido is the only daughter left in this country. She married and initially she and her husband were farming near Macheke, where she managed my herd of Charolais cattle. This was during the bush war of the 1970s. One moonlit night, in the early hours, machine gun fire was heard from the paddock below the house. The guerrillas had shot twenty young Charolais bulls being prepared for the bull sales. They fired at random and killed twelve bulls; four were so badly injured that they had to be put down. The short stretch of road from the farm to the main road was land-mined periodically.

When Diana's first baby, Catherine, was born, the risk was too great to continue and they abandoned the farm and moved into Harare. Diana started a garden nursery, growing the plants she had always loved.

Wendy and I enjoyed our travels to far-away places, and in 1997 we decided to ask ten friends to come with us to the Antarctic on a small ship, the *World Discoverer*, which carried 100 passengers. The ship followed the route of Captain Robert Scott, and it was the most phenomenal journey from the Falkland Islands right down to the Antarctic continent. We went on land and walked amongst a huge number of animals and birds. Wendy and I thought it was the best trip we had ever made. We went through the Antarctic Circle and finished up eventually on the Chilean islands.

Eighteen months later we went on a similar trip to the Arctic, in the Arctic summer. We started from Gnome with the same group of friends, and travelled up through the Arctic Circle and across the top of the world to the Russian mainland, and then down the Aleutian Islands and Kodiac Island, where the bears were monstrously large.

As a surprise for Wendy on her seventieth birthday, we hired a magnificent hot-air balloon. It was a complete surprise, and Wendy could not believe her eyes when she woke up in the morning. There below the house was a huge balloon being filled with air. Of course, all work on the farm came to a standstill. We drifted over Mount Lothian and neighbouring farms for a couple of hours before we ran out of puff and had to land.

The hot-air balloon is blown up on the farm for Wendy's seventieth birthday trip.

Wendy and I were to celebrate our golden wedding anniversary in 1996. The following is what my grand-daughter, Catherine de Swardt, wrote about this unforgettable occasion.

Ever since C.G. and Wendy built the house and stunning water gardens at Mount Lothian, they had held many glorious candle-lit dinners in the gardens, sometimes on the lawns and sometimes under marquees, with the Harare Male Voice Choir enchanting the guests with moonlit choruses, occasionally interrupted by the noisy Hawaiian geese and crowned cranes. As 1996 dawned, so did the prospect of C.G. and Wendy's golden wedding anniversary, and as a family we decided to extend Mount Lothian's repertoire and move from sea shanties to Shakespeare.

We felt that Shakespeare's wedding play, *A Midsummer Night's Dream*, would be ideal, as its magical world of fairies and forests could easily be set in the creeper-clad water-gardens at Mount Lothian. We wanted to do a professional production and so decided that the play should run for five nights, one night being a gala performance with almost a banquet to celebrate C.G. and Wendy's golden wedding anniversary, and the other four nights being open to the public. The funds generated from the four public nights could be used to cover the costs of producing a professional play with proper sound and lighting design.

The de Swardt family had long been involved with the world of dramatics in Harare and so they, as producers, gathered together a group of Zimbabwean actors who were excited by the idea of performing an outdoor Shakespeare in such a lovely setting. The experienced director and theatre critic, Dr Susan Hains, agreed to direct the play and rehearsals began in June 1996.

Actors from the theatre group Over the Edge, which in the next decade was to become Zimbabwe's best-known professional company, kindly agreed to take on the comic roles of the rude mechanicals. Bottom was played by Wina [Lucian] Msamati, who is now a professional actor in London (his recent appearance alongside Helen Mirren at the National Theatre bears testament to his talent). Every night he brought the house down with his hilarious portrayal of one of Shakespeare's best-loved characters. Shaheen Jassat played Peter Quince with great comic skill, and we were all very sad when Shaheen tragically lost his life in a car accident a few years later. Puck was played by Darren Mercer, a drama student and gymnast, who used his agile physical skills to somersault out of trees and up flowery banks. Titania was played by Marimba Wegemershaus, and Oberon by C.G.'s grandson, Nick de Swardt (the only member of the de Swardt family to take a speaking part). There is not space to name all who were involved, but the group worked tirelessly to produce a play that culminated in great success and enjoyment for all.

Dido, C.G.'s daughter, was the producer. It was her initial idea and she was the visionary for the play. She provided the energy and infectious enthusiasm for those performances, which are still talked about today. She designed the costumes and ensured the gardens captured the magic of the following words:

I know a bank where the wild thyme blows
Where oxlips and the nodding violet grows,
Quite over-canopied with luscious woodbine,
With sweet musk-roses, and with eglantine;
There sleeps Titania sometime of the night,
Lull'd in these flowers with dances and delight...
A Midsummer-Night's Dream (II. i. 249–54)

Dido also worked tirelessly to organize rehearsals, actors, drivers, meals and technical staff, and without her the whole play might never have come off.

To enable the public to enjoy the Mount Lothian experience to the full, we decided to emulate the Glyndebourne experience from Britain. The ticket price included a picnic hamper with delicacies such as smoked salmon and French cheeses, and the patrons were invited to arrive an hour before the play started to collect their hampers and buy a bottle of wine, put a rug down on the lawn and enjoy their sunset picnic in the splendour of the gardens, followed by an almost-full moon. The Mount Lothian gardens overlooked the game park and so, in addition to the swans and water gardens, patrons saw the zebra, giraffe and baby elephants coming down from the kopje to graze in the golden evening light.

Once darkness had set in, the evening's performance was announced by a loud bang and a spotlight suddenly illuminating Puck atop a tree on one of the islands. He asked the guests to move down to the lower terraces where the play was about to begin. The audience sat on stands facing the terraced stage, and between them and the actors were the moonlit waters of Goose Pond, with a pair of nesting white mute swans who gracefully and silently glided on the water during the play.

This sometimes became a bit hair-raising for poor Darren (Puck), as he had to deliver some of his lines from a rock in the pond which the swans very much regarded as their territory, and they occasionally rushed at him in a very threatening manner. Luckily Darren was a gymnast and so he was able to remain in character and elegantly remove himself with a quick back-flip – and the audience never knew the difference.

Whilst the play may not have been a technically perfect Stratford-on- Avon rendition of Shakespeare, the many letters we received afterwards tell of its success. It was the perfect way to celebrate fifty years of marriage.

Following the fun and success of *A Midsummer Night's Dream*, we had hoped to stage *The Tempest* in the same setting a couple of years later. However, sadly, events in Zimbabwe overtook us and the farm was seized before we could make these dreams a reality.

Richard Winkfield, in his column 'Bottom Line' in *The Farmer* magazine, wrote about our joint eightieth birthday party in Diana's garden.

> The week before, ... we together with another seventy invited guests went to the combined eightieth birthday celebration of an amazing couple who have probably contributed more to the past fifty years of this country's agriculture than all our politicians, past and present, put together. It was a celebration to be remembered, put on by their loving family with all the graces and values of a society which goes back in history many hundreds of years. We came away feeling proud and humble and thankful for civilized, God-fearing and ordered lives which we all so desperately nurture.

At the beginning of the farm invasions, my brother Martin and my sister-in-law Jill were severely assaulted in bed in the middle of the night at their farm near Chakari. Neighbours were quick to help. An emergency ambulance was sent from Harare to the Kadoma hospital and neighbours helped take Jill and Martin to the hospital in Kadoma. Jill died from her head injuries on the way to Harare. My brother survived, but his skull was fractured.

Jill's death brought into focus the fact that even people who had done so much for the indigenous population in their area were not spared. The Tawstock farm school had been built by Martin and Jill at no cost to government. The school could take 400 pupils, and government paid the teachers, who were supervised by Martin and Jill. They put a lot of money from farm profits into providing what was necessary to keep the school running properly. They also had one of the very early pension schemes.

One day in 2008, my sister Bridget, then aged 82, was attacked at lunchtime in her small cottage immediately adjacent to her daughter's house. The house and grounds were electrically protected, with their dogs inside. The first action of the thugs had been to throw poisoned meat over the wall and both Bridget's beloved dogs eventually died. Ten days later, with the dogs out of the way, they cut the security fence and came in. Bridget was reading quietly and was taken by surprise, beaten up and tied up with telephone wire. No bones were broken but her face was pretty smashed up. Her son-in-law was in the main house, but she could not call him. Her hands were tied, but after a while she managed to untie one of the knots with her teeth and then got help, quite an achievement for an 82-year-old.

Plans were advanced for Bridget to join her son and daughter in Australia and New Zealand, and she left as soon as she was fit to travel. Bridget had been a very active member of the Enterprise farming community and known as an excellent farmer in her own right. She has done so much work over the past few years in town, helping care for old people with food parcels.

Wendy and I were married for a splendid 58 years. After a tempestuous meeting with our war vets on 20 January 2005, she showed her despondency about the near impossibility of getting the farm back, and we were very depressed. In the car coming home, she questioned how long we could go on with stress and strain and threats. We went to bed earlier than usual that evening, and in the early hours she awoke and, as was our custom, made a pot of tea. She poured out a cup for me and was pouring out her own when she was stricken with a major heart attack and died on the spot. Unexpected, very sudden and an indication of the trauma we had been forced to endure.

There was a wonderful funeral service in the Presbyterian Church on the Enterprise Road, and I was able to have all three daughters, Elizabeth, Diana and Caroline, with me – Elizabeth from South Africa and Caroline from Australia, while Diana lives in Harare. All our grandchildren managed to travel to Zimbabwe for the funeral, from America, South Africa, Australia and the United Kingdom. David Lewis gave a short eulogy and then, one by one, most of the grandchildren made their contribution to a much-loved grandmother.

I was able to make my own acknowledgement and goodbye at the end. Because Wendy loved flowers, we asked people to bring flowers, and there was a huge bank of gorgeous blooms, which Wendy would have so loved, in the church. A friend sang 'I'll walk beside you', which was beautiful. Our relationship was typified by that old love song.

A month before Wendy died, we had discussed where our ashes should be scattered, so that whoever went first would know the other's wishes. We agreed that the huge granite kopje on which our lovely big dam is anchored and where we had the most wonderful picnics and braais on the edge of the water would be the best place. But we were prevented from going to the farm because of the threats of violence by the settlers.

Wendy's ashes are still in a cardboard box in a chest of drawers and we have agreed on an alternative, to spread them at Boulders Beach near Simonstown in the Cape, where many of our family used to have breakfast picnics at the edge of the sea among those boulders. We had bought a lovely old house on the main road fifty metres from the beach and tried to get down a couple of times a year.

Nobody could have had a better helpmate, with such love and tolerance, so prepared to enter into every new venture and to play a far greater role than most farmers' wives would ever have done. She was understanding of my work on cotton, tobacco and the Promotion Council, and other matters which took me away frequently. She was always in charge of the Jerseys, the poultry, the horses and the farm accounts.

Our three daughters are, we think, a great credit to Wendy's influence in bringing them up. All of them are different in their own careers, but all are successful and we have nine grandchildren: seven boys and two girls.

Wendy, in her later years.

– 19 –

Farming on Mount Lothian

Buying Mount Lothian • A new dam and a new house
• Seed maize • Pigs • Chrysanthemum flowers for export
• Producing chrysanthemum slips • Onions • Road maintenance
• Students' hostel • Eucalyptus • Vegetables • Nicholas joins us

In 1983 the sale of Handley Cross was imminent and at the same time we had the opportunity to buy Mount Lothian, in the Enterprise valley, 20 kilometres from Harare. We bought Mount Lothian before we had finalized the Handley Cross sale, which actually fell through, and so for that season we were farming both farms, which were 100 miles apart. The following year we concluded the Handley Cross sale and reinvested heavily into Mount Lothian.

It wasn't an easy decision to move, because a farm is a living, growing thing, and we sold Handley Cross soon after the major irrigation schemes outlined in Chapter 2 had been commissioned. The cropping programme was very well planned and balanced and, with adequate water after the construction of the Suri Suri dam, production was immense. It was very sad to sell the farm, and I remember Wendy crying all the way into town when we finally left, but it was the right decision for us.

We invested the proceeds into buying Mount Lothian, a smaller property of 550 hectares, very fertile and well watered but under utilized. We were able to develop its full irrigation potential – and it was only half an hour away from my company offices in the city.

Mount Lothian has extremely good, deep, red soil, reliable rainfall, and the advantage of being close to Harare. It was only partly developed, with two small dams and a pump

Zig Pikor, from whom we bought the farm, was a Polish lawyer who had escaped when the Germans invaded Poland and worked his way down through the Balkans to Turkey and eventually to Cairo and Britain, where he joined the Polish Free Forces. He married a Scottish girl, Margaret, and after the war they emigrated to Rhodesia and bought Mount Lothian.

out of the Mbvunzi River with portable aluminium pipelines. In our first year, we concentrated on workers' houses, tractor sheds and workshops, and the construction of sties for a thousand pigs. We had bought the entire company through a share transaction, which included all the equipment and a very fine herd of Jersey cattle, one of the best in the country. However, we did not wish to run a dairy, so we decided to concentrate on developing the irrigation potential. A couple of months after the purchase, we held an auction sale of all the cows, which went a long way towards funding the farm and the irrigation. Ignatius Mangombe, our general manager on Handley Cross, and I alternated between the two farms.

During the second year, John Hart, a water engineer, surveyed the catchment area and calculated the amount of water that would run off and the area of land it could irrigate. At the eastern end of the farm was an ideal site for a dam, which we built, and we were then able to store 1,650 megalitres of water. One side of the dam wall abutted on an enormous granite outcrop, on to which we could construct a spillway, which was a great saving because flood water was able to spill down the granite back into the river without causing erosion.

Simultaneously we contracted the irrigation firm Doré and Pitt to plan the water reticulation for the arable part of the farm, 240 hectares. Another contractor did the piping trench excavation. We bought the piping from Turnall in Bulawayo, which entailed a huge road haulage exercise.

Zig Pikor, having once been a refugee, had been reluctant to spend much capital on building a house. He had never improved his original, simple, prefabricated small house made of asbestos sheeting. Wendy and I lived in that house for the first couple of years. Once our farm priorities had been completed, we set about designing, with an architect, the house we had always wanted. We chose a site, near the prefab house, on a ridge of land that protruded into the river valley. It sloped steeply to east and to west and we built the house on that spur, with wonderful views down the valley and across the dam.

We had brought from Handley Cross a 'pug-mill', used to puddle the clay to make bricks. All the bricks for the house were made and kiln-burnt on the farm. We had a small team of building contractors, initially under the care of the architect, but when he became ill we had to finish the construction ourselves.

We had excellent contacts with the building trade, particularly with the Costain team who had built the Tobacco Sales Floor. These workers were keen to earn extra money, and we used to collect them on a Friday evening

– carpenters, plasterers, plumbers and electricians. They would work over the weekend at an attractive rate and be taken back into town on Sunday evening. It was a good mutual arrangement and the work continued apace and we were able to occupy the house shortly before the rains set in.

At the same time we started construction of the ponds around the house and on the slopes on either side for our duck and geese collection. The whole of the water-garden area and the house was enclosed in a high security fence, to keep out predators. They were always our biggest problems – wild cats and pythons, particularly. The wild cats were difficult to control, but we built a simple python trap, like a fish trap. The python would enter through a tapering funnel, but could not find his way out. The next morning we would take him twenty kilometres away and leave him in the bush. This was because we had been advised that a python will find his way home from almost that distance.

It is possible to mark a python so that, if it does come back, you can see whether you have caught a new one or a previous inhabitant who has returned. On the underside of the python surrounding the vent is a small area which is covered with scales, not skin. With a pair of nail scissors you can clip off a few scales around the vent. Those scales will never grow again, so it is a good way of identification. However, we lost a lot of birds to pythons over the years until we got the trapping perfected.

The house on Mount Lothian, surrounded by lovely trees
and overlooking the two dams and the game park.

When we bought Mount Lothian, the farm had a contract with Willards, manufacturers of potato crisps, which we were able to maintain. We grew a red-skinned variety of potato called Pimpernel, which was ideal for crisps because it had a very low moisture content, a high solid content, and was economical in its absorption of fat in the cooking process. It was one of the most profitable enterprises on Mount Lothian.

We continued with maize production but reduced the area, as a lot of green maize had previously been used to make silage for winter feed for the dairy herd, which by now had been sold. So that area was then put under seed maize. The rest of the arable land was put under commercial maize, which we continued to grow for the workers and for the pig herd.

After 1943, seed maize had become a major part of our farming on Handley Cross. Now on Mount Lothian we used an American seed maize grading system which we had built on Handley Cross thirty years earlier. We moved the equipment successfully to Mount Lothian, and it was still functioning perfectly when we were evicted. It was a three-tier rotary grader which passed the seed maize through different-sized screens from tromell to tromell, so that when the grain had reached the last screen it had been sorted into nine grades of depth – whether thick, round or flat kernels – with very small variations of $^{14}/_{64}$ of an inch. (We bought the grader from America and this was the measurement system used at the time.)

The cobs were reaped by hand direct into tip trailers and brought to the concrete standing area, where they went on to a conveyor for sorting and the removal of any diseased cobs, and were then hand-shelled by women workers; we hand-shelled to ensure that there was no chipping. The maize then went into a vertical elevator up to the top screen in the grader. Later we used a gentler sheller, which helped to eliminate any of the few chips which had got into earlier samples.

Then, grade by grade, the seed was put into an aspirator which removed any light material or fluff, and then it went straight into the seed maize dressing unit where anti-fungal and insecticide chemicals were applied. The final product came out at the other end, and the maize was weighed into 25 kg bags ready for inspection by the Seed Maize official inspector. They were very strict and we had to achieve a very high standard. The samples were then sent to the laboratory for germination tests, and finally the seed maize certification labels were added and the seed could be distributed. This quality of grading enabled us to sell a very uniform product which was necessary for the new vacuum Monocem seed planters. These planters dropped each seed with precisely the same interval in the line, which ensured the optimum plant population per hectare.

A few years ago Mount Lothian was runner up in the Seed Maize Grower of the Year competition, which was judged on all aspects of our production through the whole season from planting, ensuring correct plant population per hectare, through de-tasselling, reaping, shelling, grading and treating. We competed in a field of 80 growers.

The hybridization process required two inbred strains, which were planted at a ratio of three to one. The pollen parent was allowed to keep its tassel to produce the pollen to fertilize the silks on the cob parent. The other three had their tassels removed before they started to shed pollen, so that their cobs could only have been fertilized by the other parent. The pollen parents on maturity were removed so that there were no cobs from them to contaminate the cobs from the other three lines. De-tasselling was a strenuous job with many hundreds of thousands of plants having their tassels removed manually. If a careless worker left some tassels, the inspectors would destroy the plants around the offending one. A bad grower could have his whole crop condemned because many of the cobs would not be true hybrids. We were meticulous on this matter and proud of our high standard.

We had grown seed maize for a very long time. I am sorry that after our eviction, the new farmers did not do this highly demanding job sufficiently well and some of their crops were condemned. The farm now produces no seed maize.

A centre pivot irrigation system is far more efficient and labour-saving than movable surface aluminium piping, and we invested in two 30-hectare centre pivots. It was beautiful American equipment, and we were able to tap the water supply from the existing underground reticulation. The sprinkler pipeline extended from the centre pump base and travelled in a circle, taking eight to ten hours to complete a full circle. A hydraulic pump with one pump on each of the six towers powered the supporting wheels, which moved in a radius from the pump base. The power was so adjusted that each of the tyres moved at the correct speed to keep the overhead irrigation line straight. The whole system was so graduated that the last sprinkler on the radius applied exactly the same amount of water as the first, remembering that the whole pivot line covered a circle. We were able to put on 50 millimetres of water in a ten-hour cycle.

The irrigation was so uniform that the crops were also uniform. This system was a great success, much better than ordinary overhead irrigation, and it required only one man on duty. The other pivot, bigger, completed its circle in just under three days and then the whole pipeline was towed to the next pumping position. So we could do 60 hectares plus 30 hectares in a six-day cycle, giving a total potential of 90 hectares with our two units.

We had been running about 350 sows at Handley Cross. To match the amount of feed grain we could produce, we decided to reduce the herd size to 100. As the pigsties were built, the pedigree sows were moved up from Handley Cross. They were all in the Stud Book and we started to sell fully tested breeding stock from Mount Lothian instead of from Handley Cross. After about six months we had filled the Mount Lothian capacity and the remainder of the Handley Cross herd was taken over by the new owners.

On Handley Cross, for many years we had been selling progeny-tested stock and we continued to do this, all 100 sows being in the programme. Our Large Whites and our Landrace families, supplemented by a couple of imported gilts from Britain and from Canada, provided the basis for the new infusion of genetics into our herd. We started a small herd of the American 'Duroc' breed. They were quick-growing and extremely lean and, when crossed with the white breeds, a top-quality carcass was achieved.

The Pig Industry Board, which for many years had had an excellent testing scheme for pedigree breeders, started to deteriorate and the results they produced were inconsistent and inadequate as a basis for breed

View of the farm with two of the dams,
showing our centre pivots growing certified seed wheat.

selection. We therefore built our own testing station with 120 single pig pens. We brought in an ultrasonic unit from Britain. By placing a probe along the middle back of the pig, it was possible to measure the depth of back fat on the live animal. The requirement was for a carcass with maximum lean meat (because the consumer doesn't want too much fat), which was genetically inherited. Each pen had its own small feed bin and each pig was fed separately and the food consumed was recorded, to give us a precise food conversion figure. Food conversion from meal to meat is also a heritable and very important characteristic. With our test results, we continued to improve the herd, whilst at the same time ensuring that the strength of legs was maintained. Pigs reared under intensive systems are prone to leg weakness.

We could now select animals which passed the minimum criteria for strength of leg set down by the British authorities. We used precisely the same system as theirs and therefore our results were comparable. We sent all our data back to the British national testing scheme. They fed this information into their computer program to set the levels at which a pig might be culled, and our results compared well with those from Britain. We were the only herd in Zimbabwe producing fully tested pigs.

We were able to use the very best bloodlines by semen importation from Canada, America, Britain, Sweden and Finland. Results from the different boars used for semen were put in the computer program and we were able to select those boars which would give us the best maintenance or correction influence on key characteristics. It was exciting to see the range of genetic material available. Our herd had its first public sale of breeding stock a couple of years after the pigs got to Mount Lothian.

In our plan to intensify production on what was a relatively small farm, we started to grow flowers for export. Helped by a technical horticulturalist representing English and Dutch distributors, who also advised a number of other growers in the country, we decided to concentrate on chrysanthemums because the capital cost was so much lower than for roses. Rose root-stock has to be bought from international rose-breeders who have put an immense amount of development work into each of the many different varieties, and the root-stock is excessively expensive initially. So we established our chrysanthemum mother-stock and constructed greenhouses. Initially we built what are called Colombian houses, with timber roof supports and timber trusses clad with polythene.

The start of the operation required us to bring mother-plant cuttings from Holland of the varieties for which there was the greatest demand, in different colours and with differently shaped flowers. Fashions in flowers change frequently and we always had to have available a stock of new mother plants which were likely to be the most fashionable in the next year or two, so that we could switch to the new market requirement without much delay. These cuttings or slips were rooted in sand with a root hormone, and after about thirty days, when they had developed a good root system, they were transplanted into the flower beds in the greenhouse, where they grew on, taking about ten weeks from planting to flowering.

After planting, one of our major challenges was the control of insects such as thrips and aphids. The inspections in Harare before dispatch and on arrival in Holland, London or America were very strict and, if they found a consignment with live insects, they simply dumped the whole box, after we had paid for the freight – a serious loss. So insect control by spraying insecticides was of prime importance. We had a regular schedule with different sprays for different insects and we scouted the growing plants continuously for insect eggs to ensure that they were destroyed before they hatched and caused damage, so that we would pass the phytosanitary requirements. Chemicals were one of our biggest expenses. The insect eggs also gave us forewarning of which species would be hatching next.

The initial mother stock continued to produce cuttings and so the whole process continued week by week.

Chrysanthemums for export to Holland and Sainsbury's in the UK.

Strath Brown, a man of many attributes, grew a lot of tobacco and also had a huge crocodile farm at the Victoria Falls which produced thousands of skins for export. He also had an engineering business producing tobacco-curing equipment and erecting greenhouses. At our considerable expense, his firm erected a modern, steel-framed greenhouse, and we built our pack shed, cold room and water-storage tanks next to it. Strath had been a main board director at Tobacco Sales Limited and was deeply involved with the construction of our great new tobacco sales floor.

After several years of satisfactory production, but with the inflation of air-freight costs, we found that the flower-stem weight/freight ratio was becoming so narrow that the margin was too fragile. While six or seven hundred rose stems would fit into a carton, we could put in only two hundred and forty chrysanthemum stems. So our transport cost per stem was much greater than for roses.

When I was in Holland and discussing alternative production, it was suggested that we should change from producing cut flowers to the production of slips. In Holland, the chrysanthemum industry is very well structured: one grower will confine himself only to the production of mother plants, from which the cuttings are taken to another farmer, who does nothing else but root the cuttings in small pots. He, in turn, sells on the rooted cuttings to the end flower-grower. There was an opening for us to supply slips for the first stage of this process. A huge number of slips could go into a flower carton and therefore the freight cost was relatively insignificant, and we gradually switched to the production of slips. The mother stock was sent out to us at intervals and our slips performed well in Holland. Wendy and I were very nervous at the responsibility of consistently supplying a high-quality slip on the precise schedule required and never mixing the different varieties. Had we failed and not delivered the slips, the planting programme in Holland would have suffered. The damage suffered downstream in the next two stages would have been immense.

After we had been sending slips for some months, I went to Holland to see how our they were doing and was taken into an enormous rooting house. Apprehensively, I asked where our slips were growing and the farmer said, 'Oh, they are down in there – you'll find them.' I searched throughout to see if I could find some that were perhaps of a different quality, but the whole house was uniform. I came back and said, 'I can't see them. 'Oh, no?' he said. 'They are about ten metres away from you and are just as good as the slips produced in Holland,' which was a relief. We were very proud of our slips.

Then Affretair became more and more unreliable and failed to meet shipping dates. If our slips left a day late and arrived in Holland a day late, the farmer who was going to pot them was also late, and the same applied to the end-producer of the blooms. With such a tightly planned regime, where precision was imperative, the people who did the rooting Stage 2 warned us that, although our slip quality was excellent, they would be unable to continue taking supplies from us if we could not guarantee precise delivery. That, of course, was what Affretair were unable to do, and the Dutch growers eventually cancelled our contract because of unreliable, inconsistent deliveries.

So, having stopped chrysanthemum flowers, gone into slip production and having now stopped that, we wondered what to do with the greenhouses. With a lot of help we ventured into the production of greenhouse sweet peppers and greenhouse tomatoes for local consumption and export to South Africa. We were able to continue the limited production of chrysanthemums for South Africa, but the prices were not good.

In order to ensure that the plants had precisely the right combination of nutrients – phosphate, nitrogen, potash and trace elements – we imported from an international irrigation company called Netafim in Israel a highly sophisticated drip-irrigation system which was computer-controlled. It was complicated and difficult to manage, but Nicholas de Swardt, who was with us at that time, mastered the technique. Fertilizers were mixed in two bulk tanks and then two computer-controlled pumps drew the two different nutrient solutions. The volume and blend was automatically adjusted by our Israeli computer-controller so that exactly the right mix of nutrients was continuously passed through the pipes and applied to the plants. It was lovely equipment and very expensive, but perhaps too advanced for our workers.

We continued with our high-class greenhouse tomatoes until we were evicted. Heavy yields could be obtained on some of the new varieties. Our large steel-framed greenhouse has stood the test of time. The Colombian houses needed attention continuously and, since our eviction, yet again high-tech management has been absent. Many of the greenhouses have collapsed.

The onion market in Zimbabwe has always been volatile. Most producers who have no proper drying or storage facilities dump their fresh crop on the market, which causes a glut, and prices are depressed. Once those fresh onions have been sold, shortages push the price up considerably.

I went to Australia and got much help from the CSIR, who have done good work on drying and curing onions, and also from Tasmania. We had a lot of help from Mrs Currah, who led a team of three scientists carrying out applied research on onions in Britain. We had much help from a huge fruit and vegetable farm in Ceres, South Africa, run by the du Toit brothers, who were growing several hundred hectares of onions and several thousand hectares of apples, pears and plums. One of their advisers came to check what we were doing and to fine-tune our system, which was largely a copy of their installations.

We decided that, if we were going to make onions a main part of our horticulture, we would have to tackle it professionally with the right equipment and buildings. To this end we built six barns for drying and storing onions, which could each take 400 pockets of 10 kg each. They had a false mesh floor a metre off the ground on which the onions were put in bulk. There was a high-tech installation on each barn that provided temperature and humidity control. The unit could either recirculate the warm air within the barn, or if it was too moist the air could be blown out into the atmosphere. The air volume was controlled electronically and the heat was provided with hot water pumped from the main boilers past every barn and through a radiator/heat-exchange and fan which blew the air into the barn. The somewhat cooler water then returned into the boiler for reheating.

It was eerie to see the control valve three metres up on the outside wall with its own baffle opening or closing depending on temperature and humidity inside. It would react to a variation of between 1 and 2 per cent difference in both temperature and humidity. Probes from the control equipment went into the barns and into the mass of onions, and the temperature and humidity readings were transmitted back. This provided very accurate measurements within the mass of onions.

Initially the onions had to be dried to remove the field moisture and surface moisture, which would take anything from five to eight days. Once the onions started to 'rustle', the drying process was sufficiently advanced to start the next process, curing the onions. The equipment was set with new parameters to ensure drying right through the onion mass. After this curing process, we were able to hold the onions in perfect condition for five months.

That equipment was designed by a young electronics engineer who hoped to apply it to tobacco curing. There would have been a huge market, but, given the situation between 2000 and 2003, he decided to leave the country and we were thrown back on our own resources for maintaining and operating the plant.

The venture operated well and, when Zimbabwe would otherwise have had to import onions because of the lack of supply here, Mount Lothian for some months filled the gap. The policy of doing the job fully and properly paid dividends.

In my 2002 farm report for the family trust, I remarked that the onion operation offered the brightest opportunity of all our diversification. We therefore expanded and went from 6 barns to 12 barns, and then on to 18 and finally to 24 barns. But then the invasions began and the last 9 barns were completed only at the time of our eviction; they have never had an onion in them and have never been used to this day. They could have supplied the country's requirement for several months of the year, and were capable of further expansion, with the consequent saving of foreign currency for onions imported from South Africa.

The international demand for paprika was growing and many farmers tried their hand. It was a crop that required strict attention, particularly in insect control and in the supplementary fertilizer that had to be applied at frequent intervals. Failure to do this resulted in the pods being either damaged or not of the lovely bright cherry colour which the market demanded. We were reasonably successful until the Zimbabwean/South African group who were buying paprika direct from farmers reneged on the payment terms: they had our paprika and we didn't have the payments. Endless attempts to litigate in South Africa came to nothing and ultimately our group never got paid for that crop by the merchants. This coincided with our eviction; the danger of marketing to South Africa was also such that many farmers discontinued growing the crop.

The gravel road, administered by the national Roads Department, running through Mount Lothian and linking the Shamva and Mutoko roads, had not been maintained for many years – culverts were blocked and drains were not functioning. The road was also the drain, and during the rainy season we frequently had to pull vehicles out of the mud with our caterpillar tractor. The Roads Department asked if they could borrow our heavy equipment to remake the road. I pointed out to them that the reason they wanted to borrow our equipment was that most of theirs was unusable. If they borrowed our equipment, it would probably be mismanaged in the same way, so we refused. They had no funds.

But many years ago a huge gravel dump had been deposited nearby for building up the shoulders of the Shamva national road. This gravel was surplus to requirements and could be used for remaking the four-and-a-half kilometres of road, all of which was originally gravel. The farm was adjacent to the Ewanrigg national botanical gardens, world famous for their aloe and cycad collections, but visitors in the rainy season often could not get through.

In order to help not only ourselves but also the adjacent community and the national gardens, I offered to enter into a joint agreement. We would remake the road, from scratch, with our heavy equipment and clean out all the drains. The Roads Department, with two dump trucks, would dump the gravel at five-metre intervals along the newly remade road. We would then, with our road graders, spread the gravel and consolidate the material to complete the rebuild. It was useless to look for any payment, so we agreed in the national interest to do our side of the operation at no charge.

The Roads Department head office were very pleased with this arrangement and we had many letters of appreciation. Once the road was remade, with the correct camber, we graded it a couple of times a year to maintain its shape and to eliminate the usual corrugations. It was a good example for other farmers to do the same thing. When we were being evicted we pointed out what we had done for government, but that help was ignored and we received no credit for our contribution to the community.

I had always been critical of the educational system at most of the agricultural colleges and at the agricultural department of the University of Zimbabwe, because I felt they placed too much emphasis on the academic part of their courses and not enough on the practical side. Students would graduate with quite a reasonable academic knowledge, but had had minimal exposure to the practical aspects of farming. For example, nobody at the colleges taught the students how to erect a barbed-wire fence, or how to do comprehensive maintenance on a tractor. This may sound basic, but if these people were going into the field to help newly settled farmers they needed a strong practical base.

On Handley Cross, Wendy had managed our farm junior school, and a number of our pupils later did well at higher levels. The headmaster had been brought up on Handley Cross and, although he had no formal teaching qualification, he did an excellent job with the children until they went to the senior school on the Dalny Mine. So we decided to build a students' hostel on Mount Lothian where we would take young people from various agricultural institutions for a summer vacation on general aspects of farming or on the subject that they wished to specialize in.

The routine would be two or three weeks on seed maize and arable cropping and potatoes, a month on horticulture, a month on livestock.

We had one young agriculture-faculty student who enjoyed the livestock so much that, on her return to university, she requested, and we supported her, that she transfer to the veterinary faculty. There she came top of her course, worked at a veterinary practice in Harare and then went overseas, started at the bottom as a locum and is now a partner in a thriving practice. Our only regret was that she had to leave the country.

Our hostel provided six small bedrooms. Wendy outfitted it with beds, mattresses, tables and chairs, hot and cold water, toilet facilities and a small living room. The proof of the pudding was in the eating, because we always had a waiting-list of youngsters wanting to come to us for attachment from colleges and universities from different parts of the country.

That hostel no longer has any students. The practical training and knowledge of our government agricultural extension workers is dismal. Some of the chemical and fertilizer companies have done their best, but the technical and practical training opportunity remains abysmally low.

We had 24 hectares of eucalyptus trees and supplied the creosote plant at Marondera with poles up to six metres long for power-line transmission poles and for roofing timbers. Timber which was of the wrong size or not straight was sent to the Hunyani paper mill at Norton for pulping.

When eucalyptus trees are six or seven metres tall they are cut at thirty centimetres from the ground and will regrow over the next three or four years to the same height. If a plantation is well managed and suckers are controlled, it can be cut and will grow again at least two or three times. The settlers on our farm have bulldozed most of the small plantations to make way for crops with a quicker cash return, such as soyabeans, and they have no replanting programme.

We also had a big gum-seedling nursery on the farm where the seedlings were pricked out into small polythene pots two inches wide and six inches tall and grown on until they were nine or ten inches high, when they went to our many customers throughout the country. We grew three varieties, *Eucalyptus grandis*, *E. camaldulensis* and *E. insignis*, and hundreds of thousands of our seedlings went to farmers who were able to use for gums odd small pockets of land which were difficult to cultivate for summer crops.

We had a rotation of vegetables, carrots, cabbages, broccoli, butternut and cauliflower, between the large potato and onion crops. Some of these were grown for the dehydration plant owned by Fresca beyond Harare. That factory, for lack of raw material, has closed down and is now a big, empty shell. We also supplied the retail and wholesale markets in Harare and Mbare with fresh vegetables.

For the best fruit-set of butternut, insect pollination is important. There were two commercial bee farms which brought hives to Mount Lothian. The hives were placed at the rate of four hives per hectare throughout the crop. They were moved by night, and the next morning the bees were busy at work transmitting pollen from flower to flower. When that crop was finished the contractor moved the hives to another location.

We grew winter wheat from May to October, and in our rotation it followed seed maize, which matured during April to early May. If the seed maize was slightly too moist, our drier could take out the last two or three per cent of moisture in the kernels. This helped us to get our wheat in early and, as the seed maize crop was taken off the land, the maize stover was disced under and the wheat planted and irrigated. As a result, that land was under almost continuous cropping, and with the centre pivots providing accurate applications of water we got the best possible returns.

Wendy and I had always wanted a member of the family to take over Mount Lothian from us. At a family discussion, I asked if any of the grandchildren, boy or girl, would be interested, because, if so, we would

Harvesting winter wheat. We invested in plant and machinery all the time to make Mount Lothian as productive as possible.

be prepared to enter into a beneficial continuing lease to make it easier for them to take over the whole farm in due course. The only grandchild who was really keen was Nicholas, Diana's eldest son, who was 23, and so it was arranged that, after his honours degree in pure mathematics at Edinburgh, he would come and live with us on the farm and become involved with every aspect.

When Nicholas arrived, he designed and built a most attractive small house in the game park. It had a security fence around it so that the animals could not actually get in, but he lived there on the edge of the dam with them around him. His design was novel, with a brushed thatch roof and a part-mezzanine, to which he ascended on a circular metal staircase. He put a great deal of love, care and enthusiasm into that small house. He was able to live there only for a very short time before we were all evicted from the farm.

We had graded a rough farm air-strip on the edge of the game park and got it smooth enough for a vehicle to travel sufficiently fast to tow and launch a paraglider. Nicholas loved paragliding and would go up several thousand feet, cruising around the farm – what better way of seeing how the crops were developing? He never once had to do a forced landing and it was not long before we had a small paragliding club with a professional instructor.

Nicholas got on extraordinarily well with our workers and had many good new, innovative ideas, but once he had to deal with our settlers he found that their attitudes and their arrogance were more than he was prepared to take. They attempted to intimidate him on our half of the farm, arbitrarily interfering with labour and equipment, which was all part of their strategy to wear us down. It was not long before Nicholas asked to be allowed to opt out of the agreement.

We had always said that, if unsatisfactory and unforeseen events took place, we would be prepared to terminate the arrangement, and this is what, sadly, we had to do. He went back to Cape Town University, got his next degree, and was head-hunted by a big international Dutch bank, ABN Ambro, who sent him an air ticket to go for an interview. However, he ultimately joined another financial institution, Moody's, which offered him a great opportunity where his pure mathematical experience stood him in good stead. He was in risk-assessment of bonds in the international market. He travelled extensively – to Russia, the Far East, Saudi Arabia and various countries in Europe – looking at the security of bonds on some huge engineering projects.

It was at about this time that we were looking for a nucleus of reedbuck for the game park and there were plenty on a farm nearby. We planned to put up long nets and then to drive the reedbuck into the nets where they could quickly be put into a truck and driven to our boma. I flew in a microlight piloted by a friend to try and drive the animals towards the net. It was an exhilarating experience.

Another microlight pilot friend, Mike Laing, now sometimes takes me up. A full tank of fuel can keep us airborne for three to four hours, flying over farms, dams and mines at a very low altitude. This makes it easy to see what is happening on the ground – or, rather, what is not happening. The microlight can take off in 60 metres and only needs 150 metres to land. If need be, we can land in a clear field, or, better still, on a straight length of road. I use a digital camera and on one trip we took over 150 photographs of the area between Harare and Shamva, showing the almost complete absence of crop cultivation in the communal lands and in what was left of the commercial farming areas as a consequence of the government's 'fast-track land reform' programme.

Wildlife

Water gardens • Rhodesia/Zimbabwe Wildfowl Trust •
Importing eggs on British Airways • Wildfowl & Wetlands Trust council
• Game park • Baby elephants

Wendy and I had made water gardens on Handley Cross with a series of pools for our collection of geese, cranes and swans. When we moved to Mount Lothian we were able to expand our collection considerably. There, around the house we designed and built, we laid out a lovely water garden for our birds. Many indigenous ducks and geese would fly in during the evening for some grain and often stayed overnight on the ponds and lawns.

The snow geese, the bar-headed geese, the barnacles and the Russian red-breasted geese came from the Arctic. The black swans came from Australia and the mute swans from Europe. The endangered nene came from Hawaii: they are unsuspecting and friendly and make easy prey. The knobbilled duck, the spurwing geese, the rare Hottentot teal, whitebacked and whitefaced duck were indigenous. Crested or crowned cranes are indigenous to central Africa from Kenya down to South Africa and are the national bird in Uganda. Blue cranes, which have become an endangered species, are very rare in Zimbabwe, but there are small populations in the wetlands of Natal and our original stock came from South Africa.

The nene, from Hawaii, is probably the rarest goose species in the world. We had obtained our parent birds from Sir Peter Scott at the headquarters of the Wildfowl & Wetlands Trust (WWT) at Slimbridge in the UK, and managed to breed two clutches. The stock at Slimbridge

After my 23 years as chairman of the TSL group, Wendy and I were presented with a pair of knobbilled geese cast in silver, which I treasure. They were commissioned from Patrick Mavros and were the first knobbilled geese that he himself cast. He has now produced more, which can be found in London in his lovely silver boutique in the Fulham Road, London.

was and is being used to bulk up more nenes to release into the wild in Hawaii. They are a very quiet and somewhat timid bird.

The beautiful Russian red-breasted goose, nearly as rare as the nene, originates from the Arctic. They have a particularly raucous cry. These, too, were breeding on Mount Lothian.

I think, if I had to choose, I would say that the snow geese were my favourite. They were made famous by Paul Gallico in his epic story of Dunkirk, *The Snow Goose*, which was illustrated by Peter Scott.

We had a group of enthusiasts in the country who formed, originally, the Rhodesia Wildfowl Trust, later to become the Zimbabwe Wildfowl Trust. We encouraged our members to develop wetlands and water gardens and their own populations, principally of indigenous species.

I was the first chairman of the Trust. My deputy was a very knowledgeable ornithologist and tobacco farmer, Colin Wintle, who had a wide-ranging collection of species. He had a remarkable ability to get the foreign species to lay and hatch in his water garden at Bromley. He participated in our incubator egg imports and helped stock other people's water gardens.

The wattled crane is on the endangered species list, with only about thirty or forty pairs nesting in suitable wetland habitat in the country. In the early days of the Trust in 1983, a plane was lent to us and over two days we made a count of wattled cranes in all the wetlands in the country, and mapped nesting sites. With the ravages of small-scale subsistence settlement in recent years and the disturbance of their habitat, the population of wattled cranes has become smaller and smaller and I fear will soon be gone.

Blue cranes.

Mute swan, black swan and nene.

There were strict veterinary requirements for importing any live birds. These made it difficult to import exotic species from abroad, so we sometimes used to import eggs where the embryo was well developed. However, the small capillary blood vessels on the outside of the yolk and embryo are easily damaged by handling and vibration. The danger is less if the embryo is 75 per cent developed, but the eggs could not be put into the cargo compartments of aeroplanes because of the low temperatures.

Working on aircraft engine maintenance at British Airways was an enthusiastic bird man named Rod Hall. He and Bill Makings, of Fakenham in Norfolk, developed a tiny incubator powered by battery. This met the air-safety regulations and had excellent temperature and humidity controls.

The eggs were laid and the incubation process was begun. At 75 per cent of the time to hatching, the eggs were brought to Heathrow and put into the incubator, which had been moulded to fit an economy-class seat in a jumbo jet. There was thus no break in the continuity of temperature from land to air and, on arrival, the incubator was taken to the farm. We had excellent percentage hatchings, and by using this technique we were able to increase the range of birds in our collection on Mount Lothian.

Sir Peter Scott and his team at the Slimbridge WWT centre on the river Severn had helped us with some birds not represented in our collection, and we had been able to send birds to them. Sir Peter said he would like to put my name forward for election to the WWT council. I was duly elected and served a three-year stint with them.

While I was on the council, Her Majesty the Queen, Patron of the Trust, said that she would like to come down and spend a day at Slimbridge. When the Queen wishes to visit, it is expected that all the senior people involved should be available to greet and receive her. I was informed that she was coming but that, as I lived 6,000 miles away, the formalities of my attendance would be waived.

I made some minor changes to my schedule and was at Slimbridge with Sir Peter and Lady Scott and fellow council members where we were introduced to Her Majesty. She took a great interest and questioned me about what was happening with wildlife in Kariba.

After lunch we all walked right around Slimbridge. One of their Hawaiian nene geese decided that she would like to walk with the Queen and Sir Peter and travelled the whole circuit with us.

At the end of my term of office on the WWT council, Sir Peter gave me one of his paintings, of barnacle geese landing in the early morning sun, which we still have today.

Our house on Mount Lothian.

The view from our house.

On Mount Lothian, parts of the farm were difficult to cultivate, some rocky, some too wet. Here was an opportunity to make use of marginal land and build the game park that we had always wanted. We fenced the whole of the north and south-eastern section of the farm with 12-strand plain steel wire two metres high, supported on gum poles and with one metre of mesh fencing at the bottom to prevent small game squeezing through. The cost was only the wire mesh and labour, and we were able to use our own gum poles for the fence posts, cut from small plantations on the farm.

We built an off-loading ramp and a *boma* (enclosure) into which the animals were put after arrival for them to recover from the trauma of a long journey, which was up to a hundred miles for those from Mvuma. The boma was strongly built, with steel wire supporting black plastic three metres high so that the animals could not see outside. Once the animals were quiet and confident in the boma, they were released and soon found the perimeter of the park and settled down well. Our big new dam was in the middle of the park, so water was no problem.

The first wild animals we brought on to the farm were impala. They bred very well and at one stage we had well over a hundred. We had small populations of waterbuck, kudu, eland and giraffe. The browse foliage in the park was not really suitable for giraffe, but the other species did very well and multiplied until we had reasonable herds of them all. To supplement the giraffe feed, we built 'giraffe dining tables' three metres up in the trees. Each day fresh cabbages and sweet potatoes were put on the tables, and the giraffe waited expectantly for their next meal without competition from the other animals.

The National Parks Department carried out elephant culls in the 1980s because the population was becoming too large for the environment. In order to prevent panic in a herd, they culled the whole herd. Had some animals that had witnessed the culling operation escaped, they might have upset other herds. It is difficult to know the communication system between elephants, but there certainly is one. Just a few very young elephants were saved.

We were offered two male babies. They were only about eight weeks old, and we were warned that because they were not weaned it would not be easy to rear them. They were only about 75 centimetres at the withers when they came. We decided to bottle-feed them on cow's milk. We built a small but very strong *boma* and gradually got them on to other food; they became quiet and more confident with their handler, Stephan, a

Visitors feed the orphan elephants.

wonderful old man who had been working in our dairy. Stephan developed a really good relationship with them. He named them Big Boy and Boka. They gradually became accustomed to humans. Stephan would take them out of the *boma* for a walk, control them by voice or waving arms (as you would with cattle), and then put them back into the *boma* for supper and the night.

Gradually the period outside was lengthened until they would go out after breakfast and come back by themselves in the evening. They became very tame and didn't mind the many visitors who came to the game park. They were particularly fond of sweet potatoes. When we went into the park to see them, each visitor was given a basket of cut sweet potatoes, which also helped in the taming process.

After about ten years, when the elephants had grown very well and had developed reasonable tusks, we decided that they would have to leave us and go to a bigger game park. The Mazowe Citrus Estates had a lovely big park in the hills and we sold them to Anglo American. However, there was the problem of moving the elephants seventy kilometres from Mount Lothian to Mazowe. On many farms brute force was used to drag elephants with ropes up a ramp and on to a big vehicle, with noise and trauma. Stephan said that, if we parked a high-sided game trailer at the loading ramp, he would gradually teach them at feed time to go up day by day, bit by bit, to the top, and then later step by step into the trailer. After a month they were quite happy to go up for their meals into the trailer.

When the huge truck arrived to take our elephants, the game-capture team had brought fifteen men and ropes to drag them into the trailer. Stephan absolutely refused, told everybody to go away and he would load them by himself. The team were suspicious because it was a new trailer which they didn't want broken, and it took him half an hour to reassure them. We all went off to breakfast and during the meal a message came that the elephants were safely on board.

Boka and Big Boy travelled without mishap through Harare to Mazowe, where the next problem was that the *boma* was a couple of hundred yards away from the off-loading ramp and in strange surroundings, so the elephants might rush off into the park. But Stephan talked to his two elephants and off-loaded them quietly down the ramp and they walked obediently behind him to the *boma*.

The elephants settled down happily in the new game park. Stephan stayed at Mazowe for a month until his charges were completely at ease there, and then he returned to us, but he always pestered us to get him some more babies.

Taking the baby elephants for a walk.

At the time of our eviction from Mount Lothian, we were unable because of the suddenness of the invasion to get any of our ducks and geese off the farm. We did get the cranes and swans off late one evening and they are happily living in Darren Lança's water garden on the outskirts of Harare, the only collection to have survived the land settlement.

All our geese, including the nenes, the Russian red-breasted geese and the snow geese, were wiped out by the farm invaders.

Crowned cranes.

Russian red-breasted goose.

Part of the Mount Lothian water garden.

– 21 –

Land Resettlement and Farm Invasions

Land-acquisition legislation • Process of farm acquisition
• War Veterans • Eviction of farmers
• Cases of violence • Avril Capon, Umritsur
• World Earth Summit Conference, Johannesburg •
International Bar Association • Judiciary attacked • Jerry Grant
• Export earnings shrink • CFU statistics

Under the Lancaster House agreement, compulsory acquisition of land was put on hold for the first ten years of independence.

The United Kingdom had, in the early 1980s, provided £47 million for land reform based on willing-buyer/willing-seller. When the plan was later abandoned, three million hectares had been bought and £4 million remained in the kitty.

Land-acquisition legislation was put in place after the ten years stipulated in the Lancaster House agreement, but it was poorly administered. The Ministry of Lands required anyone buying a farm to obtain a 'Certificate of No Interest' from the government, who had first option on land for sale.

Indigenous settlers entering farming for the first time faced immense problems. The programme to develop the infrastructure in terms of logistics, supply of inputs and facilities for schools, clinics, water supplies and the like, was enormous. Without the active help of an extension officer, many of these people were lost. They were 'dumped' on pieces of land, they had to build huts, try to establish a supply of water within a reasonable distance of their huts, and clear land, which often entailed stumping to remove trees. They had neither the resources nor the skills. They did not have capital for equipment or adequate and prompt finance for inputs. And so the settlement programme stagnated.

In 1998 the government hosted a Land Conference in Harare, involving all the major international donors and the multilateral institutions. It resulted in proposals that were initially agreed to by all participants and which, had they been accepted by Zimbabwe, would have set the stage for successful land settlement, limited but active commercial farming, and a return to donor support, but there were too many conditions for government to accept.

However, urged on in 2000 by the electorate's rejection in a referendum of its proposals for a new constitution, the government then wanted farms cut up and settled for political purposes at the maximum possible speed.

> Between 1980 and 2000 Robert Mugabe's government had stymied plan after plan put forward by the Commercial Farmers Union and the Zimbabwe Tobacco Association for foreign-funded, voluntary land reform. From what happened later, I suspect this was because the government wanted to own all the land and use it to reward its political supporters.

The process was to start with a letter delivered to the farmer, designating the farm under 'Section 5' of the land acquisition legislation. This designation would then be gazetted, indicating government's intention to acquire that piece of land at some time in the future. There was to be no compensation for the value of the land, but provision was made for compensation for permanent improvements to the infrastructure, such as dams, buildings and equipment. This compensation would be paid over a period of five years, which was ridiculous in light of the steady devaluation of the currency.

In fact, very few farmers were ever paid compensation. Professional valuers were scarce and the valuations were conducted by government officials, who were largely inexperienced and arrived at values remote from reality and far below the true worth of the assets acquired. Government had five valuers to cover 6,000 farms.

In essence, a Section 5 notice would be served on a farmer and a list of farms to be taken for redistribution would be published in the press and in the *Government Gazette*. The farmer then had 30 days in which to object. If he did so, the government could then, within one year, serve on the farmer papers in terms of Section 7, setting out its case for acquiring the farm. This case had to be heard before the Administrative Court. If the Court confirmed the application, a Section 8 notice would be issued, confirming the compulsory acquisition of the farm.

Alternatively, government could, within 30 days of the service of a Section 5 notice, issue a Section 8 notice compulsorily acquiring the farm, but then, within 30 days of the Section 8 order being issued, government had to apply to the Administrative Court for an order confirming the compulsory acquisition of the farm. Once a Section 8 notice was served, the farmer had 45 days to vacate his farm.

In real terms, this sequence was seldom followed. Several farmers won their cases in the Administrative Court, but were forced off their land anyway. Refusal to comply led to police being used to evict the farmer and arrest him. Many commercial farmers were arrested and jailed, with bail initially being withheld.

Further legislation followed, denying a farmer the right to remove his movable assets, tractors and equipment off the farm. Later, this was modified to some extent, but in practice it became increasingly difficult to get transport on to a farm to remove equipment. In many cases the equipment was trashed or stolen by the settlers. Forty-five or even 100 days' notice was inadequate for a farmer who had an enormously valuable crop growing in the land.

In 2000, 77 per cent of Zimbabwe was either communal land, or was land held by the small-scale commercial farmers (formerly known as African Purchase Areas), or national land, such as game parks and resettlement areas. Twenty-three per cent of Zimbabwe was large-scale commercial land. This figure included land owned by a few black large-scale commercial farmers doing a good job; even some of them had their farms listed and seized.

In 1997, the Zimbabwe National Liberation War Veterans Association (ZNLWVA) had complained about the government's monthly pension of Z$2,000 a month. Mugabe immediately increased this to Z$50,000 and from then on the 'war vets' became a law unto themselves. They were often led by very violent and opportunistic people, and whether or not a 'war veteran' had actually been involved in the Rhodesian war seemed irrelevant. In many cases, roving mobs of people invaded a farm that had not even been designated. Many farmers were given 48 hours or less to pack up and go. This was accompanied by widespread violence, and the police were under instructions not to interfere with the war vets because the matter was said to be 'a political issue'.

As soon as the farm invasions began, a secure radio link to each farm was established, and each farmer had his own call sign. In each area, one farmer's wife took her turn every evening at six o'clock and called the numbers and received reports. This system worked well for a long time until it was corrupted. The radio link meant that, when a farm was being attacked, all the other call signs could know what was happening and possibly help.

282

War vets even invaded a sitting of the Supreme Court and assaulted court staff, who had to flee from the court for safety's sake, while the judges cowered in the corridor. In fact, the ZNLWVA developed into a political force, which was becoming a threat to government. These so-called war vets were committing crime after crime, claiming that these were 'political matters' and not ones in which the police should involve themselves.

Widespread looting took place on farms, and human rights organizations say that 400 people, including 14 whites, were killed. It is not easy to imagine the state of shock of a farming family besieged by a mob of fifty people, many high on drugs or alcohol, singing and chanting at the front door, usually invading the privacy of the household and looting the house of furniture and personal possessions.

Farmers being evicted were helped by neighbours with transport to move their belongings to a neighbouring, unaffected farm, or into the nearest town or city for safe storage. The farmers themselves had to look for accommodation. The effect on all the families, and particularly on wives and children, was traumatic. Frequently, roads leading off a farm were barricaded, and people even had difficulty in evacuating it, while the theft of furniture, stocks, stores, equipment, chemicals, fuel, harvested grain or tobacco was widespread, and cattle were rustled or slaughtered.

On a few big estates, including some of the most productive farms in the country, the theft amounted to many hundreds of thousands of US dollars. A variety of documents, said to be official but in fact often

Terry Ford, aged 51, was the tenth person to be killed in the land seizures. Besides the farmer's mutilated corpse, authorities found the man's devoted dog, a Jack Russell called Squeak, who would not leave the farmer's body. According to Meryl Harrison, of the Society for the Prevention of Cruelty to Animals, it took Ford's relatives an hour to coax the little dog into their car so that they could take him away.

forgeries, were used to gain entry to farms. Irrigation piping and equipment were removed or vandalized. War vets occupied farm homesteads and many livestock were slaughtered.

There were many violent incidents during this period. In one horrific case, on a big tea estate in the north-east, a mob arrived on the evening before pay-day. Phil Laing, the finance manager, went down at nine o'clock to investigate. He was seized, tied up and taken fifty miles away. There he was strapped to a tree trunk. His mouth was forced open and the mob poured battery acid down his throat. He died an excruciating death in the early hours of the morning.

In an incident on another farm, hay was spread over the floor of a loose box with four horses. The horses were shut into the loose box and the hay was set alight. One horse managed to get out, but the others were burnt so badly that they had to be destroyed.

On another occasion, war vets arrived on a white-owned farm. The manager and his wife were present, and so was the pregnant wife of a worker. She was seized and raped by bayonet, disembowelled, and the seven-month foetus was removed from her body and its skull smashed.

In another instance, a large farm was seized and vehicles arrived and started loading seed maize, fertilizer and grain.

Forty kilometres north of Harare is Carswell, one of Zimbabwe's biggest cattle feedlots, supplying significant numbers of slaughter cattle to the Cold Storage Commission and to the trade. When the price-slashing and price-control system was put into place, Carswell was effectively closed down, the army took over, cattle were slaughtered and the meat largely sent to army and police. Cattle numbers shrank dramatically and they are only now starting to rebuild the herd of cattle in the feedlot, which supplies the abattoir on that farm.

One of our closest neighbours, Alan Windram, who was the largest vegetable supplier in Zimbabwe (he used to send 30 tonnes of vegetables and tomatoes into Harare every day) was overwhelmed by a huge mob. His workers' houses, which were good buildings, had their front doors and windows smashed, and the houses were set on fire. The Windrams' own homestead was also set on fire and most of it destroyed. Their five dogs were cornered and severely injured; only two survived. The Windram family had to evacuate their home; the next day, their immediate neighbours, the Stobarts, suffered the same experience. That farm was taken by a senior government minister.

These incidents and atrocities were widely televised by the BBC and in the USA before the government introduced laws that made it almost impossible for the foreign media to operate in Zimbabwe. On this television exposure, some senior could be seen to be taking part in the chaos.

A sudden invasion took place at Umritsur farm adjacent to Mount Lothian. Umritsur was owned and well run by a widow, Avril Capon, and her manager, with a high-quality big Friesland dairy herd, a beef enterprise, a large amount of land under irrigation, and a dam that her late husband had built himself, which was the biggest in the Enterprise area. The head of the Agricultural Rural Development Authority (ARDA), followed shortly afterwards by Minister Didymus Mutasa and Minister Joseph Made, arrived at her door on 5 June 2005, and told her that later that very day ARDA were taking over the whole farm and its management and she was to move away.

After she moved, milk yields fell from twenty litres per cow per day to seven. Many cattle died. The wheat, which had been grown and was being combined at the time of the take-over, was seized by ARDA, who instructed the breweries that payment for the wheat was to be made to their account, although they had not had a hand in the crop except for the final combining. Substantial pressure had to be brought at a very high level to abort their attempt to take the money for the wheat, but eventually Avril Capon was paid for the crop.

Her life became impossible. She could not go back to the farm. Her bank account was frozen because of the delay in receiving the income from the wheat and milk. Shortly afterwards she decided to leave the country and went with just two suitcases in her hands.

Ultimately, a number of war vets were charged in the courts, but even those who were convicted were released. Thousands of farms were laid waste. These were the farms that had made Rhodesia and then Zimbabwe the envy of Africa and the breadbasket of the region.

> Within about ten kilometres of Mount Lothian, farms were taken over by people who were in senior positions at the time, including: Godfrey Chidyausiku (Chief Justice); Brig. E. Muzonzini (Ambassador to Kenya); David Chapfika (Deputy Minister of Finance); Herbert Murerwa (Minister of Finance); Ray Kaukonde (Provincial Governor, Mashonaland East); David Karimanzira (Provincial Governor, Harare); Olivia Muchena (Minister of State for Science and Technology); General Constantine Chiwenga (Commander of the Defence Forces) and his wife, Jocelyn. Our 'settlers' were retired army Colonel Godfrey Matemachani and Mr Justice Garwe, then Judge President of the High Court of Zimbabwe.

SMALL SURVIVOR

The rape was brutal, scorching, searing pain
And no remission. Again and yet again
The shrinking body quivered in the dust
As all the soldiers gratified their lust,
Then left the girl for dead. The nightmare scene
Was now a travesty of what had been
A prosperous village full of peaceful folk,
All fled, or dead, in shroud of evil smoke.

At last came night, with night the will to live
For hunger is a strong imperative.
She did not die. Half-crazed by many ills
She made her way in secret through the hills
To reach a distant hamlet spared from war
Where cousins lived, where she had lived before
In happier days. Up that familiar street
Starving she crawled, collapsing at their feet.

How did she do it? God alone can tell.
One in a thousand could survive such hell.
In time she bore a babe, swore he should die,
But when she saw the tiny creature lie
Helpless and crying, alien, yet her own,
She found her bitter hatred almost gone.
She put the small survivor to her breast,
Half-drowned in tears, and Nature did the rest.

Lady Angela Greenhill

Lady Greenhill said her poem could be applied to Rwanda, Burundi,
the Democratic Republic of the Congo, Zimbabwe, and also Kenya.

At the World Summit on Sustainable Development in Johannesburg in 2002, the British Prime Minister, Tony Blair, and Robert Mugabe were both present and there were angry exchanges between the two. Blair stressed, among many other points, the unacceptable situation of land seizure. Mugabe's response was that their policy was to leave no farmer without one farm. In other words, nobody would be left without one farm of the right size, and this hectarage varied from area to area, with a minimum of approximately 450 hectares. That was an empty promise made to a worldwide audience, and it had no effect on the continuing, completely ruthless, seizure of farms. Many people who owned only one farm lost everything.

Government's take-over of farms and businesses demonstrated that law and order were irrelevant to the ruling party. In 2004 the International Council of Advocates and Barristers was so concerned about the state of justice in Zimbabwe that it undertook an extensive investigation which showed that law and order had been severely prejudiced and the country's judicial system had been profoundly compromised. The team, chaired by Stephen Irwin QC, Chairman of the Bar of England and Wales, included: Conor Maguire SC, Chairman of the Irish Bar; Glenn Martin SC, President of the Bar Association of Queensland and Treasurer of the Australian Bar Association; Roy Martin QC, Vice-Dean of the Faculty of Advocates of Scotland; and Mr Justice Poswa SC, Vice-Chairman of the South African Bar. This eminent team recorded its findings in a detailed report to the Council entitled *The State of Justice in Zimbabwe*.

The report confirmed political interference with the judiciary. The team met, among others, Bharat Patel, then the Acting Attorney-General, Chief Justice Godfrey Chidyausiku, and the Minister of Justice, Patrick Chinamasa. They concluded that the executive and ZANU(PF) did not observe constitutional protection for the judiciary but had removed judges whose independence was thought to be an impediment to their policies and had compromised the integrity of the Supreme Court and the High Court by allocating farms to a number of judges.

Magistrates and prosecutors perceived to be unsympathetic to government faced violence and attacks on their property and families. Their pay was ludicrous. As more left the law, there were unacceptable delays in hearing cases and handing down judgments. Lawyers representing politically unpopular cases suffered physiological and physical intimidation, violence and torture as well as attacks on their families and properties.

Jerry Grant produced a valuable chronological record on every land incident, whether on farms or in the government ministries, showing how widespread was the acquisition of productive farms right across the country. Grant had been a long-serving and outstanding member of the staff of the RNFU, and later was deputy director of the CFU. Perhaps more than most, he had a clarity of vision of the consequences of land acquisition.

Sadly, there were strong differences of opinion within the Commercial Farmers Union council about how the it should operate in the difficult and shrinking commercial farming economy, and he left. I personally regarded this as a huge loss. His chronological record was abruptly terminated when he left the CFU. I know of no similar record compiled by anybody about the events of that time.

Export currency earnings shrank as the land seizures began. Tobacco, horticulture, seed maize, cotton and grain production tumbled. The CFU produced a table in July 2006 which showed the catastrophic effect and the decline of all commodities and livestock. A few figures extracted (and rounded off) from this table give the picture.

Production on Commercial Farms

	1998	2001	2005
	'000 tonnes		
Maize	521	385	180
Cotton	77	38	0.5
Wheat	270	281	125
Soya beans	113	162	48
Tobacco, flue-cured	210	195	55
Coffee	10	7	2
Dairy	184	173	93

THE PATRIOTS

War's a dead loss
And mocks Love on the Cross.
None the less we will strive
By land and by sea
In the air if need be
Against all men alive.

Who would tread with iron heel
On our necks, make us kneel,
Who would plot and connive
To steal what's our own,
The fields we have sown,
The towns we made thrive.

Who would ravage the earth,
The land of our birth
And of Liberty bright.
As the dead from the tomb,
As the babe from the womb,
We will rise in our might.

Make no mistake,
All bonds we will break –
We will die for our right
Or live to be free.
Brother, link arms with me,
Together we fight.

Lady Angela Greenhill

– 22 –

Thrown off Our Land

An unexpected visit • A mob at the gate
• A meeting on the football ground • The agitators return
• A statement to the police • Section 8 served, farming stopped
• A1 and A2 farmers • The 'settlers' on Mount Lothian
• Agreement with the occupants • Seed maize production
• Nicholas decides to leave • Business environment worsens
• The Utete Commission • Bill Deedes in the *Daily Telegraph*
• The occupants taken to court • Future prospects

Let me relate the happenings on Mount Lothian, our farm. Our first sign of danger was at the end of 2001, when we had a lunchtime visit one Sunday from four people who asked permission to make an assessment of the farm. They refused to identify themselves, had no documents, and we told them that the farm had not been listed for acquisition and that they must be mistaken. They denied that this was so and said that if we refused to allow them to make their assessment they would make up one from a map.

Some weeks elapsed and then, in February 2002, we had another visit, this time from a suave, well-dressed man who announced himself as Retired Colonel Godfrey Matemachani, saying that he had come to introduce himself as the new owner of Mount Lothian. We told him that we had not been served with any acquisition notices and that I was certainly still the owner. He replied that it was easy for him to go to Marondera, the provincial head-quarters of Mashonaland East province in which the farm is situated. His very senior contacts there would provide him with a Section 8 order. In other words, the decision to take the farm of his choice was his alone. He liked it. He demanded a Section 8 order on Mount Lothian from his friends in government and he got it. The legality of this order has subsequently come under scrutiny, as described by our lawyer.

Shortly afterwards, we were called to our security gate one afternoon. There was a yelling mob of about 100 people, men and women armed with pangas (broad-bladed knives) and heavy sticks, some evidently under the influence of alcohol and drugs, headed by the infamous self-appointed chief war vet, Joseph Chinotimba, a junior employee of Harare Municipality. I greeted him through the locked mesh gate and asked what he wanted.

He said that he wished to talk to me. I invited him to do so but he refused unless we opened the gate. It was obvious to me that once the gate was opened the mob would surge through, so I declined. He then, in quite a matter-or-fact way and with a pistol in his hand, told me that my choice was simple: either to let them in, or he would shoot me. He said he

An aerial view of Mount Lothian.

would then bring further reinforcements and destroy our house, equipment and tractors.

Arguments of legality went right over his head. One of our black managers said to me, 'Mr Tracey, my advice to you is to let four or five of them in and then deal with the matter'. So I agreed that Chinotimba could bring in four people to discuss the situation. We then endured

Our workforce was subsequently infiltrated by war vets and our workers were highly apprehensive and intimidated by them. They caused a withdrawal of labour and sporadic wildcat strikes, which disrupted our work.

the normal lecture of having stolen the land from their forebears, that we supported the opposition party, we were bad employers, and so on. After an hour they left, to be followed a few days later by another group, who broke down the security fence and came on to the lawn in front of the house with violent threats.

They turned to Wendy and told her to cook a meal for fifty people immediately. Hoping to buy time, I ordered a sheep to be slaughtered and the meal to be cooked in our workers' canteen. We were then over-run. I went in to telephone for help, but the phone was wrenched out of my hand and out of its socket. Eventually they dispersed. On each occasion, police were present. They stood by and provided no assistance whatsoever – on the grounds that this was a political matter and not a police one.

A few days later, at about 11 a.m., one of our black managers, Edward Hermes, said that we had been summoned to go to the lower football ground where there was to be a meeting between our workforce and the war vets. Our grandson Nicholas went down in the car with Wendy and me. We met the group of war vets in the late morning. This group was led by a particularly notorious and uneducated man named Kapesa, who acted like a madman.

Kapesa and his cronies had compelled the entire village population to assemble on the football grounds for a show of force. He addressed the whole village community – men, women and children – plus his own war vet contingent. He said that Mount Lothian was a very bad farm and that we treated our workers very badly, that Wendy and I were supporters of the opposition party, the Movement for Democratic Change. He commanded five of our management team to step forward from the group of workers: our number one, Edward Hermes, the second-in-command, Magodi Mvula, and three others.

They were told to sit down some way from the crowd and take their shoes off. This had traditionally become the start of a session of violence and flogging, as we had learned from the terrorist war. After they had called Edward and questioned him before the crowd, when he courageously told the war vets that there was no substance to any of the charges they were making, they called Magodi. The same accusations were levelled at him and, because he was responsible for allocating work, he was regarded as an enemy of the workers. They said he had subjected the workers to unreasonable tasks. They said he was a womanizer and that he would have to leave the farm. By this time, passions were extremely inflamed by mob frenzy.

Magodi was then told to lie down on the ground (all the war vets were armed with strong sticks) and they said he was going to be flogged. I stood beside him and spoke quietly and said that he had earned our loyalty and that he should not lie down and that I was not going to allow him to be beaten. We walked up to Kapesa and I told him exactly that. Then they started assaulting Magodi and beating him. Nicholas came to his aid and got soundly thrashed for his pains. They did not actually attack me but, after two or three minutes in the mêlée, they ceased hostilities.

I admonished the war vets in Shona in the strongest possible words and told them that what they were doing was illegal and would be reported to the police and the authorities. Meanwhile, the police had arrived and became interested spectators only. The war vets urged us to go back to the house to discuss their grievances. We sat down on the lawn and started to talk. Shortly, a message came from the top village, where Magodi had his house, to say that a group of war vets and some of our own hostile women employees, who were enjoying the opportunity of venting their fury on one of our two senior managers, were looting his house.

Magodi's family had a pleasant three-bedroomed home, which was well equipped with modern conveniences. The war vets were hurling the furniture, the beds, mattresses, his small electric stove, TV and refrigerator, and odds and ends on to the grass outside. Their actions were akin to a maddened swarm of bees. Magodi, his wife and small children were understandably terrified.

The war vet leader said Magodi should leave the farm immediately and that if he was not gone by sunset they would take him and he would never be seen again. They said they knew where he lived and that other war vets would be watching him at his home in the rural area. Magodi asked me if he could have the use of one of our three-tonne farm trucks to take his goods, or what was left of what had been accumulated over years, to his home in the communal lands at Centenary. He and his family left the farm to threats of retribution if he was ever to return. We renewed contact with Magodi a week later, and for 18 months we met each month in Harare. We had undertaken to pay his salary until the madness subsided.

It was rumoured widely enough to be believed that our 'settler', Matemachani had orchestrated the whole scene. It seemed that the plan was to take the farm from us and then to instil an atmosphere of fear and intimidation throughout the whole workforce to ensure compliance.

The war vets dispersed. I spoke to our own employees and their families, told them that they had our complete support and that we were farmers, not politicians, that we were well known for the way in which we looked after our workforce and that they would be supported. The next day everybody was at work until lunchtime, when the agitators returned and co-opted six of our farm-workers. These people went around the farm telling workers to leave their jobs and go home.

Early next day the war vets returned in force and said that the farm was not to operate in any way. The pigs were not even to be fed or watered, the cows should not be milked, irrigation was to cease, and if anybody was found doing those jobs they would be severely punished.

Land was not truly the issue, and the intimidation of the work force was intense. The cattle were not milked until later that night, and for 24 hours the pigs were not fed and were obviously suffering and in a bad way. A couple of loyal stockmen went out to feed and water the pigs on their own initiative after dark, when all was quiet. But we had to prevail on the war vets to allow us thereafter to deal with the livestock and general crop farming. I had to threaten them that, if there was any further interference in those two jobs, I would go directly, without hesitation, to the government in Harare. (To go to the police would have been useless.) Reluctantly they agreed and for the next few days we were able to get on with farming.

After a week, there was a resumption of sporadic strikes and we resorted to the Magistrates' Court in Harare to seek an eviction order against four women and two men, the farm-workers who had earlier been co-opted by the agitators. These were the main trouble-makers, constantly urging illegal work stoppages. The case was heard and an order was given for the Messenger of the Court to remove these six people and their belongings from our farm. The Messenger came with a removal van to execute this court order. However, the political leaders in the district were soon alerted and they intervened, telling the Messenger of the Court that his jurisdiction was no longer valid, that he should leave immediately, and that the six people were not required to leave the farm.

At this time, near Bulawayo, a ZANU(PF) leader named Cain Nkala had been abducted and killed. A ZTV news crew was present when his body was 'discovered' and exhumed. ZANU(PF) immediately blamed his murder on the MDC and launched an anti-MDC propaganda campaign, dubbed 'war against terror'. A few days later I was accused by the war vets of having taken hostage some of our workers, abducting them and, in the same way that Cain Nkala had been abducted, forcing them into the sheriff's furniture van, which had by then left the farm. There was, of course, not one shred of evidence that anything of the sort had happened.

> Cain Nkala, a previously unheard-of war veteran, was declared a national hero, and the three of the suspects spent 21 months in appalling conditions in jail before they were later acquitted in court. The judge, Sandra Mungwira, said that the state had failed to produce any evidence against them, that police witnesses were manifestly unreliable, and that confessions obtained under torture and used against them were inadmissible.

The war vets' hostility then was focused directly on me. They summoned me to a meeting at the top village. Again I was accused of abduction. They were armed with *machetes* (axes) and the leader rushed at me and was on the point of slashing me when he was restrained by some of his mates. If it hadn't been for my grandson Nicholas's quick intervention I should probably have been wounded. I told the war vets to leave immediately and that I would inform the police.

Later that week, I was telephoned by the Marondera police, under whose jurisdiction we fell, and asked to go to the charge office to make a statement about this incident. The police had a technique of asking farmers to go to a police station to make a statement on a Friday afternoon. Once a farmer arrived there, he would be charged with various alleged offences. It was often impossible to get a lawyer to come to a detainee's aid and apply for bail late on a Friday afternoon. The unfortunate individual would then have to spend the weekend in disgusting over-crowded cells, which usually had only one sanitary bucket in the corner, until a court hearing on the Monday. Sometimes ten to fifteen farmers, and sometimes their wives, were incarcerated in this way. It was a form of intimidation and harassment.

I told the police that I was otherwise occupied and that, if they wanted to see me to take a statement, I was ready to give one, but preferably at the farm or with my lawyer. On the following Monday, the CID (Criminal Investigation Department) came to the farm and asked me to give them a statement. I declined to do this unless I was in the presence of my lawyer, Alex Masterson, so we travelled the 35 kilometres into Harare. A suitable statement was prepared and this I signed. We heard no more. It was just another of the many attempts at intimidation.

After the unsettling war-vet violence on Mount Lothian and on every farm in the district, it was necessary to make a number of contingency plans. The farm was almost fully developed. The main sectors were hybrid seed maize, zero virus potatoes for seed, wheat and vegetables, all under irrigation, greenhouses for export flower production, and we had sufficient arable land to grow enough maize for our 800 pedigree pigs, and grazing for our herd of pedigree Limousin beef cattle and the Jerseys for milk.

When we were served our Section 8, which gave us ninety days to leave the farm, it appeared that the inevitable had finally come. During that time we had to close down the whole pig section. This was the oldest pedigree registered herd in Southern Africa, started in 1934. Genetics had been imported from South Africa and, subsequently, from the UK, Finland, Sweden and America. In three months, 64 years of genetics were swept away.

Our house on Mount Lothian.

As we had been ordered to cease production, all work in the greenhouses came to an abrupt halt. We were not allowed to continue during that fortnight to irrigate, fertilize or harvest the crops in the greenhouses, so it was pointless to throw good money after bad. We were then, after all, allowed to stay on, but with two settlers.

Mount Lothian is a small farm of just over 550 hectares, of which only 250 hectares are arable. Its size complied with the maximum farm size for this area, as laid down by government. But it seemed that government policy was to make farmers downsize their farms and co-exist with either A1 peasant farmers or A2 large-scale settlers who wished to farm commercially, with the previous owner farming the rest of the land.

Government policy sub-divided the settlers into two categories, A1 and A2. The former were allocated 10 to 30 hectares, depending on the Natural Region, in many cases hardly enough for their own requirements. They were grouped together to facilitate the distribution of fertilizer and seed. But there was no provision for infrastructure such as wells, boreholes and buildings. These A1 settlers were just dumped on the land and largely left to fend for themselves.

The A2 settler group consisted of people who were allocated substantial areas, sometimes part of a white-owned commercial farm, or more often the whole farm. They were given 200 to 400 hectares, depending on soil and rainfall and therefore the Natural Region division, and in theory had adequate financial resources of their own to supplement government loans. There was, however, no acreage limitation for the elite, and many simply seized a number of farms.

It was in the A2 category that every High Court judge, except two, and four of the seven judges of the Supreme Court took one farm or more, as did almost every Cabinet minister and senior official in the public service. Importantly, they were supposed, immediately on occupation, to start to build their own house, workshop and other farm buildings and facilities, and, if they were not going to live on the farm themselves, to employ a manager. But many simply used the farm as a weekend retreat. Of course, production fell dramatically. In most cases not only was the original farmer evicted but all his workers and their families were as well.

Many of the best farms in Enterprise, one of the best farming areas in the country, had been set aside for the elite. The two 'settlers' allocated our farm were the then Judge President of the High Court, Mr Justice Paddington Garwe, and a retired army colonel, Godfrey Matemachani.

Although, under Ministry of Agriculture regulations, the farm had been classified as too small for subdivision, we undertook to downsize it to half its previous area, so that we farmed half, while Garwe and Matemachani farmed the other half. The Provincial Office approved the downsizing and the subdivision of the farm. We agreed to co-exist and to help and teach the new farmers the basics of farming. But they had no experience, no equipment and minimal capital.

A civil servant in the land settlement section of the Ministry of Lands had reported on our farm and conceded that it was too small and too intensive and highly technical to downsize. He told Nicholas that he was then instructed to do a second and more critical and negative report. He was later demoted to a junior position.

We believed that if we did not downsize and co-exist we would probably lose the whole farm. It was obvious that both the settlers needed us in order to farm at all. They were quite frank about this, and admitted they had no farming experience. The judge did not have much money to invest and the retired colonel worked for the Commercial Bank of Zimbabwe in a management position.

We therefore negotiated that the farm would be subdivided on a 50-50 basis and we would do everything for them to start them off. The agreement we produced, with top legal advice on our side, took months to conclude but was eventually signed by all parties in February 2003. This formal legal agreement laid down that we would manage the settlers' section for the first year, they would pay only for direct costs and there would be no charge for my time or for overhead costs. At the same time we would try to teach them the fundamental aspects of practical agriculture. What we did was a gesture of goodwill and we hoped to provide a demonstration of what could be done. How wrong we were!

We tilled the land, we planted the land, we grew the crop, we harvested the crop, we helped them source fertilizer and chemicals for the crop. We sold the crop and they got the cheque. We deliberately did not charge for overhead costs, nor did we look for any payment for management, either for myself or for our black managers. We grew a good crop for them, which gave them a gross margin of over Z$350 million, which in 2003 was a substantial amount of money. We had kept our toe in the door, but they had simultaneously put their foot in and were using the agreement to play for time. They did not occupy our house. They bought only a minimal amount of their own equipment and did no capital development at all, although that had been required under their offer letter.

They then reneged on the terms of our agreement and in September

2003 told us to get out of the house and off the farm. They gave us 48 hours to pack up both farm houses (our own house and that of our grandson Nicholas). They refused to allow me or any of my family on to the farm to pack up, so my secretary and our two black managers had to do it all. In the haste a number of documents were damaged or lost. I was glad that Wendy was away in Australia and did not have to go through that traumatic experience. We later managed to get agreement that we could continue farming our side of the farm, and I travelled out on most days from Harare. But we still had the Section 8 hanging over us, under which we could still be displaced, invaded or kicked out at any time.

During those first twelve months the situation had gradually become more difficult, as the occupants intruded more and more on to our side of the farm. They were supposed, under the A2 scheme, either to live on the farm and run it themselves, or to employ a manager. After five or six months they had done neither, so we seconded a young man as manager, although he was far from qualified. As we were on site at the time, we were able to guide him.

Garwe and Matemachani were supposed to develop their own facilities, workshop, headquarters and houses. They refused point blank to undertake any development of any sort. I see now that they did not want to spend any money on development because they knew that the government would disown our joint agreement and give our half to them with all our infrastructure and equipment.

Despite these troubles, and in view of the serious seed maize shortage, we made a proposal to increase our seed maize production significantly, albeit at the cost of other crops, which we hoped would strengthen our case for the retention of our half of the land. It was already November 2003, time to plant the crop for that season. We discussed the matter with senior officials in the President's Office. I put the question to them, 'Are we short of seed maize?' The answer was affirmative. Then I asked if they wanted an increase in the area of seed maize to be grown. I told them that, if necessary, we could increase the seed maize crop threefold. I asked if that was what they wanted. The answer was vague, and with time constraints I needed a definite answer. Did they want us to grow the extra seed or not - yes or no? Although nothing was written down, they asked me to go ahead.

SeedCo, who marketed ninety per cent of the seed maize in the country, helped to get the increased programme under way. They put an experienced manager on the farm to mastermind the crop, in my absence. The project for that season was successful and we achieved our target. However, so aggressive and unpleasant were the two new occupants towards the SeedCo manager that, after the crop had been grown, he resigned and emigrated to the UK. That was the last seed maize crop we grew on Mount Lothian.

We had kept our side of the bargain with 'the settlers' to the letter but, whenever it was convenient, they bypassed their responsibilities. They ran up debts with us when we had purchased their inputs, and it was always difficult to secure repayments. At the end of the first twelve months, the agreement stipulated that an assessment of an extension of the facilities agreed should be re-negotiated in the light of experience, without changing the basic principles of the agreement.

Garwe and Matemachani, however, would never come together to any meeting to deal with this subject. All over the country, the tempo of farm seizures increased and we were now limited to our half of the farm, where we could maintain some production of seed maize, potatoes for crisps (potato chips), vegetables and certified seed wheat production, but with no livestock or horticulture. But by exploiting every resource, our farm business could still have been viable.

In the meantime, Nicholas, who was due to take over and lease the farm from the family trust after two years of experience, concluded that it would not be possible to build a proper working relationship with the new 'owners' as their manner was patronizing, dictatorial, hostile, demanding and arrogant. He foresaw problems associated with political attitudes, a potential new wife, children, education, currency restrictions, and a great likelihood that everything would be lost anyway, so he decided to take his second degree in financial mathematics at the University of Cape Town.

Our side of the farm ran pretty well, but it missed my grandson's presence. He had done so much, had become familiar with all aspects in a very short time, applied his computer skills, and thrown himself with enthusiasm into the continued development of Mount Lothian, and he got on well with his workforce.

The disastrous economic effects on the country of the land policy caused an accelerated deterioration on every side. Inflation was doubling every month, and interest rates soared, while as I write in 2007, ordinary borrowing and overdraft rates have fluctuated between 50 and 500 per cent and are not expected to diminish.

Fortunately our financial management was such that we seldom needed to borrow anything significant, so that did not affect us very much. But the cost of inputs in that last year on our farm was rising at an unbelievable rate. So, we decided to simplify management and limit our exposure by cutting out the whole of our potato and vegetable division, which up to then had been very profitable. Our only focus became hybrid seed maize and seed wheat crops. It simplified management, which was in any case growing slack, and by limiting the cropping programme we were able to treble our seed maize area, which could be better controlled.

Transport and spare-part costs, already high, were also escalating, and we could never be certain whether the gross return would cover both our direct and indirect costs, and give us an adequate margin. Seed maize production in the country was now falling dramatically as more and more seed maize farms were over-run by war vets and settlers, and thus we entered into the agreement mentioned earlier with SeedCo.

However, while the cuts maintained our efficiency at a very difficult time, it also meant that, by 2003, the farm operation had lost the pedigree pigs, the Limousin and Jersey herds, our greenhouse operation, and now potatoes, onions and vegetables, areas that had taken years to develop to full strength.

In addition to all these problems, labour legislation made farmers pay a very substantial redundancy package to workers who had previously been permanently employed and who now had to leave because of the farm take-overs. This package included items such as outstanding leave pay, transportation to their homes, and one month's pay for every six months worked, calculated at current wage rates with no ceiling. People who had worked for us for many years had enormous gratuities, far more than they could have expected, and this was on top of the normal pension

Worst of all was losing our Jersey herd.

scheme to which we had been contributing for them for many years. After we made these redundancy payments we still continued to employ those workers who wished to stay on, but under a new contract.

We used the Agricultural Labour Bureau negotiators to try and set at rest the workers' fear that, if we were evicted, they would get no benefits from us under the agreement and neither would they get any payment from government. At the same time they were concerned that, if we left, they would have no one to fall back on, unless the seed company gave them a similar guarantee, which they did.

Years of good relations with workers who had sometimes been with us for three generations were undermined by fear and suspicion that, one way or the other, they might miss out, and it took some effort from the National Employment Council to explain the package to them. The principle was not in question, but the amount had to be calculated, and in many cases it came to more than six months' pay. On some farms the packages were so crippling that farmers were unable to pay them even after selling their assets. We had to pay out over Z$75 million in 2003 and 2004, at that time an enormous amount of money.

It did seem, at one stage, that the President had begun to recognize the catastrophe of Zimbabwean land reform, as the country was left with fewer and fewer international friends and was economically in ruins. In May 2003, he appointed a commission to advise government on land settlement and to plan the future. In fact, it was nothing more than a delaying tactic. Headed by Dr Charles Utete, who, for many years had been the Chief Secretary to the President and Cabinet, it had some good men on it, though I would have preferred fewer academics and more practitioners. On Mount Lothian, we were visited by an uninvited but interesting team consisting of the head of the police force in Mashonaland East, an active army colonel, a member of the intelligence service, and one member from another province (to prevent bias, apparently) but no one with any farming experience.

The Utete Commission did a thorough job and exposed many people who were supposed to have only one farm but had grabbed up to half a dozen. They compiled a list of existing farmers who were prepared to subdivide and co-exist and who were working as far as possible on the original formula – one farmer, one farm – within the maximum hectarage allowed for that Natural Region. In some cases, of course, that maximum hectarage did not make for a viable farm, but at least there was a degree of flexibility.

We had two meetings with this task force, constructive, congenial and forward-looking, and they quickly realized the deficiencies of our two occupants. This task force acknowledged everything we had done for our them and that they had done nothing for themselves; that we had honoured our part of the agreement and they had not.

When they finished their report at the end of 2003, they presented it to the President, who accepted it. It was put to the Politburo and Central Committee of ZANU(PF) and eventually to Parliament, all of whom accepted its recommendations, though few were implemented.

By 2004, I was living in Harare, so unsettled and threatening had the situation become. Then we were struck another blow, Wendy, my wife of 58 years, died on 20 January 2005. A few days later the gates to Mount Lothian, the farm which we bought in 19 were finally closed. I was warned by the Judge and the Retired Colonel of violence should I attempt to get back on to the farm.

The following was written by Bill Deedes in the *Daily Telegraph* of *20 April 2003*:

> A senior Zimbabwean judge, Peta Thornycroft tells us from Harare, has just nicked a prize farm off my old friend C.G. Tracey, now in his eighties.
>
> In days when I used to visit Ian Smith's Rhodesia, and after, there was no one doing more to ease the transition to black Zimbabwe than Tracey.
>
> He had his interests (mainly farming and banking) to defend, of course, but he was tireless in seeking to bring black leaders forward in public and business life.
>
> Every time I went to Rhodesia, he arranged for me to take a meal with them. I can think of no white who deserved better of what eventually became Zimbabwe.
>
> Instead, he has been robbed of his home in old age – by a senior judge! – and treated like any other white farmer.
>
> I am still waiting for someone to explain to me the ethical distinction between Saddam Hussein and Robert Mugabe.

Few of the Utete Commission recommendations were implemented, so we found ourselves with no option but to revert to the courts to regain access to the farm and to possession and use of our equipment. We had always wanted to avoid litigation against the new occupants or government, although we had a sound case to take to the High Court. We were also concerned with the possible bias that might exist against us in the High Court because the judge to try the case would be chosen by Mr Justice Paddington Garwe, who, of course, had settled on our farm and was therefore an interested party. He thus had a major conflict of interest. As Judge President of the High Court he had taken back the power to allocate judges for cases and was an interested party in a similar case. We therefore had no confidence in obtaining a fair hearing at trial, or at any potential appeal.

However, we had no alternative but to sue Garwe and Matemachani after they refused to allow us to remove our own equipment off the farm. Under the government's own laws, we were entitled to do this. The presiding judge selected was Mr Justice Ben Hlatshwayo, who had frequently delayed judgments or remanded cases indefinitely. In our case, we had five set-down notices for court hearings that were postponed again and again before the case was ultimately heard. The defendants, who were our settlers, through their advocate, surprisingly conceded our case. However this did not mean that we were able to retain the machinery and irrigation equipment in which we had invested over years because Constitutional Amendment No. 17 gave government the right to take all land without compensation. I and others felt that the delays in passing down judgment in the High Court and Supreme Court had been either designed or orchestrated to slow down the administration of justice, particularly on land issues. These delays were therefore ultimately effective.

The damage to a once proud agricultural industry is all but irrecoverable. Our research stations such as Henderson and Grasslands are run down and produce no useful results, and less than four per cent of commercial farmers remain on the land; those that do, do so precariously. Moreover, it often happened that farms were seized just at the point when the farmer was about to harvest his crops, thus ensuring that the new settlers received all the income without having done any work.

The damage to agricultural production has been so severe that in the 2006/7 season our tobacco crop, once our main foreign-exchange earner, will probably have fallen to less than 25 per cent of its former glory. Effective control of foot-and-mouth disease, which is already endemic, is no longer possible, so we lost our very valuable EU quota of 12,000 tonnes of beef a year. The breeding herd has been drastically reduced and, as cattle breeding is a very long-term business, it will take many years to recover.

We will probably only deliver about 20 per cent of our grain requirement to the formal market at the Grain Marketing Board at a time when the firm international maize market is resulting in increases of maize price from South Africa. We shall have to import from the region at a higher price to cover our food deficit. We will need to seek support and relief from international agencies and the UN.

Strangely enough, some commercial farmers are trying to hold on to their land, or trying to regain some of their lost land. They are people who love this country and farming so much that they have devised plans for themselves and their families to try and continue. The odds are immense, but they can only be admired for their courage and persistence. Time will tell. Minister Didymus Mutasa is on record as saying that his aim is to evict evicted every single white farmer, race, not citizenship or productivity, being the criterion for eviction.

If government had really wanted a properly developed land settlement scheme, they would have organized it soon after independence, instead of waiting until their ruling party needed a topic to divert the population's attention away from government's shortcomings. What better strategy to use than to play both the race card and the land card? Superficially, it may have been politically effective in buying time for the ZANU(PF) government, but there has been little concern about the effect of this on the economy in its widest sense, in food production, foreign-exchange earning crops, tobacco and horticulture and industry. Mount Lothian is a good example, where a number of its enterprises have ceased to operate. Our horticultural exports to Europe, our 24 large onion-drying and -curing barns, which could have supplied 400,000 pockets of onions a year, stand idle. Ninety per cent of the onions consumed in Zimbabwe in 2007 are imported from South Africa.

Farmers loved their farms and the land. Many had turned their land, unoccupied at the time of purchase, into viable and productive units. They wanted to hold on to their life's work. In many instances, farms that had not been listed for acquisition were invaded by war vets and politicians. Civil servants and the police were under instructions not to assist farmers in removing these illegal settlers.

Chibvuti farm belonged to my widowed sister, Bridget Newmarch. She produced hybrid seed maize, wheat, fresh milk, and barley. Now subsistence settlers have taken over her farm, with each squatter tending his own small area and producing his own family's needs, with little, if anything, for the market. Attempts to regain occupation of Chibvuti have for the time being been abandoned. The equipment, including centre pivots for irrigation, has been either stolen or vandalized. The 20-hectare citrus orchard has been abandoned and, more recently, her lovely house was burnt to the ground by rival groups of settlers. Her extensive water reticulation and irrigation systems have been vandalized and are unused. The same has happened to her four immediate neighbours.

We are still fighting for Mount Lothian. While litigation drags on, and it became clearer after Wendy's death that it would be impossible for me to assume full day-to-day control of such an intensive enterprise, we developed a new strategy. Following the success of the one season with the Seed Company, we decided to bring in others to operate sections of the farm.

Colcom, the award-winning pork-processing company in Zimbabwe, was prepared to restock our breeding herd and guarantee food supplies for our 1,000-head pig herd. Colcom needed more pigs, as they were running at only 32 per cent capacity. Export markets were open but they did not have sufficient product. SeedCo agreed to return to the farm under the same conditions and management as before. This could have produced substantial volumes of hybrid seed maize.

For the cattle, we planned to use an entirely new concept, the technology of embryo transplants. This would have entailed modification of our dairy buildings and facilities. We would establish an embryo-transfer station in conjunction with the Ministry of Agriculture. The previous AI station had been severely affected, and there is little systematic plan to improve the genetic quality of the national herd. Little now remains of the commercial pedigree breeding herds. This concept is on hold because one of the participants, the Cold Storage Company, is insolvent and also because the then Minister of Agriculture, Joseph Made, was adamant in refusing any such development associated with white commercial farmers.

The opportunity for commercial farmers to offer assistance in this highly specialized field was lost. We would also have offered to receive batches of 40 or 50 cows or heifers from the communal areas, the best they had available, to Mount Lothian or other research stations. Here their oestrus would be synchronized, they would be inseminated and, once pregnancy was confirmed, they would be returned to their owners in the communal land. Batches of cows would follow one after another, thus improving the quality of the peasant farmers' herds. Four or five batches of cows could be dealt with in each breeding season, and similar units could be established throughout the country.

The part of Mount Lothian under eucalyptus could be restored with correct management. The biggest job of all would be the reconstruction of the greenhouse section.

Our proposals were generally well received, though unfortunately two apparently influential ministers, Made and Mutasa, opposed them, and our plans had to be abandoned.

Another twist to the story of Mount Lothian is the fact that Pioneer Seeds, a subsidiary of the giant DuPont group in America, have (without detailed knowledge of the local situation) been using some of our land and our equipment without our permission and without payment and before the eviction notices had come to fruition.

Our case is extremely complicated and not easy to condense for laymen to comprehend, so I asked my lawyer Kevin Arnott to give me a brief summary, which I have included as an appendix to this book.

Meanwhile, as the Portuguese say, 'a luta continua': the struggle goes on ...

Epilogue

This year, 2008, our winter has been cold, with a lot of frost. Some msasa trees have had their leaves frosted right to the top, but they will recover. In South Africa, it snowed in Johannesburg a couple of times, a very rare experience, and their frosts have been extremely hard.

And so I have spent a lot of my time sitting by my fire - warm and comfortable but, alas, now alone after Wendy's death. This has given me the time to ponder quietly and to think of the events of the 80 years which I have recorded in this autobiography.

This book is really a story without end. Many of us who sought a political-economic solution for Zimbabwe so that the country could get on its feet again have tired of grasping at straws. Whoever runs the 'psychological warfare' in this country has used the weapon of rumour to maximum effect. The worse the situation becomes, the more rumours abound, most of which are not true. There is a pervading atmosphere of fear, disillusionment and apprehension amongst all races. Intimidation has been widespread, against anybody suspected of being connected with the opposition party, the MDC. Corruption has become common in all walks of life. The illegal export of foreign exchange is widespread, with even the Reserve Bank buying South African rand on the street with Zimbabwe dollars, an offence for which many people have been convicted.

At the same time, government's refusal to address the root of the problems in the country means that the people's everyday lives have become more and more difficult; those in power are desperate to divert attention from the daily hardships. As a result of the government's decision to control and force prices down, the cost of living increased several-fold. Price-control legislation was carefully planned for political ends, regardless of the economic consequences. Business executives are being flung into jail for 'over charging' and often prosecuted in their personal capacities, instead of in their corporate capacities. They were only carrying out the policy and instructions of their boards, which was to stay in business, to make a reasonable profit, to have adequate funds to renew the stocks on the shelves, and in the end to make a margin for their shareholders. Police were not allowed to interfere when mobs, who might almost be described as looters, went into supermarkets and without inhibition seized goods off the shelves at the reduced prices. For propaganda purposes, prices were, at government's insistence, cut by half. As a result, the shelves are now bare.

Most retailers who have been targeted have declined to replace their stocks, as they might be forced by government to sell them at prices lower than they paid for them. Many companies have closed and unemployment is worsening. Manufacturers are not prepared to sell their products below cost. The food situation is untenable, with basics no longer available easily, if at all, except on the black market – maize meal, salt, flour, bread, meat, cooking oil, sugar.

The confusion and uncertainty in the whole country is so great, with official year-on-year inflation climbing to over 2.2 million per cent, that it is difficult to make a logical forecast of the outcome. Iraq has the next highest inflation in the world after Zimbabwe, with a figure of approximately 50 per cent. Hyperinflation has been described as a situation when inflation has been above 50 per cent for four consecutive months. Historically, this has always been followed by a change in government in other countries. We passed that benchmark a long time ago. We must ask ourselves whether the government can survive under these circumstances.

The self-inflicted damage will be very difficult to reverse, certainly in the short term. Huge problems will confront whoever is brave and capable enough to take over the reins of government to try and bring us out of the present political and economic chaos. When the political situation settles, and if there is a new and thinking government, they will find themselves up against the amalgamated evil of certain individuals in the present government. It is imperative that four major principles are non-negotiable: a return to the rule of law, the protection of property rights, freedom of information, and the elimination of corruption. These are requirements established by the international community, other countries and the IMF and the World Bank. No help will be available for balance of payments or other aid until these requirements are met.

But President Mugabe finds these terms unacceptable and an infringement of Zimbabwe's sovereign rights. The influence of SADC, South Africa and the African Union are simply brushed aside and Zimbabwe continues on its downward trend.

Looked at objectively, the situation is more than depressing and bleak and, as I write this in 2008, no one can guess what the next few months will bring. However, an increasing number of younger black Zimbabweans quietly hold views different from the government's. If there is a change at the top, either from within or from some alternative, there is hope that people of this calibre may return from the diaspora - people who are well educated, principled and realistic, who will have the courage to offer an alternative to blind political support, to apply their skills to support a new administration, and to stand up against widespread intimidation, corruption and our many other ills. A potential opportunity might be for government to allow Zimbabweans living abroad to vote, but this could change the balance of power and is unlikely to happen at present.

Such an administration would have the blessing and support, both morally and financially, of many countries and international agencies, and therein lies the opportunity. I have always regarded challenges and problems as the basis for opportunity. Is this perhaps another opening? Perhaps I am grasping at yet another straw. But, until such time as economic advantage overrides political imperatives, progress will be difficult.

I look back over the last 80 years and apply the old phrase, 'What if ...?' But that is academic. Zimbabwe is in danger of joining the ranks of derelict African countries - its agriculture, and particularly its tobacco and food sectors, have been mortally wounded. An atmosphere of mistrust and corruption is widespread. To correct these alone would be a major task.

What Wendy and I did was to produce three lovely daughters, all of them successes in their own fields and with nine superb grandchildren, of whom Wendy and I were so proud. Their successes in this country, New York, South Africa, London, and Australia give me the feeling that the Tracey family - and not forgetting my brother Martin and sister Bridget Newmarch and their children and grandchildren - have been very fortunate to have had the opportunity, and to have grasped it, and made their own contribution to this wonderful little country over the past 80 years. Those eight decades of progress cannot be taken away, although the developments of which we were proud have been so misused.

The title of this book was discussed at length. Finally we settled for Wendy's choice: *All for Nothing?*

'The future's not ours to see. Que sera, sera.'

C. G. Tracey
Harare, August 2008

Appendix
Events regarding ownership of Mount Lothian:
A summary prepared by my lawyer, Kevin Arnott

(This paper refers to Mount Shannon, which was the name of the original farm. Mount Lothian was the name given to one subdivision of this farm.)

A Farmer, a Colonel and a Judge

PART 1

As a practising lawyer in Zimbabwe, it has for no less than the last seven years been a challenge for me to represent the interests of many farmers in Zimbabwe. At the heart of the challenge is the harsh reality that is clear to all: that the furtherance by legal argument of any interests of a farmer will be extinguished by the promulgation of another tsunami of legislation that is then backdated.

And perhaps the ultimate prohibition to date of access by farmers to the courts and their constitutional rights is Constitutional Amendment No. 17 which was promulgated on 14 September 2005 and which effectively declared that ownership of any farms listed in prior *Gazettes* are to vest in the State. The effect of this law is variously described by Advocates Jeremy Gauntlett S.C. and Adrian de Bourbon S.C. in their Heads of Argument filed in the Supreme Court case of Campbell two weeks ago to include the following:

> Thus the legislative endeavours to which this application relates are without modern parallel in any constitutional democracy worthy of the name. They set Zimbabwe apart, so far as we are aware, from all member states of SADC, the British Commonwealth and the African Union which function as constitutional democracies. They violate Zimbabwe's international law obligations, most immediately through its membership of the African Union. They entail the abrogation of constitutionalism and elevate the fiat of the

executive and legislature over the entrenched core provisions of the Constitution. They certify the existence of a totalitarian state.

It is with this reality in mind that I now turn to recount in broad summary the tragic demise of C.G. Tracey's farming empire.

No person in the agricultural community in Zimbabwe will take issue with the fact that C.G. had, with the unfailing support of his late wife, Wendy, from 1983 to 2000 developed Mt Shannon Farm from virtually undeveloped land into a state-of-the-art, high-tech and intensively diversified farming enterprise. Indeed, Mt Shannon was, without parallel, one of the most diversified farms in the country.

In February 2002 a retired colonel and banker, Godfrey Matemachani, introduced himself to C.G. as the 'new owner' of Mt Shannon. He produced an offer letter dated 25 February 2002 but stamped 13 March 2002. When he was advised that the farm was not the subject of a Section 8 acquisition order and had not been acquired, he simply stated he could 'organize one'. He promptly did.

Government then applied in July 2002 to the Administrative Court to confirm its right to acquire Mt Shannon. This was opposed. In August 2002, C.G. sought permission from Government to downsize. There was no clear or satisfactory response to this request.

What followed between September 2002 and February 2003 were a series of intensive negotiations between C.G., Colonel Matemachani and the then Judge President of the High Court, Honourable Justice Paddington Garwe, to agree on the terms of a co-existence agreement in respect of Mt Shannon. A detailed written agreement was signed by the parties.

In essence the agreement permitted C.G.'s company to farm the Eastern portion of the farm. The Colonel and Justice Garwe had rights to farm the Western portion. C.G.'s company assisted with the farming operations on the Western section. The agreement was effective to the end of September 2003.

Colonel Matemachani then, in April 2004, proceeded to encroach on C.G.'s portion of the farm. He claimed that the acquiring authority would not recognize either the agreement concluded or any extension thereof. And, despite his written undertaking to assist C.G. in obtaining the consent of the acquiring authority to allow C.G. further rights of occupation, the Colonel simply ignored this obligation.

C.G. and his wife, under threat of physical violence, moved off Mt Shannon in September 2002. But the beginning of the end was to commence in June 2004. Attempts made by C.G. either to regain access to the farm or to acquire possession of his many movables and equipment on the farm were to be denied by Colonel Matemachani. This resulted in the filing by C.G. in October 2004 of a High Court Application to regain access to Mt Shannon and to possession and use of his equipment.

The application was opposed by Colonel Matemachani. He raised spurious defences such as the contention in his affidavit filed in the High Court that 'the process of acquiring the movable equipment on the farm had been initiated by the acquiring authority and will be completed presently'. On this basis he refused access to the farm or equipment. Yet it was only in January 2006 that Government first served upon C.G. a notice of intention to acquire equipment.

The application was heard before Justice Hlatshwayo on 14 February 2006. The judge granted an order in open court to the effect that by consent Colonel Matemachani was prevented from interfering with C.G.'s rights of ownership and possession of his equipment. However, shortly thereafter the judge called the lawyers to his chambers and said he felt that the order required details of specific items of equipment before he could formalize it. By this time there appeared to be a prospect of settling disputes over the equipment amicably and thus the need for the order became redundant. But what is noteworthy is that the Colonel had, by consenting to the order, effectively succumbed to concede that his resistance to the application had been futile from the outset.

Having been served in January 2006 with a notice to acquire his farming equipment, C.G. and I entered into an intensive phase between February 2006 and August 2006 of negotiating with the acquiring authority to resolve disputes over the extent of compensation offered for the equipment that Government required.

Because of the promulgation of Constitutional Amendment No. 17,

C.G. then took the painful decision to not resist acquisition of the farm but to seek compensation for improvements. Compensation was finally settled by agreement and paid in August 2006. Given his age, the delay in contesting compensation through the courts, the remote prospect of persuading a court to reject the sum assessed by Government valuers and the opportunity of wisely investing what was offered, C.G. was constrained to settle the issue of compensation. The amount paid was no more than 25% of the true market value. At this time invaluable opinions were obtained from Advocate Adrian de Bourbon S.C. on various aspects of the equipment legislation. C.G. generously offered those guidelines to other farmers suffering a similar plight.

After compensation was paid, there remained on Mt Shannon Farm numerous items of equipment not required or acquired by the Government. I accompanied C.G. in the presence of Miss Hove (the Colonel's lawyer) and Jason Ridley of CC Sales (appointed by C.G. to value equipment) to Mt Shannon. The visit was for the purpose of identifying and implementing the removal from the farm of the items of equipment not required by Government. What emerged was the horrifying realization that much equipment (including many irrigation pipes) could not be accounted for and some was in very bad condition.

The missing and damaged equipment is now the subject of pending litigation in the High Court where the Colonel is being sued for damages for
    i) the value of the missing equipment; and
    ii) the use of the equipment without C.G.'s consent.
A claim is also made for damages depriving C.G. of his use of the farm for the period up to the promulgation of the Constitutional Amendment.

We also sued the American Pioneer Seed Company, one of the biggest seed maize producers in the world. They relied on a signed statement from Matemachani that the land on which he was going to grow a partnership seed maize crop was free and had been offered to him, which was not the case. Pioneer were unaware of what they had done in good faith.

C.G.'s story is a unique one. It has witnessed every aspect of the compulsory acquisition of improvements and of farm equipment. It is unfinished; many more chapters will soon unfold. C.G. has, in traversing the turbulent and traumatic experience of compulsory acquisition suffered, confronted, co-existed, conceded, overcome and simply never given up. In the process he has lost his wife, his farm and his equipment. But through all this he has maintained his dignity, his self-esteem, and, given in particular his age, his courage and fortitude are legendary.

In short, C.G. gives credence to the universal truth that: 'it is better to light a candle than curse the darkness'.

K. J. Arnott
8 February 2007

Since Kevin Arnott wrote the above, a lot more water has flowed under the bridge and our case has been largely concluded and we await judgment. So I asked him to write a second piece covering that stage. He writes:

PART 2

A deep shadow of darkness was to suddenly overwhelm C.G. He was rushed to hospital on 15 February 2007 and appeared to be suffering from internal bleeding. I visited him there on several occasions. I was very humbled and moved to see a legendary and great pillar of our society and heritage very ill and delirious. I feel strongly that the trauma of the events in the two preceding years had much to do with this setback. It seemed that his last candle was about to succumb and surrender. But C.G. would have none of it. Beneath the rapid physical appearance of deterioration arose his unique strength and defiance. He would live to fight another day. Indeed, he was true to his favourite Winston Churchill saying: 'Never give in, never, never, never ...'

Several pre-trial conferences were held in the High Court before Judge President Makarau concerning the claims against Colonel Matemachani. The purpose of the conferences in this case were essentially to define the issues for determination by the trial court. An interesting aspect of these conferences was the concern of the judge as to whether Justice Garwe should be joined as a party to the proceedings or whether he should be served with all pleadings and invited to respond. Neither C.G. nor Matemachani claimed anything from the judge. At this time Matemachani did not say that the judge was in possession of any of C.G.'s equipment. Instead the Colonel pointed fingers at Seed Co and C.G., saying that they had taken the equipment. At the last pre-trial conference the judge

President announced that she had discussed the litigation with Justice Garwe (who was by this time a Judge of Appeal in the Supreme Court) and the latter indicated that he did not want to be cited as a party but would be happy to give evidence for either party.

The trial in the matter was set down before Justice Bhunu from 4 to 7 September 2007 in Court 'J' of the High Court. Advocate de Bourbon S.C. flew from Cape Town to represent C.G.'s company.

Prior to trial, procedural requests were made by us to the Colonel's lawyers to provide details of his farming operations and documents in this regard. They were denied. This resulted in a claim for costs of the trial being made against the Colonel's lawyers. It was argued on behalf of C.G. that every attempt was being made to cover up the truth. As the trial was about to commence a letter was received from the Colonel's lawyers. It stated that an inspection of the farm by the lawyers revealed that certain items of the disputed equipment were seen on the part of the farm occupied by Justice Garwe. This was the first time this had been made known.

A memorable moment during the trial was the first question asked of the Colonel by Advocate de Bourbon S.C.: 'Did you, Mr Matemachani, have lunch with the Chief Justice on the first day of this trial?' He replied: 'Yes', but went on to deny that anything had been discussed about the pending trial.

The following is an extract from portion of the closing submissions made to the trial judge by Advocate de Bourbon S.C. The Plaintiff is Mt Lothian Estates (Private) Limited and the First Defendant is Colonel Matemachani. I am in respectful agreement with these submissions:

1. Two witnesses gave oral testimony during this trial, and to only a limited extent is it necessary for the Honourable Court to make an assessment as to credibility. It is the submission on behalf of the Plaintiff that any conflict in the evidence must be resolved in favour of Mr Tracey, rather than Mr Matemachani.

2. Much has been made during the course of this trial of the fact that the Plaintiff did not cite Judge Garwe as a party. There is no requirement to join all joint wrongdoers, other

than the risk set out in section 6(1)(a) of the Damages (Apportionment and Assessment) Act [*Chapter 8:06*]. Under the common law joint wrongdoers are liable jointly and severally and any one of them can be sued for the whole amount of the alleged claim, see *Toerien* v. *Duncan* 1932 OPD 180; *Naude and Du Plessis* v. *Mercier* 1917 AD 32 at 38–40. In terms of section 6(1)(b) of that Act it lay within the power of the First Defendant to join Judge Garwe. Indeed, at the pre-trial conference the learned Judge President advised the parties that she had spoken to Judge Garwe who told her that he did not want to be involved as a party, but would come as a witness if either party called him. The First Defendant has chosen not to call Judge Garwe to support his assertions and has tried to implicate the Judge in this matter, and the obvious inference to be drawn is that the Judge would not support him. In this regard it must be borne in mind that it was only at the very last minute that the First Defendant disclosed the existence of an offer letter in favour of Judge Garwe.

3. It is respectfully submitted that Mr Tracey, subjected as he was to a challenging cross-examination for a person of his age and health, showed only confusion on dates and an obvious tiredness. He was not shaken at all in cross-examination and his evidence is consistent with the affidavits that he swore at the time of the relevant events. It is respectfully submitted that he showed himself to be a kind and honest man who somewhat naively believed in co-existence, and did not properly measure the type of person that Mr Matemachani clearly is.

Throughout the affidavits Mr Tracey has been consistent in his evidence. Furthermore, the letters that he wrote, especially that at page 52 of Exhibit 2, correctly set out a factual situation. With particular reference to that letter he would have no motive to falsely accuse the First Defendant of attitude and behavioural issues if these had not occurred. Those attitude and behavioural issues show the dominant personality of Mr Matemachani, confirming that he was the prime mover in evicting the Plaintiff from the farm.

Mr Tracey can therefore be believed when he told this Court that it was indeed the First Defendant who required him to vacate the farm in April 2004 and that it was the First Defendant who was the major player in the occupation of the farm.

4. On the other hand, Mr Matemachani showed himself to be a witness who would say whatever was necessary to deal with a particular question. He is undoubtedly a person of a very strong personality, and indeed admitted it in an affidavit, although he tried in evidence to suggest he did not understand what was being put to him in this regard, see Exhibit 1, page 53, paragraph 31.

His failure to produce records and his failure to make a proper discovery and to give proper particulars is again indicative of his attitude that matters must be done according to what he thinks the rules of litigation should be, and his decision as to what is or is not an issue. As a result he swore affidavits that were at the very least inaccurate, and despite the undertaking to provide by affidavit a correction and explanation for the apparent misdescription of documents in the affidavit filed on 4 September 2007, he did not. Even the affidavits he filed in the application proceedings he then challenged in giving evidence when it seemed convenient to him to retract what is contained in those affidavits.

There can be no doubt that the First Defendant in asserting that he was the new owner of the farm was acting unlawfully, and with the intention of intimidating Mr Tracey. If it is remembered that this allegation was made by Mr Matemachani to Mr Tracey less than a month after the initial publication in the *Gazette* of 8 February 2002, the impact of his claim for ownership must have been overwhelming. But being the person that he is, Mr Tracey agreed to co-existence, and to achieve his ends Mr Matemachani agreed to support of the Plaintiff and Mr Tracey in their endeavours to retain a portion of the farm, see Exhibit 2, page 14, clause 1.2. The reality is, as admitted by Mr Matemachani, that he did nothing to further the hopes of Mr Tracey. In fact, he did the very opposite. As set out by Mr Tracey in his affidavit in Exhibit 1, page 5, paragraphs 13 and 14, Mr Matemachani used his influence with the Marondera Provincial Office to have a Section 8 order served on the farm. This allegation was not denied in the affidavits, see Exhibit 1, page 49, paragraph 9. When cornered with this situation, Mr Matemachani resorted to the ridiculous statement that any matter that he disputed he did not have to deny in his opposing papers, but he never in fact denied that it was through his efforts that the Section 8 order was issued at the end of June 2002. This is a good example of the fact that Mr Matemachani would say whatever was necessary, when under oath, to get out of a situation.

The denial in evidence by Mr Matemachani that he took steps to prevent the removal of items from the farm by Mr Tracey did not stand up to scrutiny as against his affidavits, see in particular Exhibit 1, page 47, paragraph 3, page 48, paragraph 6 and page 55, paragraph 37. Significantly, in the paragraph headed Ad 4 he said he was powerless to give access to land. But this was not based on any allegation of the presence of Judge Garwe, but on the pending litigation in the Administrative Court. Thus he clearly contradicted himself on a very material aspect of his evidence. The very fact that he opposed the application which sought access to the eastern portion of the farm belies his claim that the eastern portion was controlled by Judge Garwe. Mr Matemachani's claim that he was powerless was not based on the fact that that section was occupied by Judge Garwe. In any event, if it were truly the situation that the eastern section was occupied by Judge Garwe, it does not explain why the First Defendant opposed that aspect of the relief being sought in the application.

Throughout his evidence the First Defendant made it clear that he relied on one form of document from the Government to give him his rights in respect of the farm. He made no attempt to have those rights adjudicated by a court, and in effect he despoiled the Plaintiff of its rights to undisturbed possession of the farm. He made no attempt to determine the extent of his rights, but merely used his dominant personality to force a situation where Mr Tracey had to co-exist with him. Having reached that position he then did nothing to assist Mr Tracey retain possession of a portion of the farm.

The admission by Mr Matemachani that the supplementary discovery affidavit filed on 4 September 2007 was produced to support the documents he intended to rely upon in respect of his evidence is significant. First of all it shows that where it suits him he will make a false or inaccurate affidavit. Secondly, it shows that he will not disclose documents which might have a bearing on the case that support the other side. In the end, he has kept this Honourable Court in the dark as to the true factual situation regarding his presence on the farm. He has sought to involve a Judge of the Supreme Court with no evidence other than the last-minute production of an offer letter. But his actions in defending the issue of movables, see his affidavit and the correspondence in Exhibit 2, and in disputing the court application in respect of the eastern portion must raise considerable doubt as to the veracity of his claim against Judge Garwe. It is respectfully submitted that caution should be exercised before this Honourable Court makes a finding against a judge based solely on the evidence of Mr Matemachani.

On a number of occasions Mr Matemachani simply did not answer the question put to him.

The bottom line so far as his evidence is concerned is that he selected this particular farm and sought to be settled on it. Once he obtained the offer letter he asserted his rights (as he saw them) and having co-existed for a period, then took over the farm as a whole. The role of Judge Garwe was at best a limited one in all this, bearing in mind the evidence of Mr Matemachani that Judge Garwe did not want it publicly known that he had been granted rights in respect of a farm as he was handling litigation brought by other farmers. It is respectfully submitted that the First Defendant did not establish that Judge Garwe played any significant role in the unlawful occupation of the farm.'

The above submissions and lengthy Heads of argument were handed to the court by Advocate de Bourbon S.C. at the end of the trial. I believe the following key points arose, or were exposed, after evidence had been concluded at the trial:

a) Colonel Matemachani was evasive and arrogant when giving evidence. Advocate de Bourbon S.C. described him in court as a 'cherry-picker' who 'muscled' his way on to the whole of Mt Shannon.

b) The Colonel obtained a Section 8 order for the farm at will and virtually overnight. He could just as easily have obtained permission for C.G. to retain the eastern portion of the farm. Despite his written undertaking in the co-existence agreement to do so, Matemachani admitted at the trial that nothing was done to obtain such permission.

c) The Colonel tried to make out in evidence that he had never prevented C.G. from access to his farm or equipment. When it was pointed out to him that he had expressly denied access under oath three years ago he was unable to respond.

d) C.G. clearly emerged as a person who sought to comply with government policy, who assisted the other settlers and who, in a bona fide manner, had every right to expect Colonel Matemachani to honour his promises and under-takings. To the extent and degree that C.G. conducted himself in good faith the Colonel conducted himself in bad faith.

The judge has reserved judgment. It is uncertain when a judgment will in fact be given.

A letter has now been addressed to Judge of Appeal Garwe attached to which is a copy of the letter received from Matemachani's lawyers just prior to the trial. The latter letter indicated that the lawyers representing Matemachani physically saw certain items of equipment on Justice Garwe's half of the farm a week before the trial. The judge is being requested to decide whether he wishes to purchase the items and if not to advise when they may be collected.

Whatever judgment is given in the matter I am respectfully of the view that C. G., in instructing that the trial proceeds, has:

a) Exposed the bad faith and true agenda of the Colonel; and
b) Upheld the principle that the tenacious pursuit of the truth in any set of circumstances must never be surrendered because of politics, might or economics; and
c) Provided a novel and unique precedent for litigation in a politically sensitive and emotional sphere that has been, and is so overwhelmingly prevalent, in our society and which will be invaluable to many other farmers; and
d) Demonstrated most unequivocally that the Government and those in powerful political positions who commended him for his approach of co-existence cannot be taken seriously, and in so doing has heeded a clear warning to those wishing to or being forced to adopt similar approaches.

In a most profound way C. G. has in completing his trial closed another door in his life. May the door that opens be a place of serenity and calmness. May that place provide a meaningful opportunity to reflect and dwell on his many achievements and successes. May it afford many more happy moments with his family and friends. That an icon of his stature deserves nothing less can permit of no doubt.

K. J. Arnott
28 September 2007

Index of Names